Library of
Davidson College

Schoenberg's Twelve-Tone Harmony
The Suite Op. 29 and the Compositional Sketches

Studies in Musicology

George Buelow, Series Editor

Professor of Musicology
Indiana University

Other Titles in This Series

The French Cantata: A Survey and Thematic Catalog	Gene E. Vollen
The Spanish Baroque Guitar, with a Transcription of de Murcia's Passacalles y obras	Neil D. Pennington
Foreign Influence on the Zarzuela, 1700–1770	William M. Bussey
The Keyboard Concertos of Carl Philipp Emanuel Bach	Rachel W. Wade
Compositional Origins of Beethoven's String Quartet in C Sharp Minor, Opus 131	Robert S. Winter, III
Francis Poulenc: A Study of His Artistic Development and His Musical Style	Keith W. Daniel
Walter Piston	Howard Pollack

Schoenberg's Twelve-Tone Harmony
The Suite Op. 29 and the Compositional Sketches

by
Martha M. Hyde

UMI RESEARCH PRESS
Ann Arbor, Michigan

Copyright © 1977, 1982
Martha M. Hyde
All rights reserved

Produced and distributed by
UMI Research Press
an imprint of
University Microfilms International
Ann Arbor, Michigan 48106

Library of Congress Cataloging in Publication Data

Hyde, Martha M.
  Schoenberg's twelve-tone harmony.

  (Studies in musicology ; no. 49)
  Revision of thesis—Yale University, 1977.
  Bibliography: p.
  Includes index.
  1. Schoenberg, Arnold, 1874-1951. 2. Schoenberg, Arnold, 1874-1951. Suites, piano, clarinets (3), strings, op. 29. 3. Twelve-tone system. I. Title. II. Series.
ML410.S283H9 1982   781.3   81-16369
ISBN 0-8357-1279-6   AACR2

Contents

Preface   *vii*

1 Twelve-Tone Harmony   *1*
   Schoenberg's Conception of Twelve-Tone Harmony
   Past Views of Twelve-Tone Harmony

2 Schoenberg's Sketches for the Suite op. 29 (Septett)   *25*
   The Harmonic Structure of the Basic Set
   The Harmonic Organization of Individual Row Forms
   The Harmonic Organization of Two or More Row Forms
   Reorderings of the Basic Set
   Combinatoriality As Exhibited in the Sketches

3 Harmonic Organization in Music from
   the Suite op. 29   *61*
   The Harmonic Organization of Individual Row Forms
      Pitch Repetitions and Doublings
   The Harmonic Organization of Two or More Row Forms
      Noncombinatorially Related Row Forms
      Combinatorially Related Row Forms
         Aggregates containing exactly twelve elements
         Aggregates containing more than twelve elements
         Absence of aggregate formation
   Schoenberg's Use of the Combinatorial Property
      I, RI, T, and RT Hexachordal Combinatoriality
      Trichordal and Tetrachordal Aggregates
      Aggregates Displaying Unequal Row Partitioning
      Definition of an Aggregate
   Reorderings of the Basic Set

4 A Theory of Twelve-Tone Meter   *111*
    The Problem of Twelve-Tone Meter
    A Model for Twelve-Tone Meter
    Application of the Model for Twelve-Tone Meter

Appendix   *143*

Glossary   *147*

Notes   *151*

Bibliography   *159*

Index   *161*

Preface

This essay grew out of my conviction that a better understanding of Schoenberg's theoretical statements would serve to correct widespread misconceptions and answer commonplace criticisms of his method of twelve-tone composition. These misconceptions and criticisms take issue with his repeated claim that not only the melodies of his music derive from the basic set, but also "something different and more important is derived from it with a regularity comparable to the regularity and logic of the earlier [tonal] harmony."[1] His critics have commonly maintained that while the tonal system orders and integrates both horizontal and vertical dimensions of a composition, the twelve-tone system can order only a single dimension and therefore cannot in itself produce an integrated musical texture. In this view, Schoenberg's twelve-tone music contains many harmonic events unrelated to the basic set and therefore fails to justify his claim that the twelve-tone row provides a method for determining harmonies as well as their successions.

Two sorts of answers to this problem have emerged. Skeptics assert that Schoenberg's use of harmonies containing nonadjacent segments of the basic set, as well as other "licenses" such as pitch reorderings and repetitions, results in many events unrelated to the basic set and that these events expose serious weaknesses in his twelve-tone method. This skeptical argument began during Schoenberg's lifetime and is still current. The other answer belongs perhaps to the Longinian strain in art criticism. Schoenberg's genius was too great for rules, even his own rules. This argument interprets Schoenberg's licenses as evidence of genius rather than of weaknesses in his method and tends to ignore his claims for the completeness of the twelve-tone method. The appeal to creative genius has prevented true believers from explaining how such licenses are regulated by the basic set.

The history of this debate may be easier to follow in critical writings, but more recent developments in the twelve-tone method show that composers have been equally troubled by the problem of structuring twelve-tone harmony. The common view now sees Webern as a more progressive composer than Schoenberg and as a greater influence on the development of twelve-tone music. And what in Webern's method seems most innovative to contemporary composers are exactly those techniques which aim to unify all dimensions of harmonic structure. One need only reflect on the most recent trends in twelve-tone theory and composition—such as the use of source sets, the serialization of rhythm and dynamics, the extensions of aggregate structures, and the formalization of the combinatorial property—to appreciate that what we might call the "harmonic problem" has been and remains the major problem in both the theory and the practice of twelve-tone composition.

This essay undertakes to justify Schoenberg's claims for his system and to resolve the harmonic problem, first by reinterpreting some key passages in his essay "Composition with Twelve Tones," and then by analyzing portions of the Suite op. 29, with the help of his manuscript sketches. It became clear early in my research that Schoenberg's essay, which has been taken as a kind of manifesto, is incomplete and cryptic by design, and that Schoenberg himself is largely responsible for the misconceptions and criticisms of his method that followed. Comparison of early drafts of the essay shows him deleting or changing key passages, passages which often point toward specific techniques that would have helped to substantiate his claims. But even the fuller versions of "Composition with Twelve Tones" still leave much ambiguous. Shortly after beginning my research, I was fortunate enough to be given access to Schoenberg's manuscript sketches. Although the Schoenberg Institute in Los Angeles had not yet opened, its director, Leonard Stein, and archivist, Clara Steuermann, were kind enough to make special arrangements for me to study the sketches. Schoenberg's autograph manuscripts had been catalogued and described, but few of his twelve-tone sketches had been analyzed and their importance had been greatly underestimated. I could see very quickly that they exposed and clarified the specific techniques that Schoenberg used to derive harmonic structure from a single basic set, techniques which he apparently chose to keep secret from friends and critics alike.

My problem then became one of deciding which sketches to analyze. Limits on time and scope, as well as the vast quantity of sketch material in the archives, restricted my study to a single composition. After considerable debate, I chose the Suite op. 29, even though it is not a particularly well known work. It seemed most useful for several reasons. First, and most important, its sketches were extensive and reflected a self-consciousness often not apparent in those for the later works. Second, even though it is an early twelve-tone work, it uses a combinatorial row—a feature characteristic of later works. Unlike many of the later combinatorial works, however, it has many sections where the combinatorial property is not used to form aggregates or secondary sets. I anticipated that juxtaposition of combinatorial and noncombinatorial sections would prove useful in comparing Schoenberg's techniques for structuring harmony in both types of situations. Third, Schoenberg finished the Suite before writing "Composition with Twelve Tones," so that it might be expected to exhibit the techniques hinted at in the essay. In fact, it did seem to exhibit all the features that Schoenberg felt distinguished his twelve-tone from his earlier atonal works. In his essay, Schoenberg stresses that the twelve-tone method solved the problem of generating larger forms, a problem he had found insoluble with his earlier atonal procedures. All the movements of op. 29 are large and they also bear the classical titles which began to appear only with the larger forms of his twelve-tone compositions. The Suite, then, was attractive not only because it was combinatorial, but also because it seemed to fairly represent the early twelve-tone pieces which Schoenberg was describing in his essay. These reasons suggested that even though the scope of my research had to be limited, my conclusions would have a broader application. My more recent research has borne out this hypothesis even more than I anticipated.

Three other decisions also directed my research. First, I decided to omit a thorough description of the manuscript material for the Suite since most of it is available in the secondary literature and will eventually appear in the *Collected Works*. Second, while it was tempting to analyze all the manuscript material for the Suite, I decided to limit myself to those sketches that pertained to Schoenberg's method of structuring harmonies within one or between several row forms. Before I understood these procedures, I reasoned, interpretation of sketches dealing with larger formal aspects would be impossible. Most of my examples come therefore from loose sketch sheets and not from the material that appears in *Skizzenbuch V*. Third, I avoided discussing sketches which confirmed compositional procedures that other Schoenberg scholars had already discussed—such procedures as the use of invariant pitches or segments to associate row forms, inversional balance, hexachordal levels, and typical combinatorial or aggregate structures. The reader of this essay will find therefore neither analyses of all the sketch material for op. 29, nor a complete analysis of the composition. But, as I hope will be evident, the analyses of the sketches I have chosen, despite their restricted focus, significantly alter what we have commonly understood to be Schoenberg's procedures for organizing twelve-tone harmony.

The final chapter of this essay sets forth a theory of twelve-tone meter, a topic which evolved naturally from my research. As with the sketch material, I am primarily addressing metrical structure within one or between several row forms; most of my examples, then, show how Schoenberg uses harmony and meter to delineate discrete phrases. By expanding my research in this direction, I have tried to lay the groundwork for a study of Schoenberg's larger forms. I still feel, as I did in the beginning, that work on larger forms, without prior understanding of harmony and meter on the smallest scale, would have been premature.

In retrospect I think the sketch material for the Suite fairly represents Schoenberg's typical method of composing. My later research has shown, though, that just as Schoenberg experimented with different compositional procedures, he also varied the way he went about composing. As I began studying the sketch material for op. 29 I wondered why there were more sketches for the first movement than for the other three, a fact which the examples in this essay reflect. My more recent work shows this preponderance to be common in the sketches for many other works, but I slowly realized that the reasons for it are quite different than one might expect. In the initial stages of composition Schoenberg appears to have worked out certain harmonic structures or designs that he used again in varied forms thoughout the composition. Therefore, even though these early sketches often appear to focus on the beginning of a composition, they often continue to be relevant, though with different surface features, throughout the piece. In op. 29, the harmonic designs set forth in sketches for the first movement continue to appear in varied forms later.

Excerpts from compositional sketches by Schoenberg are from the collection of the Arnold Schoenberg Institute, University of Southern California, Los Angeles, California. I am able to reproduce them here through the courtesy and assistance of the Institute. Special thanks are due to the Institute's director, Leonard Stein, and archivist, Clara Steuermann, for the help they have given me over the past several years. Examples from op. 29 itself (Copyright 1927 by Universal Edition, Copyright renewed 1954 by Gertrud Schoenberg) are reproduced with the kind permission of Belmont Music Publishers, Los Angeles, California. This book was prepared for publication with the assistance of the Frederick W. Hilles Publication Fund of Yale University.

Among the many friends and colleagues who in one way or another have helped me with this project, I want to thank especially my husband Thomas Hyde, who has read portions of the manuscript and made many useful suggestions. Finally, I thank Allen Forte, as my teacher, supervisor, colleague and friend, without whose insight, guidance and encouragement this book would not have been written.

1
Twelve-Tone Harmony

Until recently it has been assumed that Schoenberg's only major public statement about his new method of composition is the lecture "Composition with Twelve Tones," first delivered at the University of California, Los Angeles in March 1941 and subsequently published in the collection *Style and Idea*.[1] In fact, Schoenberg delivered an earlier version of this lecture, written in January 1934, at Princeton University on March 6 of the same year. The earlier version, transcribed from Schoenberg's handwritten draft and texts and recently published, contains significant information which does not appear in the later version.[2]

"Composition with Twelve Tones" and its earlier version both discuss similar twelve-tone techniques and contain the same musical examples drawn from Schoenberg's twelve-tone compositions. The later statement is somewhat more general, containing several examples from the tonal and atonal literature, while the earlier tends to include more extensive and precise descriptions. Most interesting are the differences in the way various techniques are described and the relative emphasis they receive. For example, in "Composition with Twelve Tones" Schoenberg stresses inversional combinatoriality at the lower fifth, thereby giving rise to the common view not only that he preferred this type of combinatoriality, but that it was the only type he used. (For the definition of combinatoriality and other technical terms refer to the Glossary.) Analysis of his earlier twelve-tone works clearly dispels this view. His earlier version gives a historically more accurate description which refrains from specifying a preferred interval of inversion. A second interesting difference between early and later versions is that the later version, in general, emphasizes avoidance of octave doubling more than the earlier version and in several instances these cautionary remarks in the later lecture have obscured more important issues.[3]

In the following section, I summarize Schoenberg's statements on his new method of composition in both versions. Because Schoenberg's English is more awkward in the earlier version, I have quoted "Composition with Twelve Tones" whenever possible. I do not intend to investigate all the differences and similarities between tonal theory and practice and the theory and practice formulated by Schoenberg in "Composition with Twelve Tones," but rather to clarify what Schoenberg actually says in that essay. Although it is possible to analyze Schoenberg's twelve-tone music in a number of different ways, it would seem most fruitful to do so on the basis of a clear understanding of his own concepts of musical organization. Indeed, without that understanding it is quite possible to overlook or misinterpret important aspects of his music. By clearly formulating what Schoenberg says about twelve-tone composition and by analyzing the examples he provides, I show what kind of techniques Schoenberg uses for organizing harmonic structure, techniques which until now have not been fully understood.

In the final section I discuss how theorists have traditionally analyzed Schoenberg's harmonic structure and indicate important ways in which their theories have been inaccurate and misleading.

Schoenberg's Conception of Twelve-Tone Harmony

Schoenberg believes that the extensive use of chromaticism in the late nineteenth century led to dissolution of tonal harmonic procedures. One crucial aspect of tonality, "the idea that one basic tone, the root, dominated the construction of chords and regulated their succession," became a mere theoretical issue with little relevance to contemporary composition.[4] Use of ambiguous harmonic progressions and impressionistic or nonfunctional harmonies led to a radical change in compositional technique, ending in what Schoenberg called "emancipation of the dissonance."[5] Degree of "comprehensibility," Schoenberg claims, not relative beauty or aesthetic value, distinguishes consonances from dissonances. While he does not define precisely what the term "comprehensibility" means, he asserts that it is determined by use alone; as dissonant harmonies become familiar, they cease to sound dissonant and can be used similarly to consonant harmonies. With the emancipation of dissonance, dissonances and consonances become equally comprehensible.[6]

For Schoenberg, emancipation of dissonance characterizes a style which "treats dissonances like consonances and renounces a tonal center."[7] Compositions in this style, first written around 1908, differ from earlier music in their harmonic and motivic procedures and their extreme brevity—a feature resulting from the nature of these procedures. In tonal compositions, harmony serves to generate extended forms, but in the new atonal method equally developed forms "could scarcely be assured with chords whose constructive values had not as yet been explored."[8] For this reason, it was impossible to compose pieces of complicated organization or of great length.

According to Schoenberg's own account, after many unsuccessful attempts over a period of twelve years he formulated a new compositional procedure to replace the structural differentiations formerly provided by tonal harmony.[9] His new procedure, "Method of Composing with Twelve Tones Which Are Related Only with One Another," is based on repeated use of what he calls a basic set, a specific ordering of all twelve tones of the chromatic scale. The basic set is not a chromatic scale because it consists of varying intervals. However, it does function in twelve-tone music the way the tonal scale functions in tonal music: it is the source of all melodic and harmonic figurations. According to Schoenberg, ordering of pitch classes determines both harmonies and their succession with a regularity comparable to that of tonal harmony. Because the basic set also functions as a motive, every piece requires a new basic set. A basic set is not a motive in precisely the tonal sense, for it fulfills a motivic function independently of such features as rhythm and phrasing. For this reason, Schoenberg claims that it makes little difference whether at the beginning of a composition the set appears as a linear melody or occurs in a more complicated or concealed fashion.[10]

In describing the basic set Schoenberg repeatedly stresses two points. First, all of its pitches function similarly and should be equally emphasized. Any procedure which emphasizes individual pitches, such as doubling, should be avoided. Although elements of a basic set "appear separate and independent to the eye and ear, they reveal their true meaning only through their cooperation," that is, through their specific intervallic relation to adjacent pitches.[11] Thus, the most important feature of a basic set is not its pitch content or ordering, but its specific succession of intervals, a succession determined by the initial ordering of its pitches.

The second point Schoenberg stresses evolves directly from his emphasis upon the intervallic succession of the basic set. He asserts that the "two-or-more dimensional space in which musical ideas are presented is a unit" and stresses that every element of a musical idea occurs in a unified musical space.[12] A musical event, regardless of whether it occurs in the vertical or horizontal dimension, can function simultaneously in the other dimension and affect all events occurring in the other dimension. Thus, each melodic event possesses harmonic implications, and each harmonic event similarly retains a melodic identity. "A musical idea,... though consisting of melody, rhythm, and harmony, is neither the one nor the other alone, but all three together.... The mutual relation of tones regulates the succession of intervals as well as their association into harmonies; the rhythm regulates the succession of tones as well as the succession of harmonies and organizes phrasing."[13] Schoenberg's unitary conception of musical space allows linear unfolding of a basic set to be regarded as identical to simultaneous sounding of the entire set; it allows simultaneous independent development of multiple harmonic and melodic ideas, and it allows the internal ordering of the pitches. The interaction of associated vertical and horizontal dimensions "explains why... a basic set of twelve tones (BS) can be used in either dimension, as a whole or in parts."[14] Schoenberg's notion of "dimension," which at first may appear to be metaphysical or to have a geometrical analogy, will prove to have concrete musical meaning and will become clearer as the musical examples are discussed.

Related to the concept of a multidimensional musical space is Schoenberg's view that the unity of musical space demands an absolute and unitary perception.

> In this space... there is no absolute down, no right or left, forward or backward. Every musical configuration, every movement of tones has to be comprehended primarily as a mutual relation of sounds, of oscillatory vibrations, appearing at different places and times.[15]

Just as we recognize physical objects from any perspective and can reproduce them in our imagination in every possible position, the composer comprehends the unique qualities of a musical idea regardless of the direction or planes in which they appear. According to Schoenberg, the unity of musical space is a feature that has been exploited by many tonal composers, and this explains, for example, why in the seventeenth and eighteenth centuries fugue subjects frequently appeared in their inverted or retrograde forms. The principle of the "unitary perception of musical space" allows Schoenberg to use retrogression, inversion and retrograde inversion of the basic set without destroying its motivic identity.[16]

To appreciate the uniqueness of Schoenberg's new compositional method we must clearly understand what constitutes a basic set and a legitimate twelve-tone harmony. In formulating the concept of the basic set, Schoenberg consistently describes it as a succession of intervals rather than as a series of individual pitches. He stresses that each tone does not function independently since each "appears always in the neighborhood of two other tones," that is, each functions only in relation to its adjacent pitches.[17] (Because the first and last pitches are associated only with one adjacent pitch, Schoenberg uses special techniques for handling these harmonies; these techniques are discussed in Chapters 2 and 3.) He makes clear that he has included all twelve pitches in the basic set so that no single pitch is repeated more frequently than any other and all pitches are equally emphasized. In naming his new technique "Method of Composing with Twelve Tones Which Are Related Only with One Another," Schoenberg indicates that the twelve tones are mutually dependent and, most important, that they are perceived primarily in terms of each other. Since he thus regarded the basic set as a series of intervals with every pitch necessarily associated with at least two others, it is misleading, with respect to Schoenberg, to define the basic set as a series of twelve ordered pitch-classes. Rather, it is a group of *harmonies,* set forth by a series of twelve ordered pitch-classes, each containing at least two successive intervals (that is, three pitch-classes) of the basic set. As I shall demonstrate, this notion of intervallically defined harmony can be extended to refer to the *total* intervallic content of harmonies of the basic set.

According to Schoenberg, listeners will recognize a twelve-tone harmony regardless of the ordering of its pitches. Because musical ideas are recognizable in inverted and retrograde forms, the identity of a musical idea is determined by the absolute relation of its elements, that is, by its intervallic content and not primarily by the ordering of its pitches.[18] Schoenberg also implies that while the pitches of the basic set must maintain their normal ordering, the harmonies of the basic set are not similarly restricted. In discussing several examples from the Suite op. 25, each of which partitions the basic set into three tetrachords with the third tetrachord appearing before the second, he states

> In [the Gavotte and Intermezzo]... a group of the tones appears too soon—9-12 in the left hand comes before 5-8. This deviation from the order is an irregularity which can be justified in two ways. The first of these has been mentioned previously: as the Gavotte is the second movement, the set has already become familiar. The second justification is provided by the subdivision of the basic set into three groups of four tones. No change occurs within any one of these groups; otherwise, they are treated like independent small sets.[19]

In other words, the harmonies of the basic set do not have to occur in the order in which they appear in the basic set, but can function independently.

To summarize, the basic set consists primarily of a group of harmonies; these harmonies are identified primarily by their *total* intervallic content and not merely by the ordering of their pitches; and they can function as unordered, independent small sets.

A final property of the basic set is that the harmonies which define it need not be restricted to a fixed pitch-class content. Theoretical writings on Schoenberg's twelve-tone composition have not recognized this property and have therefore failed to fully comprehend his method of unifying harmonic structure. Although Schoenberg never discussed this property explicitly, it is implicit in his lecture "Composition with Twelve Tones" in three ways: in the musical examples, in his discussion of how harmony functions, and in his description of how his harmonic procedures are related to tonal harmonic procedures. To show that Schoenberg does not restrict the harmonies of the basic set to a fixed pitch-class content, I shall take up the latter two of these issues first and then show how his examples bear out my conclusions.

As Schoenberg defined it, a twelve-tone harmony differs from a tonal harmony in two ways. First, unlike a tonal harmony it has no conventionally determined intervallic structure; its structure is determined only by the succession of intervals in the basic set. This succession is made up anew for each composition. Second, twelve-tone harmonies need not be simultaneous, that is, occur only in the vertical dimension. In Schoenberg's conception of space in two-or-more dimensions no differentiation exists between the vertical and horizontal dimensions.

> I... arrived at the concept whereby the vertical and the horizontal, harmonic and melodic, the simultaneous and the successive were all in reality comprised within one unified space. It followed from this that whatever occurs at one point in that space, occurs not only there but in every dimensional aspect of the spatial continuum....[20]

Harmonies are no longer defined primarily by vertical configurations but rather by pitches occupying any similar dimension of the "spatial continuum." These dimensions are delineated primarily through rhythmic association: "The rhythm regulates the succession of tones as well as the succession of harmonies...."[21] Thus, musical ideas are delineated by rhythmic association and are considered harmonies regardless of whether they unfold vertically or horizontally.

Schoenberg's descriptions of his own compositions consistently reflect that fact that "harmony" pertains to both horizontal and vertical dimensions. It follows that what he meant by the term "harmony" depends upon which compositional style he was referring to. A comparison will make this distinction clear. Describing tonal compositions in "Composition with Twelve Tones," he states that pitches function in one of two ways: either thematically or harmonically.[22] In this context, he clearly associates the concept of harmony with the vertical dimension. However, in discussing twelve-tone composition he differentiates, not between melody and harmony, but between melody and accompaniment, and refers to the "separate selection of the tones for their respective formal function, melody or accompaniment."[23] In his list of the four possible types of accompaniment, only the first represents a "harmony" in the strict tonal sense, that is, as a vertically defined structure:

> [In deriving themes] not every tone of a set be [that is, is] employed in the melody or in the principal voice, but only some of them... In all these cases the remaining tones, not employed in the melody, can be used in the following manners [:]
> 1st   they are concentrated to form chords
> 2nd   they form coordinate or subordinate voices of contrapuntal importance
> 3rd   they form subordinate voices of only local importance and
> 4th   accompanying voices and accompanying figures, etc.[24]

Thus, Schoenberg's use of the term "harmony" in differentiating between the primary function of tones in a tonal and a twelve-tone context indicates that an important difference between a twelve-tone harmony and a tonal harmony is that the former is not defined by its vertical structure, nor regarded exclusively as a simultaneity.[25]

Before analyzing Schoenberg's musical examples and showing why harmonies of the basic set cannot be restricted to their original pitch-class content, I must develop two remaining points. First, Schoenberg asserted not only that a harmonic event could occur in any dimension, but that a single event necessarily affects *more* than one dimension:

> [A]ny particular melodic motion—for instance, a chromatic step—will not only have its effect upon the harmony, but on *everything* subsequent that is comprised within that spatial continuum. This circumstance... enables the composer to assign one part of his thinking to... the vertical, and another in the horizontal domain.[26]

More important, he implies that because it is impossible for a musical idea to affect only a single dimension, a complete musical texture necessarily contains two or more dimensions:

> A musical idea... though consisting of melody, rhythm, and harmony, is neither the one nor the other alone, but all three together. The elements of a musical idea are partly incorporated in the horizontal plane as successive sounds, and partly in the vertical plane as simultaneous sounds.[27]

Second, he maintains that his method of twelve-tone composition regulates harmonies and their successions with a precision comparable to the regularity and logic of tonal harmony,[28] that the method is capable of sustaining equally complex formal structures,[29] and that through the basic set *all* aspects of the composition are integrated.

> From the [basic] set are built the themes, the motives, the phrases, figures, voices and harmonies of a composition...[30]

He repeatedly emphasizes that the main advantage of his method is the unity it produces because all aspects of the composition are derived from one source, the basic set.[31]

I shall briefly summarize the principal points developed in the preceding discussion.

1. The basic set is best described not as a group of twelve ordered pitch-classes, but as a group of harmonies determined by an ordered set, each containing at least two adjacent intervals.
2. The harmonies of the basic set are identified primarily by their *total* intervallic content and not by the ordering of their pitches.
3. The harmonies of the basic set can function as unordered, independent small sets.
4. "Harmony" in a twelve-tone context does not necessarily imply a simultaneity or the vertical dimension.

5. All musical ideas represent "harmonies"—regardless of whether they unfold vertically or horizontally.
6. All musical ideas, that is, harmonic events, affect more than one dimension; a complete musical texture normally consists of more than one simultaneous dimension.
7. The harmonic structure of a twelve-tone composition is totally unified because every feature is derived from a single source, the basic set.

If we examine these points closely they lead, as we shall see, to an apparent contradiction. This contradiction, in turn, can be resolved only if we assume Schoenberg did not intend the harmonies of the basic set to be restricted to a specific pitch-class content.

If the harmonies of the basic set are restricted to the specific pitches from which they are initially derived, and if the ordering of pitches in the basic set determines only the constituent harmonies and not the succession of these harmonies, then the basic set can control at most only one dimension of harmonic structure. Two of Schoenberg's assertions contradict this conclusion: the first is that his compositions project a multidimensional harmonic structure, and the second is that all harmonic dimensions are derived from and integrated by a single basic set. If, however, any harmony of a basic set is restricted only to a specific intervallic content, and not to a fixed pitch-class content (as Schoenberg strongly implies), no contradiction arises.

To verify this argument I shall analyze several of the musical examples provided by Schoenberg in both "Composition" and "Vortrag" and show how he uses a single basic set to integrate a multidimensional harmonic structure. In delineating the harmonic segments of these examples, I adhere to Schoenberg's conception of a twelve-tone harmony: that it consist of at least two successive intervals of the basic set; that the ordering of its pitches does not have to adhere to the ordering of the basic set; that it can occur in either the vertical or horizontal dimension; that it is delineated by rhythmic or registral association, or by functional similarity (melody or accompaniment); and that it overlaps and occurs simultaneously with other harmonic events. His examples in fact confirm that an important premise of his compositional method is that the harmonies of the basic set are defined primarily by their total interval-class (ic) content and are not limited to a specific pitch-class (pc) content.

I begin by discussing how the harmonies of the basic set are derived. As previously explained, a twelve-tone harmony must consist of at least three pitch-classes; consequently, any segment containing only two pitch-classes is not considered a harmony of the basic set. Moreover, a harmony cannot contain more than nine pitch-classes because, according to Schoenberg, all segments (or partitioned segments as they are often called in current usage) project harmonies of the basic set. That is, if the basic set were partitioned into two segments, the first containing ten pitch-classes and the second containing two, the second segment, according to Schoenberg, would not represent a legitimate harmony. An examination of Schoenberg's twelve-tone works shows, in fact, that if a harmony appears to contain only two pitch-classes, it is almost always extended or associated with at least one other harmony usually containing two pitch-classes. (For example, while a row partitioned into dyads often occurs, these dyads almost always appear in pairs.) Thus, any segment containing from three to nine contiguous pitch-classes represents a harmony of the basic set.

In addition, the complements of each linear segment of the basic set themselves represent harmonies of the basic set. These complements contain all the pitch classes not appearing in the original linear segment. This conclusion follows from Schoenberg's statement that pitches of the basic set function within one of two principal harmonic dimensions, either as part of the melody or as part of the accompaniment. Since any linear segment of the row can be used as the principal voice, the accompaniment always contains the complementary set, a set frequently composed of two nonadjacent linear segments—that is, a nonlinear segment.[32] Thus, because complementary sets of the basic set delineate the two principal harmonic dimensions, the harmonies of the basic set include all linear segments and their complements.

In addition, two recurring compositional procedures indicate that Schoenberg regarded complementary sets as legitimate harmonies of the basic set. The first involves the simultaneous presentation of the inversion and retrograde inversion of the basic set. Referring to Example 1.1,[33] Schoenberg states "you can... see in what manner the accompaniment is constructed by the same [basic] set as the melody; Always from these tones [that is, pitches], which [the] melody has not yet used or which it has already leaved [that is, left]."[34] Notice that as both permutations (I and RI) simultaneously unfold, the unfolding vertical harmonies project nonlinear complements of linear segments (mm. 1-3). (See the Glossary for the explanation of pc "set-names" and the labelling of "complements.") Thus, Schoenberg controls the harmonic structure of two *horizontal* dimensions (I and RI) by the regular ordering of the basic set and structures the vertical dimension primarily with complement-related sets.

The second of Schoenberg's techniques that shows he viewed complementary segments as harmonies of the basic set involves the reordering of the basic set by rotating its partitioned segments, a technique which breaks up linear segments and replaces them with their complements. For example, in "Composition with Twelve Tones" Schoenberg gives one example from op. 26 showing the rotation of hexachordal segments.[35] (See Example 1.2.) The

10 Twelve-Tone Harmony

Example 1.1 Wind Quintet, op. 26, Scherzo

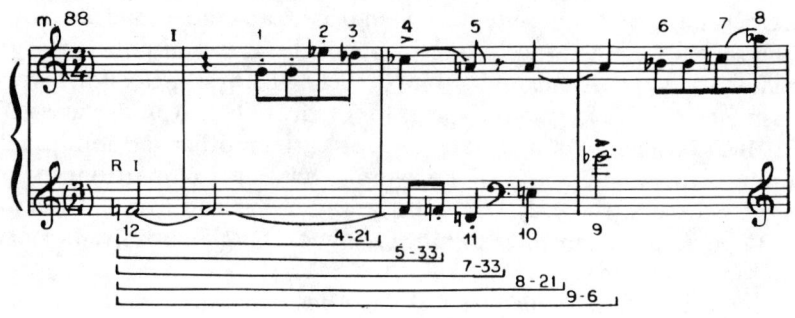

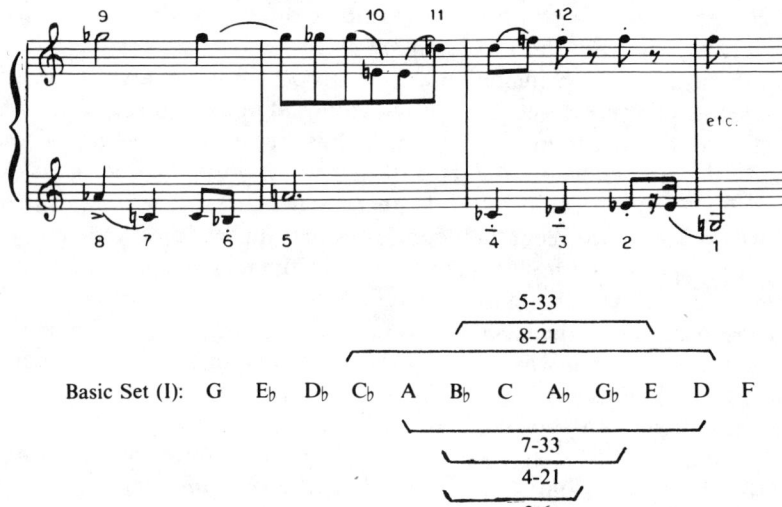

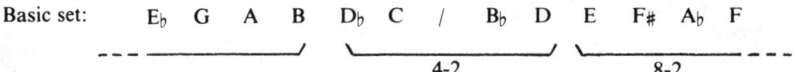

Example 1.2 Wind Quintet, op. 26

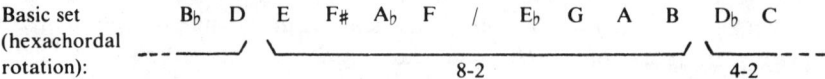

regular ordering of the basic set, for example, contains pc set 4-2 as a linear segment (order numbers 5-8) and pc set 8-2 as its nonlinear complement. Hexachordal rotation reverses this relationship: pc set 8-2 becomes a linear segment and pc set 4-2 represents its nonlinear complement. Because Schoenberg states there should only be one basic set for each composition, it is doubtful he would alter the original ordering had he not believed the most essential feature of the basic set, its harmonies, remained unchanged.

Example 1.3

pc set	ic vector
4-z15	[111111]
8-z15	[555553]

A final reason to regard complement-related sets as harmonies of the basic set is more theoretical and pertains to Schoenberg's twelve-tone and atonal compositional method. If one compares, for example, the interval vectors of the two complementary sets 4-z15 and 8-z15, one finds that each entry in the interval-class vector of 8-z15, with the exception of ic6, is larger by exactly 4 than the corresponding entry in the ic vector of 4-z15 (Example 1.3). The arithmetic difference between corresponding vector entries is equivalent to the difference in the size of the sets, with the exception of the entry for ic6. Since ic6 represents its own inverse, the difference between its corresponding ic entries is half of the difference between remaining corresponding ic entries. This invariant correspondence between ic vectors is a general property of all complement-related pc sets.[36] "In view of this intervallic proportionality it seems reasonable to regard the complement of a set as a reduced or enlarged replica of that set," a feature which justifies on compositional and theoretical grounds the association of complement-related sets.[37]

I shall now show how Schoenberg uses the harmonies of the basic set to integrate two-or-more simultaneous dimensions of harmonic structure. While only about half of the musical examples appearing in "Composition with Twelve Tones" are to be discussed here, the compositional techniques they illustrate are characteristic of the entire group of examples.

Schoenberg describes two methods of deriving themes from the basic set; the first makes use of pitches representing a linear segment, and the second includes pitches representing a nonlinear segment.[38] Though he gives an example of the second method, he states, "I cannot demonstrate through an example, because the explanation would be too complex."[39] In other words, Schoenberg says the second, more complicated technique is not obvious from the example alone, but is at the same time too complex to explain. An analysis of this example (Example 1.4), however, seems not impossible and may clarify the nature of this technique.

12   Twelve-Tone Harmony

Example 1.4 Wind Quintet, op. 26, Andante

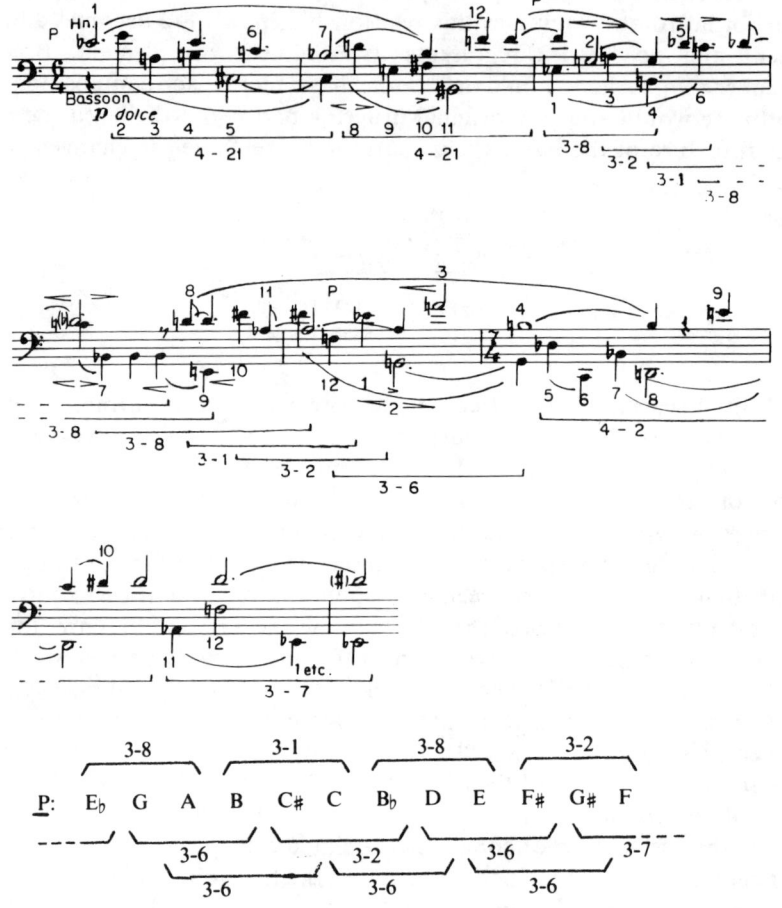

Example 1.4 contains the opening bars of the Andante (3rd movement) of the Wind Quintet op. 26.[40] It consists of three repetitions of a single row form displaying at least three discrete dimensions of harmonic structure; the first dimension displays all the harmonies of the basic set (P) with their original pitch-class content, and the second and third display harmonies *equivalent* to those formed linearly in the ordered set, but here comprised of nonadjacent pitches. (In this chapter and those following, two pc sets are termed "equivalent" if they are related by transposition or inversion followed by transposition, but do *not* contain identical pitch-classes.) The first dimension arises naturally from the regular ordering of P. The second and third

dimensions are set forth by two distinct voices (horn and bassoon). These two harmonic dimensions (that is, voices) are further delineated by separate stemming, rhythmic and registral association, orchestration and motive function (melody and accompaniment). Both voices contain successive pitch-classes that are nonadjacent in the basic set. The upper voice (horn), consisting of exactly twelve pitches, spans all three row forms and contains every order number of the basic set. Consequently, it duplicates the ic content and pc content of the entire basic set. In describing this example, Schoenberg claims that "There is a definite regularity in the distribution of tones," a rather vague assertion which suggests that the pitches within each voice have not been randomly extracted from P.[41] If one analyzes the harmonic structure of the nonlinear segments in the lower voice, one discovers that they also do indeed follow a "definite regularity."

The first two harmonic sets of the bassoon (clearly indicated by phrase markings) represent linear segments and both project pc set 4-21. After this point, nonadjacent pitch-classes are associated until the next linear segment in m.6 (pc set 4-2). Examination of the nonlinear segments shows a pattern of eight overlapping trichords; only four different trichords are represented and each occurs as a linear segment of P. Notice that because each trichord in the lower voice contains nonadjacent pitches of P, each contains different pitches from those appearing within the corresponding linear segment of P. Thus, each nonlinear trichord is regarded as *equivalent* but not identical to its corresponding linear occurrence within the basic set. One remaining nonlinear segment occurs in m.7 (pc set 3-7) and again projects a trichord representing a harmony of the basic set. In this case, the harmony is complementary to a linear segment of P (pc set 9-7, order numbers 2-10). (The equivalent trichords are indicated by set names on both the musical example and the basic set.) Thus, this harmonic dimension relates to the basic set through equivalent harmonies, harmonies defined not by pitch-class content but primarily by total interval-class content.[42] This example clearly shows how Schoenberg uses the basic set to effectively integrate three simultaneous dimensions of harmonic structure: one dimension displayed by the ordered presentation of P, and the second and third projected by two discrete voices and structured by harmonies equivalent to linear segments of the basic set.

In the examples containing only single row forms, Schoenberg repeatedly uses this technique of constructing discrete voices containing nonsuccessive order numbers whose partitioned segments project sets equivalent to those appearing in the basic set. To show the various ways he applies this technique, two further examples have been included. Both examples represent variations of the theme in Variations for Orchestra op. 31.[43] The first example (Example 1.5) again demonstrates how Schoenberg constructs segments of discrete voices composed of nonadjacent order numbers to present successive

14   Twelve-Tone Harmony

Example 1.5   Variations for Orchestra, op. 31, Var. VI

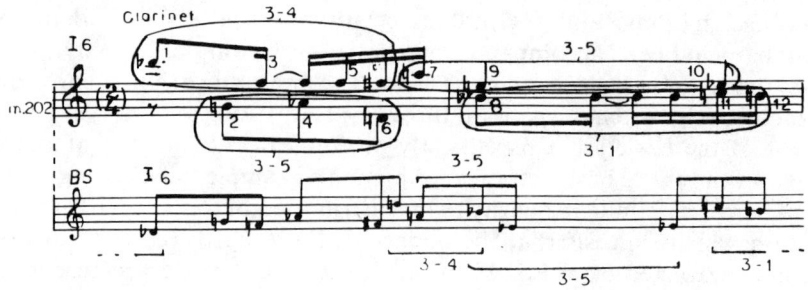

trichords equivalent to those of the basic set. The rhythmic pattern clearly partitions two trichordal segments in the lower voice (pc sets 3-5 and 3-1), both of which occur as linear segments of P. Similarly, the harmonic segments of the upper voice consist of trichords equivalent to linear segments of P, pc sets 3-4 and 3-5. Thus, because both voices are composed of trichordal harmonic segments equivalent to those appearing in the basic set, the basic set effectively integrates all dimensions of harmonic structure.

Example 1.6   Variations for Orchestra, op. 31, Var. VI

The second example (Example 1.6) shows a pair of complement-related sets integrating a multi-dimensional harmonic structure of a single row configuration. These sets contain nonadjacent pitches but again are equivalent to linear segments of the basic set. Similarly to the previous example, there are three overlapping dimensions of harmonic structure; the first is delineated by the regular ordering of the basic set, and the second and third are marked by two independent voices set forth by distinct rhythms and registers. The pitch-class content of the lower voice is 4-z15 (order numbers 2, 4, 6, 9), a set which occurs as a linear segment of the basic set (order numbers 8-11), and the pitch-class content of the upper voice is 8-z15, the non-linear complement of 4-z15.

Thus, in each of the previous three examples the harmonies of the basic set integrate three simultaneous dimensions of harmonic structure. While each example displays a slightly different method of structuring the harmonic dimensions composed of nonlinear segments (overlapping sets, successive sets, complement-related sets), the general procedure is essentially the same. These examples clearly show, then, that within single row configurations Schoenberg does not restrict the harmonies of the basic set to their original pitch-class content, but associates them on the basis of their total intervallic content. Notice, further, that equivalent sets need not set forth the same succession of intervals; for example, the interval-class succession in the linear row segment 4-z15 is 1-6-2 (measured in semitones), while in the nonlinear presentation it is 6-1-3 (Example 1.6).

Example 1.7 Suite, op. 25, Intermezzo

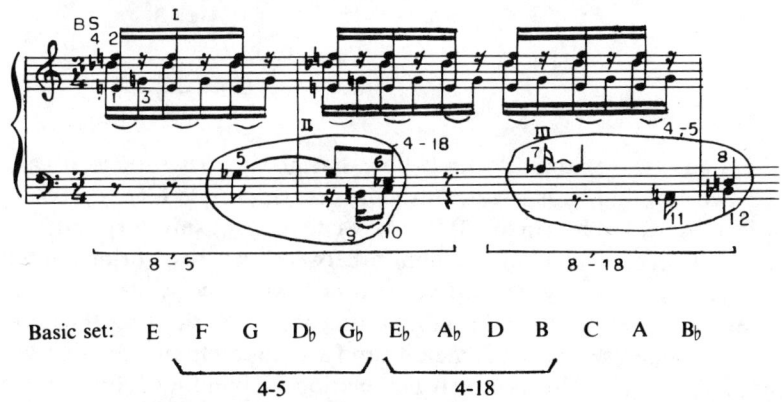

Example 1.7 contains the opening bars of the Intermezzo from the Suite op. 25 and has been mentioned previously in reference to the use of partitioned segments as independent small sets (see p. 5). Schoenberg claims that the presentation of tetrachord III (order numbers 9-12) before the completion of tetrachord II (order numbers 5-8) is justified because the basic set has already become familiar and because partitioned segments sometimes function independently.[44] The question arises as to what conditions might allow independent usage of this type. If one examines the harmonies projected by the simultaneous occurrence of tetrachords II and III, it becomes apparent that by associating order numbers 5, 6, 9 and 10 and order numbers 7, 8, 11 and 12, Schoenberg creates a new integrated dimension of harmonic structure. Notice that the harmonic tetrachords 4-18 and 4-5 represent linear segments of the basic set, and that the entire harmonic structure, associating elements from all three tetrachords, projects their complement-related sets 8-18 and 8-5. This example differs from previous ones in that the separate voices contain adjacent rather than nonadjacent elements of the basic set. The formation of pc sets equivalent to linear segments of the basic set by the association of nonadjacent elements from three ordered segments creates a multidimensional, integrated harmonic structure.

16 Twelve-Tone Harmony

Example 1.8 Variations for Orchestra, op. 31, Theme

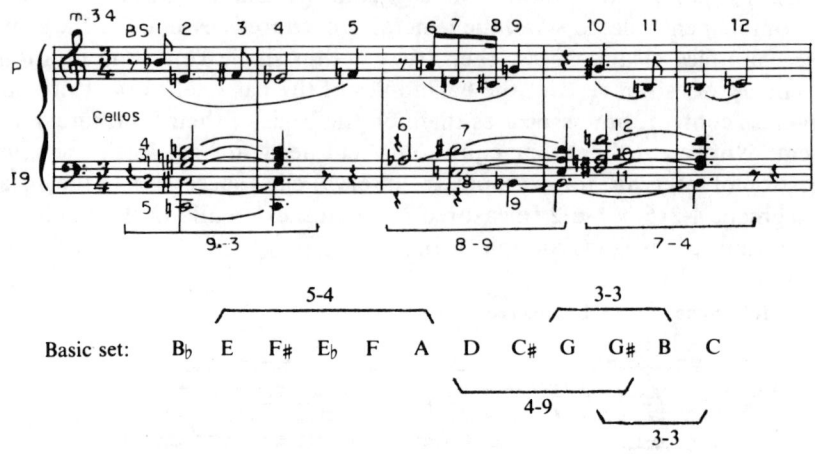

The final two examples show how harmonic structure is organized between two simultaneous row forms. The first (Example 1.8), the Theme of the Variations for Orchestra op. 31, shows Schoenberg using harmonies of the basic set to organize harmonic structure between two row forms related by inversion (P, I_9).[45] The regular ordering of the basic set controls the harmonic structure of the melody (P) and accompaniment (I_9). Notice how the first two partitioned segments of *both* the melody and accompaniment contain five and four pcs, respectively. This symmetrical relation is abandoned, however, with the final partitioning: the final segment of P contains three pcs and the final segment of I_9 contains four pcs. The vertical harmonic sets (9-3, 8-9, 7-4) indicate the reason for this change; each is equivalent to a complement of a linear segment of P and thus represents a harmony of the basic set. If the final segment of I_9 had contained three pcs, similar to P, the vertical harmony of the third phrase would not have represented a harmony of the basic set. Thus, Schoenberg disrupts the identical partitioning of two simultaneous row forms in order to integrate the vertical and horizontal harmonic dimensions by harmonies of the basic set.

The final example (Example 1.9) shows the opening measures of the Suite op. 25 Prelude and contains a use of tetrachordal segments similar to that which appeared in Example 1.7.[46] In addition, the association of tetrachordal segments from two row forms related by transposition (P, P_6) further integrates the harmonic structure. The imitative entrance of the lower voice is delayed until its initial dyad forms a harmony of the basic set with the upper voice (pc set 4-12); a similar vertical formation occurs with its second dyad (pc set 4-z15). The second phrase, similar to Example 1.7, associates tetrachords

Example 1.9 Suite, op. 25, Prelude

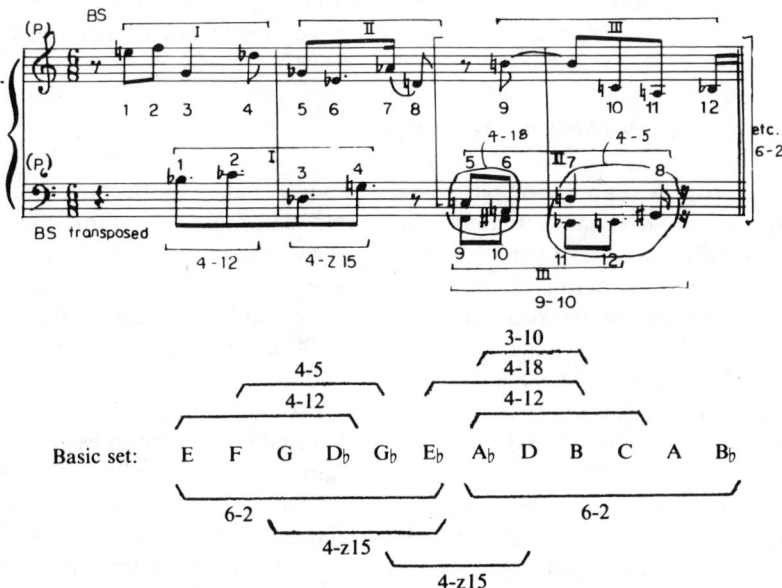

II and III from P_6, creating the vertical harmonies 4-5 and 4-18, a clear indication that this association is not unintentional. This is an excellent example to illustrate how Schoenberg usually avoids using dyads as independent structural units, but combines them with other partitioned segments (see p. 9). In addition, tetrachordal segments harmonically join both row forms by the formation of pc sets 9-10 and 6-2, the principal hexachord of the basic set. Notice how the formation of 9-10 excludes the final pitch of the upper voice (P), a segmentation justified by the rhythmic design and by the simultaneous use of B_b (order number 12) as the initial pitch-class of the following permutation. In comparison to the first phrase, the second contains two added dimensions of harmonic structure delineated by the registral formation of pc sets 4-18, 4-5 and 9-10. This example is particularly interesting for two reasons: first, the formation of vertical harmonies containing noncontiguous elements controls the rhythmic structure and entrance of an imitative voice, and second, it shows how an increase in the number of independent voices is complemented by an increase in the number of integrated harmonic dimensions.

The previous examples show how Schoenberg uses harmonies of the basic set to integrate all dimensions of harmonic structure. By expanding the definition of harmony to include nonsimultaneous events occurring in both horizontal and vertical dimensions, by allowing harmonic events to overlap,

18   Twelve-Tone Harmony

and by identifying the relating harmonies primarily by total intervallic content, Schoenberg legitimately asserts that his twelve-tone compositions are totally integrated, because every feature is derived from a single source, the basic set.[47]

Past Views of Twelve-Tone Harmony

In his lecture "Composition with Twelve Tones," Schoenberg made one claim for his method that has seemed to many composers and critics unjustified: that not only the melodies of his music were derived from the basic set, but that also, in his words, "something different and more important is derived from it with a regularity comparable to the regularity and logic of the earlier [tonal] harmony."[48] And he goes on to claim, "The association of tones into harmonies and their successions is regulated (as will be shown later) by the order of [the pitches of the basic set]."[49] The problem is that Schoenberg never really showed later how the basic set regulates harmonies and their successions, and what we might call "the harmonic problem" remains as the major problem in the theory of twelve-tone music. The common view now maintains that while the tonal system orders and integrates both horizontal and vertical dimensions of a composition, the twelve-tone system can order only a single dimension and consequently, in itself, cannot produce an integrated musical texture. In this view, Schoenberg's twelve-tone compositions contain many harmonic events unrelated to the basic set and therefore fail to justify his claim that the twelve-tone row provided a method for determining both harmonies and their successions—a method comparable to that of tonal harmony.[50]

In order to reveal the important misconceptions that arise from an incorrect understanding of Schoenberg's concept of a basic set and a twelve-tone harmony, I need to characterize more fully the common view I seek to controvert. One of the best representatives of this view is George Perle, author of the valuable and widely used textbook *Serial Composition and Atonality*.[51] I will briefly argue that because Perle does not understand the essential nature of a twelve-tone harmony or of the basic set, he is forced to conclude that it is "impossible to formulate in a simple rigorous manner...[how the twelve-tone] relations of a given context may be described as based on a twelve-tone set" (p. 2). In addition, one example discussed by both Perle and Schoenberg will be analyzed to show that Perle's failure results directly from restricting the harmonies of the basic set to a specific pitch-class content.

Perle considers the set to be "for harmonic purposes, a collection of segments of specified but unordered content" (p. 96). It is clear from his discussion that the "specified content" refers to pitch-class content, and thus he regards the basic set as a group of twelve ordered pitch-classes. It follows that when a melodic idea contains nonadjacent elements it has no relation to the linear structure of the basic set, and in such a case the basic set "is no longer recognizable as a serial structure" (p. 69). Moreover, he ignores Schoenberg's stipulation that harmonies must consist of at least two intervals and that its elements are freely ordered, and argues that a harmonic formation (simultaneity) consisting of two adjacent pitch-classes is most closely related to the basic set since the original pitch-class adjacencies are maintained. As the size of the simultaneity increases therefore, it will have progressively less relation to the basic set. A simultaneity containing twelve pitch-classes, he concludes, has no relation to the basic set since it could represent a verticalization of any set (pp. 86-87). Perle's conclusion however, denies Schoenberg's premise of an absolute and unitary perception of musical space. Perle goes wrong by assuming, despite Schoenberg's description of a twelve-tone harmony, that a harmony of the basic set is defined by pitch-class content and is more legitimate if the ordering of pitch-classes is maintained.

Perle is aware that there are many simultaneities comprised of nonadjacent elements of the basic set in a twelve-tone composition. But because he considers only vertical simultaneities as harmonies and recognizes only one determinant of simultaneity—"that elements which are adjacent to each other in a set may be vertically combined" (p. 85)—he can neither delineate an harmonic event nor account for most simultaneities containing nonadjacent elements. He explains the latter problem by a critique of the whole method: "the inadequacy of the verticalization of linear adjacencies as a method of harmonic ordering" is a result of the "haphazard and fortuitous adjacency relationships generated by the general set" (pp. 109-110). Schoenberg's basic sets offer too many harmonic possibilities, he implies, and he querulously concludes that the linear adjacencies of the set should appear in a more "coherent, systematic arrangement" (p. 109). The problem becomes more acute when he discusses the harmonic structure of a texture containing two simultaneous row forms. The problem of harmonies containing nonadjacent elements is increased with the simultaneous employment of two permutations, he argues, and this problem arises from the "absence of a precompositional standard of harmonic reference" (p. 99). Perle's argument shows that unless harmonic events are considered in multidimensional space, Schoenberg's compositions will necessarily seem random and unintegrated.

Perle's original misconception has serious consequences concerning even the most simple twelve-tone operations. In his discussion of cyclical rotation, for example, he analyzes an example (Example 1.10) discussed by Schoenberg in "Composition with Twelve-Tones." It contains six forms of the theme (P) of the Rondo from the Wind Quintet op. 26: a)P, b)RP, c)RP with hexachordal rotation, d)RP, e)RI with hexachordal rotation. Perle maintains that "thematic statements of the set may be modified by means of cyclical

20 Twelve-Tone Harmony

Example 1.10 Wind Quintet, op. 26, Rondo

permutations" (p. 64), an operation which produces "an approximate transposition of the theme originally derived from the set" (p. 65). He concludes that Schoenberg's use of this technique proves that thematic character resides "primarily in the rhythmic configuration of the thematic set" (p. 64).

Concerning this same example Schoenberg says:

> [T]he principal theme... shows a new way of varying the repetitions of a theme.... While rhythm and phrasing significantly preserve the character of the theme so that it can easily be recognized, the tones and intervals are changed through a different use of the [basic set]...[52]

Twelve-Tone Harmony   21

In "Vortrag / 12 T K / Princeton," which appeared after Perle's book, Schoenberg's comments are more extensive:

> This example shows 5 different forms of one and the same theme.... The rhythm, the character and the construction of the phrases are here not very much varied. But the intervals are new, and not only regarding the size, but also regarding direction. Very new and interesting variations of the theme [arise] by this method.... But don't think that these variations can be got in a mechanical way. On no account: forced to invent the theme every time anew[,] you will find it necessary to devote some delicacy and not less fancy to such a purpose.[53]

According to Schoenberg, the example shows five different forms of *one and the same theme*, while for Perle it contains *approximate transpositions of the theme*. What Perle means by "approximate transpositions," is perhaps not entirely clear, but Schoenberg's description clearly does not indicate that any transposition has occurred. The reasons for these varying descriptions become clear if we examine the harmonic structure of the basic set.

Example 1.11   Wind Quintet, op. 26

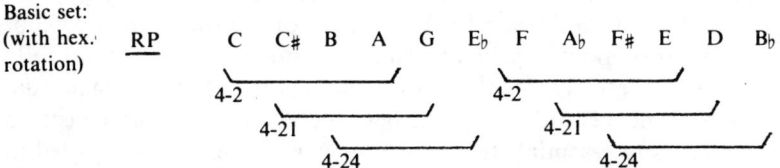

The basic set for op. 26 contains a similar, but not identical, interval succession in both hexachordal segments; the first four intervals of both hexachords are identical and the final interval differs. In addition, both hexachords contain an identical succession of overlapping equivalent tetrachords, 4-24, 4-21, 4-2. The cyclical rotation of hexachordal segments therefore maintains the same succession of tetrachords within the basic set. (See Example 1.11.) Moreover, since complement-related sets are considered harmonies of the basic set, the rotation of hexachords does not change any of the harmonies of the basic set. Thus, Schoenberg is justified in saying both

22 Twelve-Tone Harmony

forms represent one and the same theme because 1) both project an identical tetrachordal pattern which spans the entire basic set, and 2) both contain identical harmonies.

Example 1.12 Wind Quintet, op. 26

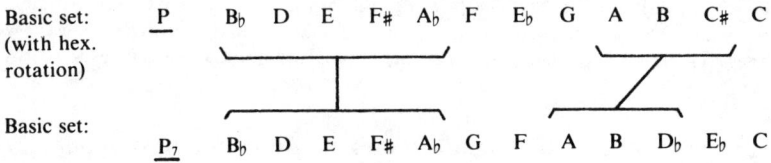

Perle describes the rotated basic set as an "approximate transposition" most likely because of the invariant ordered segments (order numbers 1-5, 8-10) that occur between the rotated basic set and a transposition of the basic set (P_7). (See Example 1.12.) Again, Perle's misconception of the basic set as a group of twelve ordered pitch-classes whose harmonies are restricted to their original pc content together with its corollary, his failure to accept complement-related sets containing nonadjacent elements as harmonies, prevents him from recognizing the essential similarity between the basic set and its rotated form. In this particular case, the similarity is emphasized by the identical tetachordal structure of both hexachords.

Failure to recognize the structural similarity between the basic set and its rotated form causes Perle to overemphasize surface features such as phrasing and rhythm. He goes so far as to argue that Schoenberg's use of cyclical permutations *proves* that thematic character resides "*primarily* in the rhythmic configuration of the thematic set" (p. 64). While Schoenberg agrees that rhythm and phrasing preserve the character of the theme, he does not suggest that rhythm defines its primary features. Schoenberg has rhythmically partitioned the set into dyads, thus accentuating the similar tetrachordal structure of both hexachords. Rhythm here merely serves to emphasize a preexisting and more essential structural property. Perle, however, is led to the following erroneous generalization: "The *theme* of a twelve-tone work ... is not in general characterized by its intervallic structure but by attributes that formerly performed a subsidiary, though essential, role: rhythm, texture, dynamics, color, shape" (p. 126).

Perhaps we can now understand what Schoenberg means in the passage quoted above (p. 21) when he says, "But don't think that these variations can be got in a mechanical way." In this example rotation of a segment containing two, three, four, or five pcs would not have preserved any harmonic pattern appearing in the original basic set and consequently would not have allowed Schoenberg to treat both forms "as one and the same theme."

Perle's failure to clearly define twelve-tone harmony and to understand the essential features of a basic set is typical of most theoretical writings on Schoenberg's twelve-tone music. Perle accepts the consequences of his argument more bravely than many, however, going on to contradict Schoenberg's claim that the harmonic structure of a twelve-tone composition is totally integrated. He is forced to divide twelve-tone harmonies into two groups, those which derive their meaning from the basic set and those which have "independent meaning" (p. 90). This distinction leads him to the unavoidable conclusion that in twelve-tone composition the basic set "is not necessarily a sufficient integrative means. Elements derived from the set may tend to function independently and to disestablish the set as a primary referential structure" (p. 81). On the contrary, Schoenberg's sometimes cryptic remarks show how thoroughly he understood the implications of his own method and how justified his claims for it were.

2

Schoenberg's Sketches for the Suite op. 29 (Septett)

The examples and theoretical statements in "Composition with Twelve Tones" strongly suggest that this essay, which has been taken as a kind of manifesto, is incomplete and cryptic by design and that Schoenberg himself is largely responsible for the misconceptions and criticisms of his method that have followed. But even with the help of his earlier drafts, much still remains incomplete and ambiguous. This chapter undertakes to investigate more fully Schoenberg's techniques for structuring twelve-tone harmony by analyzing portions of the manuscript sketches for the Suite op. 29.

While Schoenberg's autograph manuscripts have been catalogued and described, few of his twelve-tone sketches have been analyzed and, as the following analyses show, their importance has been greatly underestimated. The sketches, in fact, go far towards clarifying the specific techniques that Schoenberg used to derive harmonic structure from a single basic set. Several reasons prompted me to analyze first the sketch material for op. 29. First, its sketches are extensive and it seems unlikely that any have been lost. Second, even though it is an early twelve-tone work, it uses a combinatorial row—a feature characteristic of later works. But unlike many of the later works, there are numerous sections where the combinatorial property is not used to form aggregates or secondary sets. The juxtaposition of combinatorial and noncombinatorial sections thus proves useful in comparing Schoenberg's techniques for structuring harmony in both types of situations, and puts into sharper relief the stylistic developments in his later works. Third, the Suite was composed before "Composition with Twelve Tones" so that it should exhibit those techniques hinted at in the essay. It also makes use of those larger forms which Schoenberg felt distinguished his twelve-tone from his earlier atonal works. The Suite, then, is attractive not only because it is combinatorial, but also because it seems to represent fairly the early twelve-tone pieces which Schoenberg was describing in his essay.

In this chapter I have selected for analysis only those sketches that pertain to Schoenberg's method of structuring harmony within one or between several row forms. Before these procedures are clearly understood, the interpretation of sketches dealing with larger formal aspects would seem impossible. Consequently, most of the examples come from the loose sketch sheets which appear to represent the earliest stages of composition; but since most of these sketch sheets are not dated, this impression remains somewhat subjective. I have also avoided analyzing sketches which confirm compositional procedures that have already been discussed in the secondary literature—such procedures as the use of invariant pitches or segments to associate row forms, inversional balance, hexachordal levels, and typical combinatorial or aggregate structures.[1] The following analyses, then, clarify new aspects of Schoenberg's compositional method and, as I hope will be evident, significantly alter what we have commonly understood to be Schoenberg's procedures for organizing twelve-tone harmony.

The first sketch for the Suite is dated October 28, 1924.[2] It contains only mm.5-12 of the "Ouverture" and shows that Schoenberg did not include the piano in the original instrumentation. Schoenberg evidently stopped working on this movement and on January 1, 1925 began the second, "Tanzschritte," which was completed on June 13, 1925. The third movement, "Thema mit Variationen," was composed between July 19, 1925 and August 15, 1925. During this summer he returned to the "Ouverture" (June 17) and started the fourth movement, "Gigue" (August 17), but set them aside in the autumn of 1925 to compose *Vier Stücke für gemischten Chor* op. 27 and *Drei Satiren für gemischten Chor* op. 28 (except for the *Anhang* which was completed in the spring of 1926). The "Gigue" and "Ouverture" were not completed until March 1, 1926 and April 15, 1926, respectively. Consequently, the Suite bears a later opus number than the *Vier Stücke* and *Drei Satiren,* even though much of it was written earlier. This detailed dating reveals the Suite to be among Schoenberg's earliest twelve-tone compositions.

In order to describe more precisely Schoenberg's method of organizing twelve-tone harmony, let us first review what he considered to be a legitimate twelve-tone harmony and how he defined the basic set (see Chapter 1). On the basis of the information he provides in "Composition with Twelve Tones" we can draw the following conclusions:

1. The basic set is best described not as a group of twelve ordered pitch-classes (pcs), but as a group of harmonies determined by an ordered set, each containing at least two adjacent intervals.
2. The harmonies of the basic set are identified *primarily* by their total intervallic content and not by the ordering of their pitches.
3. The harmonies of the basic set can function as unordered, independent small sets.

4. "Harmony" in a twelve-tone context does not necessarily imply a simultaneity or the vertical dimension.
5. All musical ideas represent "harmonies"—regardless of whether they unfold vertically or horizontally.
6. All musical ideas, that is harmonic events, affect more than one dimension; a complete musical texture normally consists of more than one simultaneous dimension.
7. The harmonic structure of a twelve-tone composition is totally unified because every feature is derived from a single source, the basic set.
8. The harmonies of the basic set are not restricted to a specific pitch-class content.
9. The harmonies of the basic set include all linear segments containing three to nine pitch classes and their complements.

As discussed in Chapter 1, Schoenberg does not conceive of harmony in only the traditional sense of pitches sounding simultaneously, but suggests that each melodic event possesses harmonic implications, and each harmonic event similarly retains a melodic identity.

> I... arrived at the concept whereby the vertical and horizontal, harmonic and melodic, the simultaneous and the successive were all in reality comprised within one unified space. It followed from this that whatever occurs at one point in that space, occurs not only there but in every dimensional aspect of the spatial continuum, so that any particular melodic motion... will not only have its effect upon the harmony, but on *everything* subsequent that is comprised within that spatial continuum.[3]

He proposed that a legitimate harmony comprises all pitches, either simultaneous *or* successive, which have some sort of temporal association, that is, are comprised within the same "spatial continuum." This conception of musical space allows linear unfolding of a basic set to be regarded as identical to simultaneous sounding of the entire set and it allows highly varied configurations of a basic set without losing the internal ordering of the pitches. The interaction of associated vertical and horizontal dimensions "explains why... a basic set of twelve tones can be used in either dimension, as a whole or in parts."[4]

A few examples can clarify those aspects of harmonic structure which will be of particular interest in studying the sketch material for op. 29. To facilitate the forthcoming discussion a complete row table for the basic set, op. 29, is given in Example 2.0.[5] In both noncombinatorial and combinatorial works, Schoenberg frequently partitions the basic set into segments containing three or four consecutive pitch-classes. Consider, for example, a trichordal partitioning of the row in op. 29 which appears near the end of the first

Example 2.0 Suite, op. 29, Row Table

	P₃ =	E♭	G	F#	B♭	D	B	C	A	A♭	E	F	D♭	
	I₃	7	6	10	2	11	0	9	8	4	5	1		
P₃		E♭	G	F#	B♭	D	B	C	A	A♭	E	F	D♭	RP₃
11		B	E♭	D	F#	B♭	G	A♭	F	E	C	D♭	A	
0		C	E	E♭	G	B	A♭	A	F#	F	D♭	D	B♭	
8		A♭	C	B	E♭	G	E	F	D	D♭	A	B♭	F#	
4		E	A♭	G	B	E♭	C	D♭	B♭	A	F	F#	D	
7		G	B	B♭	D	F#	E♭	E	D♭	C	A♭	A	F	
6		F#	B♭	A	D♭	F	D	E♭	C	B	G	A♭	E	
9		A	D♭	C	E	A♭	F	F#	E♭	D	B♭	B	G	
10		B♭	D	D♭	F	A	F#	G	E	E♭	B	C	A♭	
2		D	F#	F	A	D♭	B♭	B	A♭	G	E♭	E	C	
1		D♭	F	E	A♭	C	A	B♭	G	F#	D	E♭	B	
5		F	A	A♭	C	E	D♭	D	B	B♭	F#	G	E♭	

RI₃

Example 2.1 Suite, op. 29, Overture

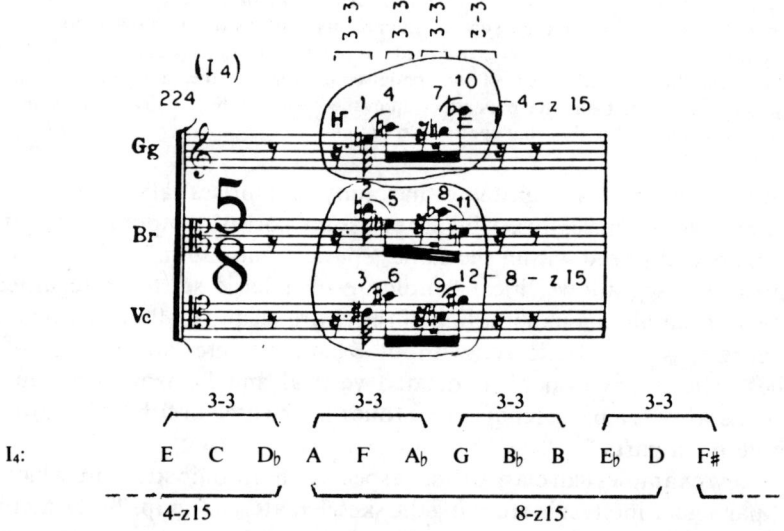

movement (Example 2.1). Here, the ordered succession of vertical trichordal segments (pc sets 3-3) maintains the original ordering of I₄. By indicating the principal melodic voice (H⁻), Schoenberg divides the configuration into two horizontal harmonic sets which are delineated by textural function (melody and accompaniment). Notice that the melody unfolds four pitch-classes representing nonconsecutive order numbers (order numbers 1, 4, 7, 10) and displays pc set 4-z15; the accompaniment contains the remaining eight pitch-classes, similarly representing nonconsecutive order numbers, and projects pc set 8-z15, the complement of 4-z15. If we examine the harmonic structure of the basic set, we find that 8-z15 appears as a linear segment spanning order numbers 4-11 (inclusive), and consequently represents a harmony of the basic set. Because complements of linear segments must, in Schoenberg's view, represent harmonies of the basic set (see Chapter 1), 4-z15 also represents a harmony of the basic set.

In Example 2.1, then, there are two independent harmonic dimensions (vertical and horizontal) derived from the linear set structure of P. The first consists of the trichordal partitions of P and projects the ordered harmonic sets (3-3) which, of course, are *identical* to linear segments of P; the second contains nonadjacent pcs and projects sets *equivalent* to linear segments of P (4-z15/8-z15). (See the Glossary for the definition of identical and equivalent pc sets.)

Example 2.2   Suite, op. 29, #1185

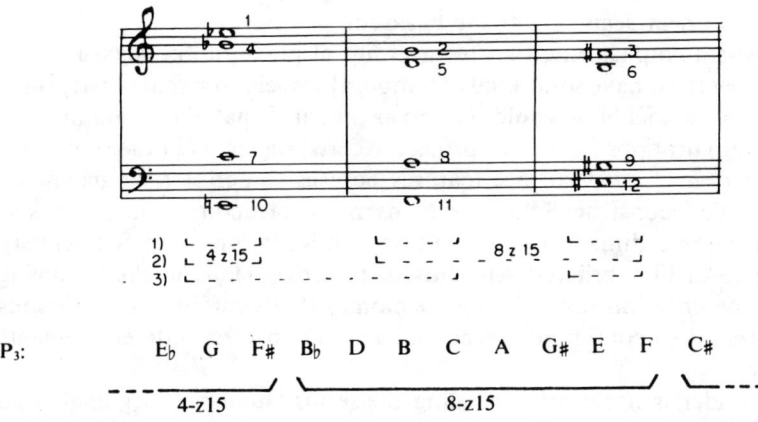

In the sketches for op. 29, Schoenberg constructs a simplified model for the configuration appearing in Example 2.1. The sketch, shown in Example 2.2, consists only of a series of chords displaying a trichordal partitioning of P_3; no rhythmic patterns or melodic voices are indicated.[6] While the original ordering of P_3 controls the horizontal harmonic dimension, there is no indication as to which segments constitute the vertical harmonic dimension. As shown by Example 2.2, there are three possibilities: 1) three harmonic segments, each containing one vertical chord, 2) two harmonic segments, the first containing the first chord and the second containing the final two chords, and 3) two harmonic segments, the first containing the first two chords and the second containing the final chord. The rhythmic pattern of the sketch favors each possibility equally, but only the second segmentation projects pc sets equivalent to linear segments of the basic set, 4-z15/8-z15.

As demonstrated by Example 2.1, when Schoenberg uses this model in op. 29 he clearly delineates pc sets 4-z15 and 8-z15 as separate harmonic dimensions. Even though in Examples 2.1 and 2.2 the horizontal and vertical dimensions have been switched, both display the same two independent harmonic dimensions based on the linear set structure of P. Thus, in deriving the model for the trichordal partitioning of P, Schoenberg clearly was concerned with using the harmonies of the basic set to integrate more than one simultaneous dimension of harmonic structure.

In my analyses of the sketches for op. 29, I examine the techniques Schoenberg uses to construct multidimensional harmonic structures. I am most interested in his use of harmonies that contain nonadjacent pitches of the basic set and in how these harmonies relate to the linear segments of the basic set. Schoenberg's sketches indicate that he attempted to interrelate *all* dimensions of harmonic structure by limiting the number of different sets that occurred as harmonic segments and by using only those sets that were equivalent to linear segments of the basic set.

It is worth emphasizing that for a group of pitches to be regarded as a harmony they must have some kind of temporal association, that is, they must occur in what Schoenberg would refer to as the same spatial continuum. The types of configurations he uses to project ordered segments of the row give a good indication of what surface features he uses to define a single spatial continuum. To reconstruct Schoenberg's harmonic structures, then, I mark as discrete harmonic dimensions only those configurations that Schoenberg might use to display ordered segments of the row. Thus, in the following analyses, one criterion for isolating harmonies that contain noncontiguous pitches is that their configurations could be used to project ordered segments of the row.

A reminder is necessary regarding the terms "nonlinear segment" and "linear segment." As in Chapter 1, harmonic sets can contain either contiguous elements from a single row or noncontiguous elements from *one or more* rows. I use the term "linear segment" to refer to a harmonic set that contains contiguous pitches of the row, and "nonlinear segment" to refer to a harmonic set that contains noncontiguous pitches from *one or more* rows. The *exact* structure of a "nonlinear segment" thus may change with each example.

In the following discussion, any linear segment of P containing between three and nine pitches (inclusive) *and its complement* represents a harmony of

P. (The terms "harmony of P" and "linear segment" are synonymous.) The harmonies of P occur with every ordered statement of P. A harmony of P is defined primarily by its interval-class content and is not restricted to a fixed pitch-class content. The "primary harmonic dimension" simply means the twelve successive pitches of the basic set. It therefore contains adjacent elements of the basic set and occurs with each of its ordered statements. A "secondary harmonic dimension" contains pitches nonadjacent in the basic set, but is equivalent to one of its linear segments. "Equivalent" here does not mean identical, but rather related by transposition or inversion or both. A "primary harmonic set" represents any harmonic segment (that is, linear segment) of P. For a harmonic set to be termed "secondary harmonic set" it must represent a harmony of P *and* occur simultaneously in more than one harmonic dimension (that is, in a secondary harmonic dimension). The principal function of a secondary harmonic set is to integrate (that is, interconnect) two or more simultaneous dimensions of harmonic structure.

Unless otherwise noted, all of the following sketches maintain the original ordering of the basic set. Consequently, they share an identical harmonic dimension defined by the harmonic sets of P. On these examples I have marked *only those sets that delineate secondary harmonic dimensions;* the marked sets, then, are equivalent to the harmonic sets of P. In other words, all of the indicated pc sets represent harmonic dimensions that contain noncontiguous elements and project harmonies equivalent to linear segments of P. Thus, all simultaneously occur in more than one harmonic dimension and represent secondary harmonic sets.

My discussion is divided into five sections. The first describes the internal set structure of P and the harmonic sets of P that are used as secondary harmonic sets. The second section analyzes sketches that treat configurations of individual row forms. These clearly indicate that Schoenberg's conception of harmonic structure was multidimensional—even in the configuration of a single row—and that nonlinear segments are derived directly from the harmonies of P.

The third section requires more explanation. It concentrates on sketches that deal with two or more row forms and shows that an important consideration in the association of specific row forms is their potential for forming interlocking harmonic sets that are equivalent to the harmonies of P. The following example will illustrate this concept.

Consider the simultaneous occurrence of the first tetrachord from P_3 and P_0:

P_3: [E_b G   F# B_b]   4-17
P_0: [C   E E_b G   ]   4-17

                   4-17   4-17

The first linear tetrachord of both row forms represents two forms of pc set 4-17. The association of the first dyads from both row forms again produces a form of pc set 4-17, as does the pairing of the second dyads from both row forms. Thus, a configuration that associates the first tetrachords of P_3 and P_0 in this way displays two dimensions of harmonic structure, vertical and horizontal, which are connected by a set representing a harmonic set of P; here, then, pc set 4-17 is a secondary harmonic set. This example offers a simple but cogent instance of how harmonic sets containing elements from more than one row form can be derived from the harmonic sets of a single row form. (Here the elements of the secondary harmonies comprise identical order numbers from both row forms, but it is important to remember that this is *not* a requirement for the formation of secondary harmonies.) Whether the potential of two row permutations for creating interlocking secondary harmonic sets is realized, is, of course, dependent upon surface features such as rhythm, dynamics, and register.

The sketches treated in the third section are particularly interesting, for they indicate the methods Schoenberg uses to associate row forms. Very often he writes down the first row form horizontally and then proceeds to write down four or five row forms directly beneath the first. He then considers the vertical nonlinear segments connecting each pair and crosses out the ones he considers unacceptable. So the sketches give us not only the pairs he selects, but also all the ones he rejects, giving us at the same time a very good indication of his criteria. Consistently, the possibilities rejected are row forms that, when combined, *fail to produce pc sets that represent linear segments of the row.*

Research into this aspect of Schoenberg's compositional method is virtually nonexistent. Theorists, such as Rufer and Perle, imply that the succession or pairing of row forms is controlled primarily by the association of invariant segments; however, Schoenberg's sketches show that the potential two row forms possess for forming secondary harmonic sets is equally and perhaps more important. In fact, as will be shown in the following chapters, Schoenberg often uses invariant segments primarily to *limit* the number of pitch classes within a discrete harmonic dimension.

The fourth section discusses sketches that involve the internal reordering of the row. Reorderings, which occur frequently in Schoenberg's twelve-tone compositions, are usually treated as local events, inspired by aesthetic considerations that have no long-range structural significance. But the sketches show that this view is inadequate. Deviation from the original ordering of the basic set often contributes to the generation of additional harmonic dimensions composed of secondary sets.

The fifth section includes sketches that show how Schoenberg understood the property of combinatoriality. Theorists often assume not only that

Schoenberg employed only hexachordal inversional combinatoriality, but that in his early twelve-tone composition he was unaware of any other types. The sketches, however, refute both of these assertions. Schoenberg not only was aware of, and used, *all* types of hexachordal combinatoriality, but also experimented with using tetrachordal and trichordal segments to form aggregates.

My objective in the following analyses is to show that in Schoenberg's early twelve-tone composition his concept of harmonic structure was multidimensional, that he interrelated these dimensions by limiting the harmonic sets to sets equivalent to linear segments of P, and that his method of organizing harmonic structure in a noncombinatorial situation did not significantly change in the presence of the combinatorial relation.

While Schoenberg used an all-combinatorial row in op. 29 and was aware of *all* its combinatorial properties (as his sketches indicate), he often used techniques for organizing harmonic structure that were not based on the combinatorial property. This clearly suggests that he regarded these alternative techniques as equally effective means of organizing harmonic structure. It also explains why he employed more extended formal structures with his earliest twelve-tone compositions, and why he never referred to them as exploratory or embryonic in nature.

The Harmonic Structure of the Basic Set

A most important development in Schoenberg's method of twelve-tone composition was the discovery of the property of some rows by which the operation of T, RT, I, or RI, applied to the first hexachord, produces a new hexachord the pitch-content of which is exclusive of the original. The combined pitch-content of both hexachords produces an aggregate representing the universal set of twelve pitch-classes. This represents a specific instance of the property termed "combinatoriality," which was named, rigorously formulated and generalized as a compositional technique by Milton Babbitt during the 1940s.[7]

Combinatoriality is a property dependent upon segmental pitch-class content but completely independent of the ordering of elements within those segments. This property allows for the formation of *aggregates* between two or more combinatorially related row forms. "Semi-combinatoriality" indicates the property of creating aggregates between a specific pair of permutations, for example between P and I. "All-combinatoriality" denotes the possibility of constructing such aggregates between all possible pairs of permutations at one or more transpositional levels. The Suite employs an all-combinatorial row (Example 2.0) and uses all types of hexachordal combinatoriality.

The Suite's all-combinatorial row creates combinatorial relations at three transpositional levels for I, T, RI, and RT permutations. This means that out of the twenty-four possible permutations of the row, there will be two groups—each containing twelve row forms—whose hexachords have identical pitch-class contents. If one examines the structure of P, the features which cause such a high density of combinatorial relations are immediately apparent.

The principal hexachord of P is pc set 6-20 (C, C♯, E, F, A♭, A). A unique feature of this hexachord is its extremely limited intervallic content—it contains no whole steps or tritones. Of the fifty possible hexachords, 6-20 is the only one to omit exactly two interval-classes, and there is only one hexachord which omits three (the whole tone hexachord 6-35). Another property of pc set 6-20, resulting from its limited intervallic content, is its extremely small number of subset-types. While many hexachords contain thirty or more subset-types, 6-20 contains only nine: pc sets 5-21, 4-7, 4-17, 4-19, 4-20, 3-3, 3-4, 3-11 and 3-12. (Dyads are not included since they are not regarded as independent harmonies of the basic set.) This property necessarily limits the number of set-types occurring as linear segments of P.

Another important property of pc set 6-20 is that it can be derived at least once by each of its four trichords (3-3, 3-4, 3-11, 3-12). This means, for example, that the combined pitch-class content of two forms of the trichord 3-3 can produce the hexachord 6-20. Pc set 6-20 can be derived in one way by pc set 3-12, and in three different ways by pc sets 3-3, 3-4, and 3-11. It is the only hexachord that contains six forms of pc set 3-11. All other hexachordal supersets of 3-11 contain 3-11 fewer times.

The internal structure of both hexachords of P is very similar. Except for the switching of the pcs represented by order numbers 7 and 8, the second hexachord of P relates to the first by RT_2. This relationship is indicated in the following example for P_3, the principal permutation for the first movement. Notice that when RT_2 is applied to P_3, the first hexachord of P_3 appears in retrograde form as the final hexachord of P_5, except for the switching of pcs D and B.

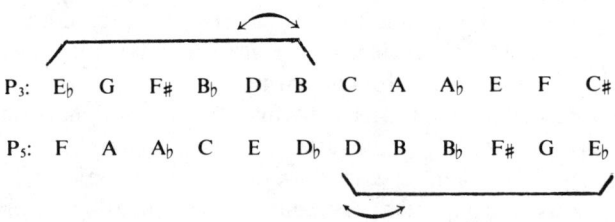

The similarity in hexachordal structure results in the symmetrical occurrence of trichord and tetrachord pc set-types:

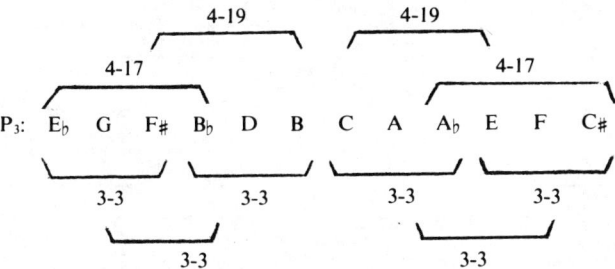

Notice that every successive trichord represents pc set 3-3 and that the first and last tetrachords represent pc set 4-17. Pc set 4-19 also occurs in a symmetrical position as the last tetrachord of the last hexachord, as do two further occurrences of pc set 3-3 (G, F♯, B♭, and A♭, E, F).

With the exception of pc set 3-3 which occurs six times, pc sets 4-19 and 5-21 appear more frequently than any other set-types. Pc set 5-21 is, in fact, the only set-type of cardinality 5 contained in pc set 6-20, as indicated above.

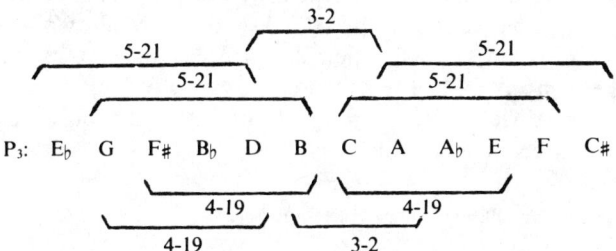

There are three occurrences of pc set 4-19 and four occurrences of pc set 5-21. The only other set-type that occurs more than once is pc set 3-2, a trichord that links both hexachords but does not represent a subset of 6-20.

In op. 29 Schoenberg uses all of the sets that occur more than once as linear segments of P as secondary harmonic sets, that is, he frequently uses them simultaneously in more than one harmonic dimension. The remaining secondary harmonic sets that Schoenberg uses most often—all of which occur only once—are given in the diagram on p. 36.

Schoenberg, in addition, uses some complements of the above sets. A complete list of these harmonies and their complements which Schoenberg uses most often as secondary harmonic sets appears in Example 2.3. Of the fifty-eight nonequivalent harmonic sets contained in P (this number includes all linear segments and their complements), Schoenberg primarily uses only thirty-three to provide harmonic structure for the entire composition. (The number of nonequivalent harmonic sets is reduced here by the frequent

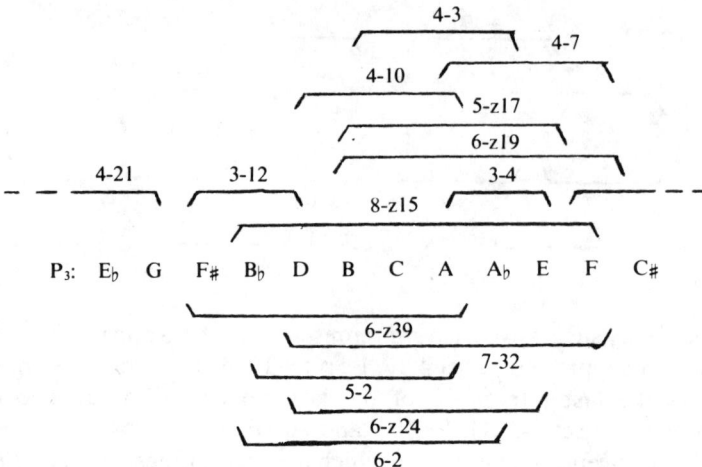

repetition of sets within the row.) Among the sets listed in Example 2.3 there is only one that Schoenberg consistently uses as a secondary set which does *not* represent a linear segment of P, pc set 3-11. As will be shown by Example 2.4, Schoenberg gives pc set 3-11 special status because of its relation to the principal hexachord 6-20; for as noted above, not only can pc set 6-20 be drived in three different ways by 3-11, but it is the only hexachord that contains six different forms of 3-11.

Example 2.3   Suite, op. 29, Secondary Harmonic Sets

3-2/9-2	4-19/8-19
3-3/9-3	5-2/7-2
3-4	5-z17
3-11	5-21/7-21
3-12/9-12	5-32/7-32
4-3	6-2
4-7	6-z10/6-z39
4-10/8-10	6-z19/6-z44
4-z15/8-z15	6-20
4-17	6-z24/6-z46
4-21/8-21	

In my analyses of the sketches, I am particularly interested in the occurrence of harmonic sets containing pcs representing noncontiguous order numbers. But if two row forms are combinatorially related, and if a secondary harmonic set which interconnects them is derived from hexachords with identical pitch-class contents, then it is very likely that such a set will represent a linear segment, that is, a harmony of P. In the Suite the probability of this occurring is increased by the small subset content of pc set 6-20. Therefore, I have tried to avoid indicating secondary harmonic sets derived from hexachords with the same pitch-class contents. However, whenever hexachords from *more than two* combinatorially related row forms are grouped together, and one of these hexachords has a different pc content, I have indicated the use of secondary harmonic sets. This is justified since in such a case the presence of a hexachord containing a different pc content means that the secondary harmonic set is extracted from the universal set, and thus, there is no limitation imposed by the small subset content of 6-20.

The Harmonic Organization of Individual Row Forms

Example 2.4 Suite, op. 29, #1188

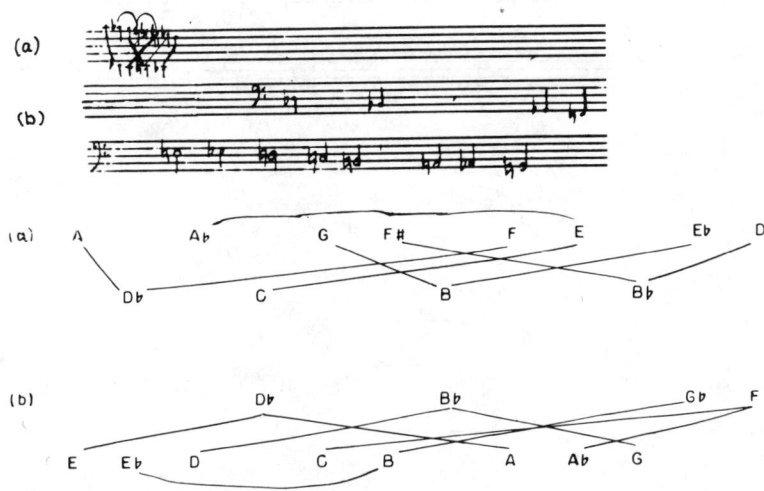

As I discuss in Section 2.1, Schoenberg consistently uses only one pc set as a harmony which does not represent a linear segment of P, pc set 3-11. Pc set 3-11 is given this special status, as the sketch appearing in Example 2.4 demonstrates, because of its relation to the principal hexachord 6-20.[8] In the upper portion (a) of this sketch Schoenberg has drawn lines connecting four discrete forms of pc set 3-12 (C E A♭, D♭ F A, D F♯ B♭, E♭ G B) whose combined pc content represents the universal set (see transcription below sketch). Notice that the lower voice contains exactly one pc from each form of 3-12. In the lower sketch (b) Schoenberg constructs a similar model to derive the universal set by four forms of pc set 3-11 (C F A♭, D♭ E A, D G B♭, E♭ B G♭). As in the upper sketch (a), one pc from each trichord 3-11 appears in a separate voice (D♭ B♭ G♭ F). While he does not use lines to connect the individual forms of trichord 3-11 in (b), his use of a model similar to the one appearing in (a) indicates that in (b) he is working out how to derive the universal set by 3-11.

Example 2.5   Suite, op. 29, #1192

Schoenberg's interest in emphasizing the derivational property of pc set 6-20 is demonstrated by the sketch appearing in Example 2.5 which represents an early draft of m. 15 from the Overture. Notice that in the upper two voices the rhythmic pattern creates two harmonic segments, both of which project pc set 3-4 and contain noncontiguous pitches of RP_3. A third occurrence of 3-4 in the lowest voice (F G♯ A) represents a linear segment of RP_3. Thus, by rhythmically controlling the unfolding of two ordered trichordal segments (each projects pc set 3-3) Schoenberg has emphasized the derivation of pc set 6-20 by pc set 3-4. Of special interest is the way in which the texture isolates the two nonlinear occurrences of 3-4 from the single linear occurrence of 3-4 and how it effectively saturates the horizontal harmonic dimension with multiple forms of pc set 3-4.

Example 2.6 Suite, op. 29, #1193

Example 2.6a contains one of the most revealing sketches for op. 29; it represents the methodical working out of a three-dimensional harmonic structure based on the derivational property of pc set 6-20. The sketch contains repetitions of one row form, I_7; the first measure presents both hexachords of I_7, the second measure gives the first hexachord twice, the third measure gives the complete form of I_7, and the last measure again presents only the first hexachord. The original ordering of I_7 is maintained throughout, thus presenting a repeating succession of pc sets 3-3. Notice that in each repetiion of I_7 the upper voice (stemmed separately) presents a form of pc set 3-11, as does the lower voice. (See transcription of sketch in Example 2.6b.)

Thus, two harmonic dimensions are projected; one displays successive forms of pc set 3-3, and the second, represented by noncontiguous pitches of the row, contains repetitions of pc set 3-11.

Only one feature, registral organization, changes with each repetition of I_7. Notice that if one separates registrally the upper three pcs from the lower three, a new derivation of pc set 6-20 occurs. In the first hexachord (m.1) registral segmentation displays two forms of pc set 3-11 which are equivalent, but not identical to the two occurrences of 3-11 presented by the individual voices. In the second measure registral segmentation presents two forms of pc set 3-12. Notice that in m.2 the repetition of the first hexachord changes the register for one pitch class (B), but that this does not affect the sets projected by the upper and lower registers. In the third measure changes in register delineate two new forms of pc set 3-3 (1st hexachord) and 3-4 (2nd hexachord). The final hexachord presents two forms of pc set 3-3 in the upper and lower registers.

Because of the derivational property of pc set 6-20, the placement of three pcs in each register will always produce two forms of the same trichord, but what is significant about each of the sets delineated by register in Example 2.6 is that they *never* represent a linear segment of I_7 or coincide with the sets projected by the separately stemmed voices. If at any point registral segmentation did coincide with either of the two other dimensions, the analysis of this sketch would be less convincing. This sketch thus shows Schoenberg working out three independent dimensions of harmonic structure: 1) the original ordering of I_7 projects successive forms of pc set 3-3, 2) individual voices project forms of pc set 3-11, and 3) registral segmentation always projects new forms of pc set 3-3, 3-11, 3-4 or 3-12. This sketch clearly demonstrates Schoenberg's preoccupation with the organization of multidimensional harmonic structures based on the linear structure of P.

Example 2.7 shows a preliminary sketch of m.52, Theme with Variations, which contains a dyadic partitioning of I_4. Notice that the registral association of alternating dyads delineates the secondary harmonic sets 6-z19/6-z44. This configuration thus projects two dimensions of harmonic structure; the first represents the original ordering of P and the second displays registral harmonic sets containing noncontiguous pcs that duplicate linear hexachords of P. This configuration will be discussed in greater detail in Chapters 3 and 4.

A configuration similar to the one shown in Example 2.7 appears in Example 2.8. This sketch represents an early draft of mm.19-20, Gigue, and is very similar but not identical to the final version which appears below the sketch. The revisions are significant; the registral and notational changes serve to delineate more clearly the nonlinear harmonic sets 6-z19/6-z44. In the earlier version, a similar harmonic segmentation is suggested, but is made more pronounced by the subsequent revisions.

Example 2.7   Suite, op. 29, #1192

Throughout the sketches for op. 29 Schoenberg frequently experimented with dividing one row form into two simultaneous voices whose nonlinear harmonic segments represented sets equivalent to linear segments of P. An instance of this appears in Example 2.9 which shows the derivation of a characteristic configuration for the theme of the Gigue. This is a particularly ingenious design, for it creates five nonlinear harmonic segments (delineated by the separate stemming of two voices) which represent secondary harmonic sets (pc sets 3-3, 3-11, 4-19, 6-z10, 6-z39). Of special interest is the linking of the two principal hexachords by pc set 3-3 (E♭ B C), the trichord which derives each form of 6-20 in the basic set and is associated exclusively with discrete statements of 6-20. Notice how Schoenberg initially places the A, C♯, and E in the upper voice of RI$_8$, but then changes their position to the lower voice, thus creating two horizontal secondary harmonic hexachords.

The Harmonic Organization of Two or More Row Forms

The following discussion concentrates on sketches which deal with two or more row forms and shows that an important consideration in the association

42 Schoenberg's Sketches for the Suite op. 29 (Septett)

Example 2.8 Suite, op. 29, #1202

of row forms is their potential for forming interlocking harmonic sets which duplicate harmonic sets of P. The first group of examples includes the association of row forms whose hexachords have identical pitch-class contents. I describe row forms that are related in this way as being combinatorially related. In some cases individual row forms may require the application of the R operation to conform to the strict definition of combinatoriality. I am using the term combinatoriality in this broader sense because in op. 29 the primary feature Schoenberg considers in the association of row forms is their membership in one of the two groups of twelve row forms whose hexachords contain identical pitch-class contents. Their potential for forming aggregates is, in general, a less crucial consideration. Consequently, when I describe row forms as being combinatorially related, individual row forms may require the R operation to fulfill the strict definition of combinatoriality.

There is considerable evidence in the sketches to suggest that Schoenberg applied the same procedures for obtaining multidimensional harmonic

Example 2.9 Suite, op. 29, #1202

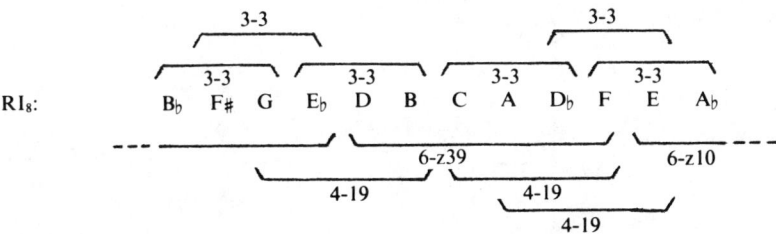

structures to groups of combinatorially related permutations as he did to a single permutation. Moreover, the sketches indicate that the application of these procedures was not significantly altered by the presence or absence of the combinatorial relation. The following examples substantiate this claim.

The sketches that appear in Examples 2.10-14 contain row forms which make up one of the principal row groups for the entire composition, $P_3:I_8:I_{10}$. In Example 2.10 Schoenberg has experimented with the simultaneous unfolding of the hexachordal segments of P_3 and I_8. The notation—especially the use of bar lines—suggests that vertical tetrachordal simultaneities are treated as harmonic segments. Each vertical tetrachord contains one pc from each of the four occurences of 6-20 in P_3 and I_8; thus, the combinatorial property has little effect on their harmonic structure. The hexachords in the upper sketch (a) maintain their original ordering. Notice that the alternating tetrachordal simultaneities form the secondary harmonic sets 4-17, 4-10, 4-17—a set succession that represents the succession of tetrachords in P. In the lower sketch (b), which Schoenberg has crossed out, the R operation has been applied to the second hexachord in each row form. Here, only one vertical harmony, pc set 4-10, projects a secondary harmonic set. Schoenberg most likely found this configuration less desirable because P_3 and I_8 were linked

44   Schoenberg's Sketches for the Suite op. 29 (Septett)

Example 2.10   Suite, op. 29, #1185

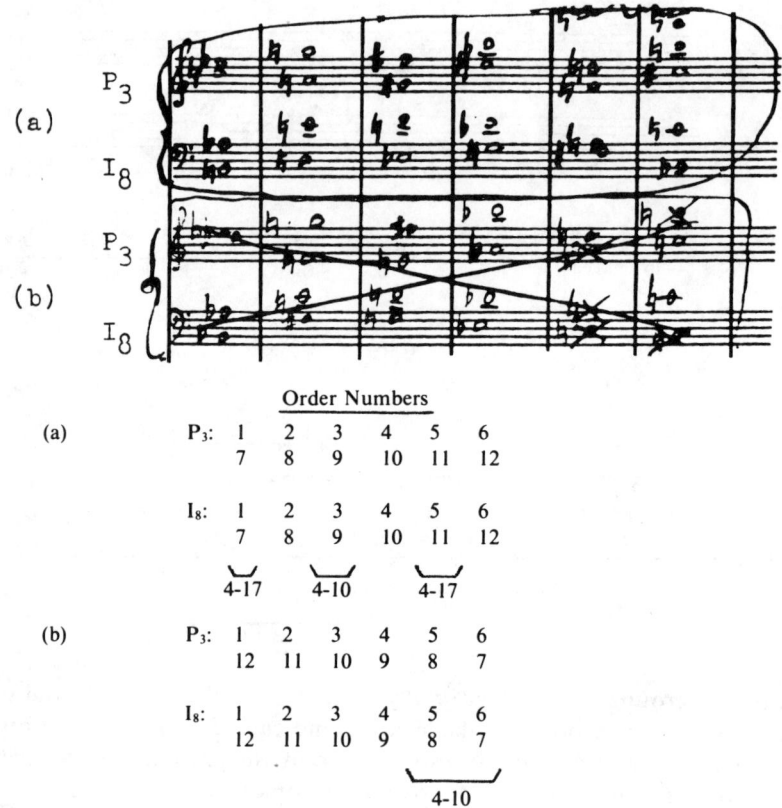

together by fewer secondary harmonic sets, and thus it produced a greater number of nonlinear harmonic segments not directly related to the harmonies of P.

The sketch that appears in Example 2.11 shows the simultaneous unfolding of I_{10}, P_3, and I_8. Schoenberg has carefully marked the dyads, trichords, and tetrachords in each row form. Notice how the dotted lines marking the dyads emphasize the vertical harmonic segments—a clear indication that he was concerned with the harmonic sets that intersected all three permutations. The entire configuration is linked together by secondary harmonic sets; pc sets 6-z10, 6-z46, and 4-10 associate the first hexachords from all three permutations, and two occurrences of pc set 9-3 link together the final hexachords. While Schoenberg's notation fails to indicate which vertical sets he favors, analysis of op. 29, as I show later, indicates he prefers those that set forth harmonies equivalent to linear segments of P.

Example 2.11 Suite, op. 29, #1183

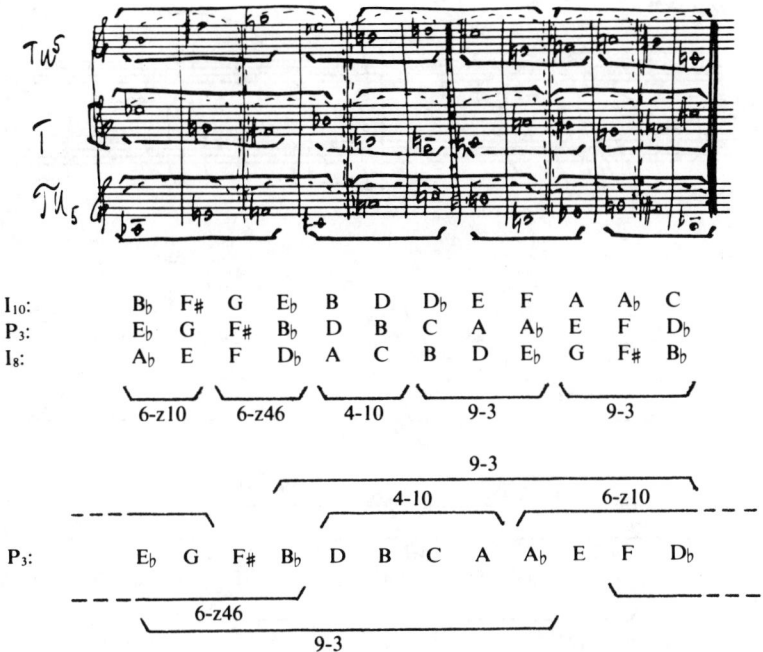

Configurations including two combinatorially related row forms associated by aggregate formation often display additional dimensions of harmonic structure. Such a configuration appears in Example 2.12 which contains the simultaneous linear unfolding of P_3 and I_8. Here, the rhythmic configuration systematically groups together dyads occupying corresponding order positions in both row forms and thus creates a succession of vertical secondary harmonic tetrachords (pc sets 4-7, 4-10, 4-17, and 4-19). These tetrachords provide an added secondary dimension of harmonic structure to a configuration already connected by aggregates.

Example 2.13 shows two identical configurations applied to RP_3 and RI_8 of a principal theme of the Gigue. Schoenberg indicates two discrete voices within each configuration whose nonlinear harmonic segments project the secondary harmonic sets 3-3, 3-11, 4-19, 5-32, and 7-32.

Example 2.12 Suite, op. 29, #1186

Notice how Schoenberg's notation strongly suggests that RP_3 and RI_8 unfold simultaneously, a conclusion supported by the extensive formation of secondary harmonic sets between corresponding segments of both row forms (pc sets 4-17, 8-17, 4-7, and 4-10). Thus, two dimensions of harmonic structure, one vertical and one horizontal, containing nonlinear segments project secondary harmonic sets, and consequently, all nonlinear harmonic segments are derived from the linear structure of P.

The sketch displayed in Example 2.9 shows how Schoenberg uses invariant segments from two row forms to construct multidimensional harmonic structures based on the harmonies of the basic set. The sketch contains two row forms, RI_8 and RP_{11}, which share four invariant trichords (unordered). While the two row forms are presented simultaneously, RP_{11} does not begin until the second trichord of RI_8. Notice that the first vertical harmonic segment, pc set 6-2, and the linear statement of pc set 6-2 in RI_8 contain identical pitches (see Example 2.14). A similar structure occurs with each successive vertical hexachord. The formation of the hexachords 6-2 and 6-20 which harmonically link two combinatorially related row forms, is dependent upon invariant trichordal segments. If both row forms had begun

Example 2.13 Suite, op. 29, #1202

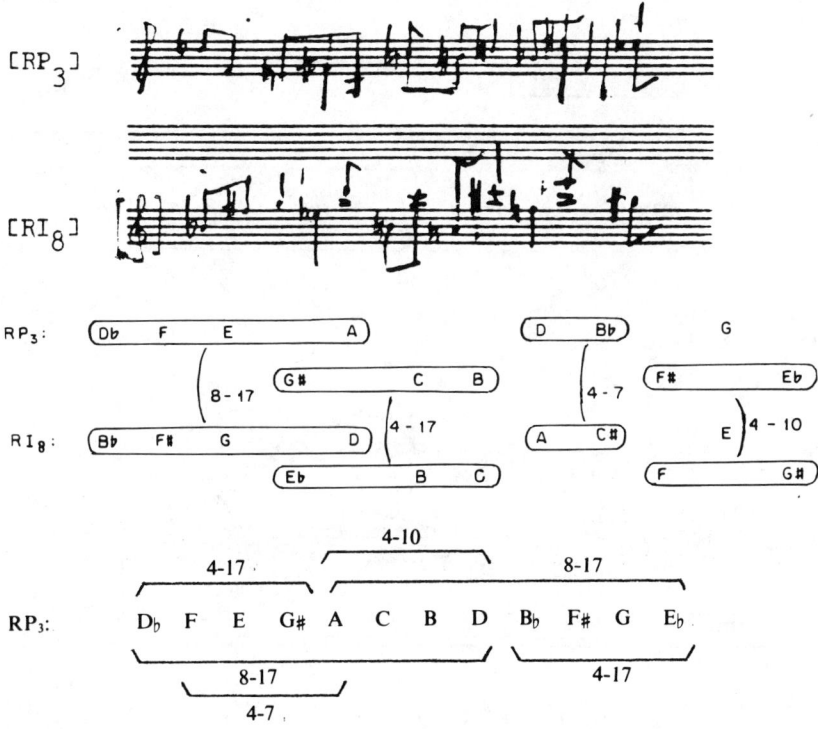

simultaneously, no secondary harmonic hexachords would have been formed; instead, the rows would have been joined by only three secondary harmonic tetrachords, a structure that would not have emphasized the special invariant properties of I_8 and P_{11}. In this instance Schoenberg has chosen not to realize the potential for aggregate formation and has used these other techniques for providing harmonic structure.

Example 2.15 contains a sketch which conclusively demonstrates that one criterion Schoenberg used to associate row permutations was their potential for forming interlocking secondary harmonic sets. In this sketch Schoenberg has circled each vertical occurrence of the secondary harmonic trichord 3-12 between P_4 and P_0. In addition, when pc set 3-12 does not occur as a vertical set, he has circled every vertical subset of pc set 3-12. The first circle encloses the initial dyads from both row forms, delineating pc set 3-12 (C E A♭). The second circle indicates the second occurrence of 3-12 and includes the next three pcs from both row forms (G B E♭ and E♭ G B). The third circle includes only one pc from both row forms (C and A♭) which represents a

48   Schoenberg's Sketches for the Suite op. 29 (Septett)

Example 2.14   Suite, op. 29

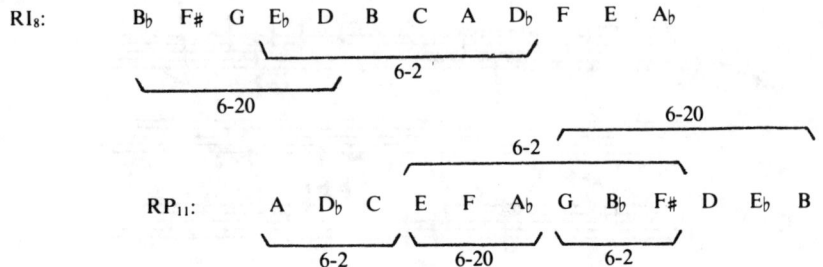

Example 2.15   Suite, op. 29, #1200

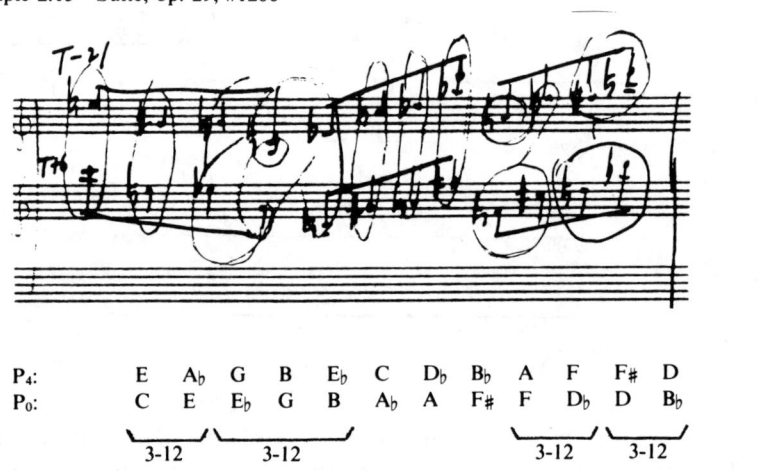

subset of 3-12. The next two circles also enclose subsets of 3-12. The circling of the final two pairs of dyads marks the last two occurrences of 3-12 between P_0 and P_4. Notice how Schoenberg has used lines to connect invariant pcs within the second and third occurrences of 3-12. It is not surprising that Schoenberg is especially interested in the formation of pc set 3-12 as a nonlinear harmonic segment, for it represents (1) a linear segment of P, (2) the most important structural difference between the principal hexachords of P, and (3) the invariant set between any two hexachords from row forms whose hexachords do not have identical pitch-class contents.

On the original sketch sheet that contains the sketch appearing in Example 2.15, there is a small chart which lists all the combinatorially related row forms (see Example 2.16). Schoenberg lists only the row label and the initial pitch of each permutation. The order in which the row forms appear is

Example 2.16 Suite, op. 29, #1200

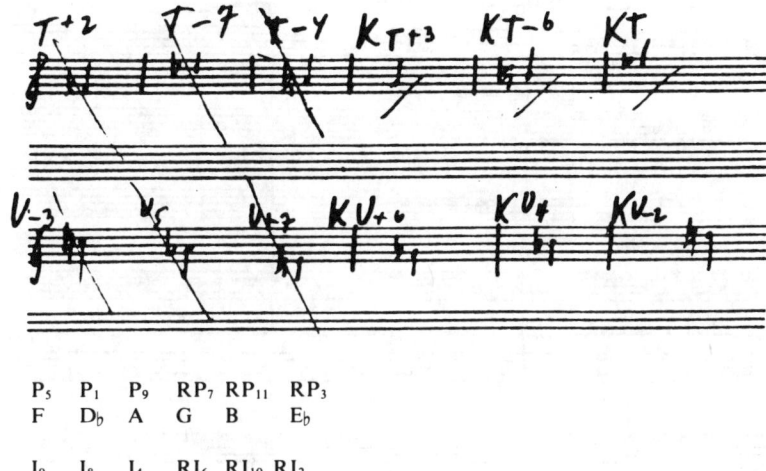

| P_5 | P_1 | P_9 | RP_7 | RP_{11} | RP_3 |
| F | D♭ | A | G | B | E♭ |

| I_0 | I_8 | I_4 | RI_6 | RI_{10} | RI_2 |
| C | A♭ | E | G♭ | B♭ | D |

based on the formation of pc set 3-12 by their initial pitches. For example, the first three row forms are P_5, P_1 and P_9, whose initial pitches (F, D♭, A) represent pc set 3-12. A similar relation occurs with the grouping of RP_7 RP_{11} RP_3, I_0 I_4 I_8 and RI_6 RI_{10} RI_2. Thus, Schoenberg constructs four three-row groups on the basis of their potential for forming a harmony of the basic set, trichord 3-12.

The sketch appearing in Example 2.17 offers further proof of Schoenberg's special interest in the association of row forms whose interlocking harmonic segments produce the linear segment 3-12. Schoenberg here has listed all twelve I permutations and crossed out all but three, I_0 I_8 I_4. If one considers these three row forms as unfolding simultaneously, as the notation strongly suggests, a highly unified vertical harmonic structure appears. Because the trichord formed by their initial pcs forms pc set 3-12, each successive vertical trichord also forms 3-12. In addition, there are four successive occurrences of pc set 6-20. While the regularity of vertical harmonies results from the internal symmetry of P, it is significant that Schoenberg emphasizes this symmetry by associating these specific row forms.

The sketch appearing in Example 2.18 displays two new row groupings: P_3 I_4 I_0 and I_8 P_3 I_4 I_0. The notation is somewhat unclear, but it appears that Schoenberg initially intended to associate P_3 I_4 I_0 (indicated by the circles) and then included I_8 (suggested by the darkening of bar lines similar to those in P_3

50 Schoenberg's Sketches for the Suite op. 29 (Septett)

Example 2.17 Suite, op. 29, #1182

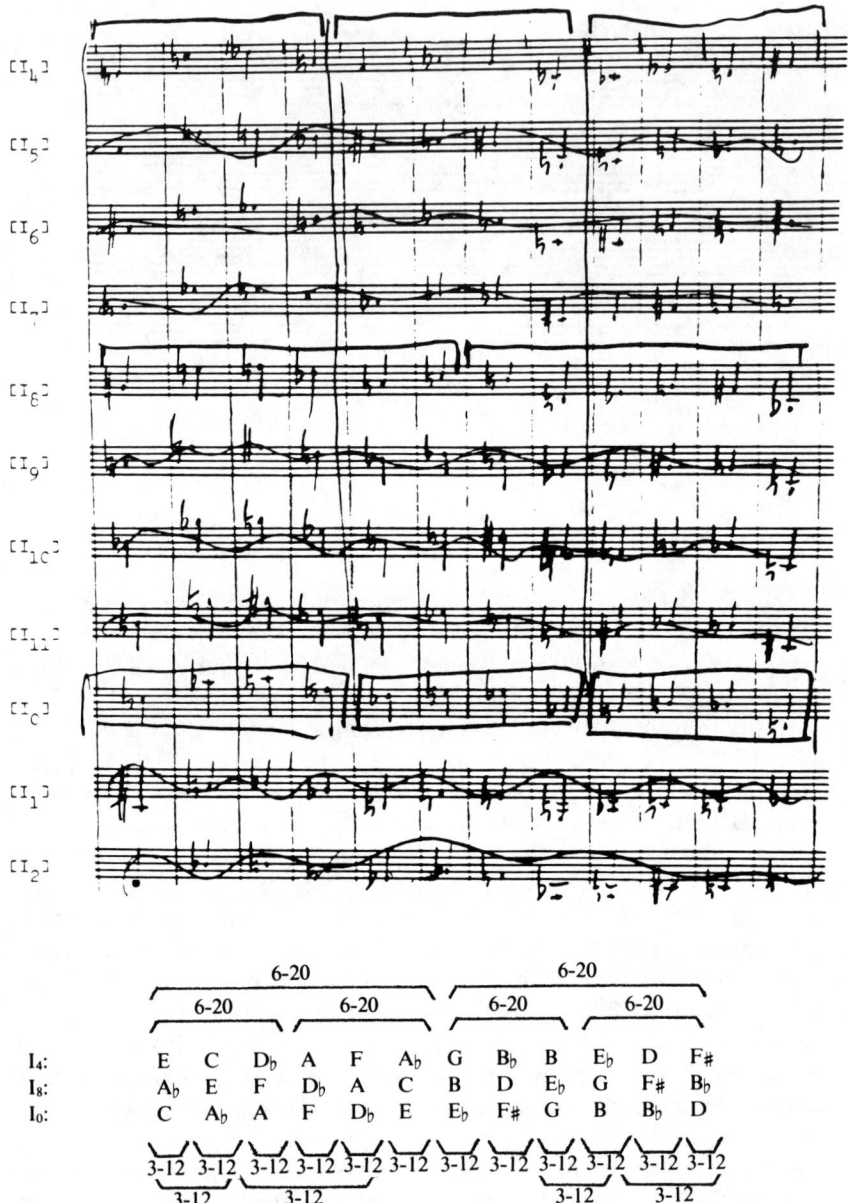

Example 2.18 Suite, op. 29, #1181

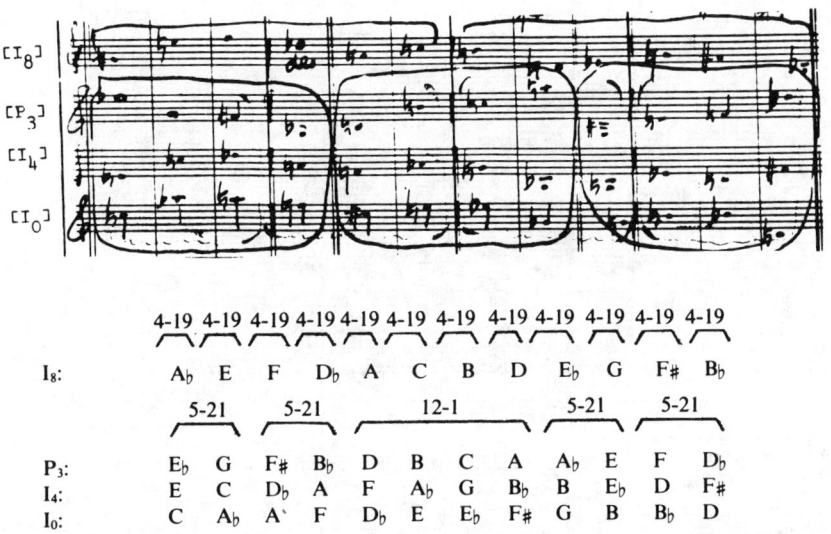

I₄ I₀ and by the downward brackets placed over the hexachords of I₈). Within the first row grouping (P₃ I₄ I₀) Schoenberg has circled all corresponding trichords and tetrachords. The secondary harmonic sets which interconnect this group include four occurrences of 5-21 and one occurrence of the universal set 12-1, a harmonic segmentation that reinforces a tetrachordal partitioning. (This may explain why the corresponding tetrachords are circled more darkly than the trichords.) This row grouping thus is structured by an aggregate and the pentachord that occurs four times as a linear segment of P. If I₈ is associated with P₃ I₄ I₀ twelve vertical occurrences of the secondary tetrachord 4-19 appear, a tetrachord formed by three linear segments of P. Schoenberg has thus derived the two row groupings that produce equivalent forms of pc sets 4-19 and 5-21, the tetrachord and pentachord that appear most frequently as linear segments of P.

The sketches for op. 29 strongly indicate that Schoenberg used the same criteria for associating noncombinatorially related row forms as he did for associating combinatorially related row forms. The sketches appearing in Examples 2.19 and 2.20 show the association of noncombinatorially related row forms whose nonlinear harmonic segments consistently form secondary harmonic sets. The sketch appearing in Example 2.19 displays a listing of nine permutations. The notation does not clearly indicate which specific row forms are being associated, however three row pairs maintain the same relationship: P₀ P₉, P₂ P₅, and I₂ I₅. Thus, it seems likely that Schoenberg was considering

Example 2.19 Suite, op. 29, #1181

the harmonic sets formed between row forms related by T_3. This conclusion is substantiated by the number of secondary harmonic sets that interlock each of these paired row forms. As the following diagram shows, their simultaneous presentation projects five occurrences of pc set 4-17, three occurrences of pc set 4-3, two occurrences of pc set 5-10, and one occurrence of pc set 4-7. Schoenberg's interest in row forms related by T_3 is not surprising, for no other pair of noncombinatorially related row forms produces as many interlocking secondary harmonic sets.

Schoenberg's Sketches for the Suite op. 29 (Septett)   53

```
           4-3        4-17       4-3        4-3        4-3
         ┌─────┐    ┌─────┐    ┌─────┐    ┌─────┐    ┌─────┐
P₀:  C    E    E♭   G    B    A♭   A    F♯   F    D♭   D    B♭

P₉:  A    D♭   C    E    A♭   F    F♯   E♭   D    B♭   B    G
     └─────┘   └─────┘   └─────────┘   └─────┘   └─────┘
       4-17      4-17        5-10         4-17      4-17
                         └─────────┘
                             5-10
```

The sketch shown in Example 2.19 contains a second row grouping associating noncombinatorially related row forms, $P_3 \; I_3 \; I_8$. In this instance, the notation clearly indicates that these three row forms are being considered as a discrete group. At the same time, however, the trichord markings in I_3 and I_8 suggest that Schoenberg also may have been considering independently the association of these two row forms. As the following diagram indicates, both row groupings, $P_3 \; I_3 \; I_8$ and $I_3 \; I_8$ are strongly interconnected by secondary harmonic sets:

```
          5-21
        ┌─────┐
P₃:  E♭   G    F♯   B♭   D    B    C    A    A♭   E    F    D♭

I₃:  E♭   B    C    A♭   E    G    F♯   A    B♭   D    D♭   F

I₈:  A♭   E    F    C♯   A    C    B    D    E♭   G    F♯   B♭
     └─────────┘   └─────────┘   └─────────┘   └───┘ └───┘
        7-21           9-3           9-12       3-4   3-11


I₃:  E♭   B    C    A♭   E    G    F♯   A    B♭   D    D♭   F

I₈:  A♭   E    F    C♯   A    C    B    D    E♭   G    F♯   B♭
     └─────────┘   └─────────┘   └─────────┘   └─────────┘
        6-z44         6-z44         6-z44         6-z44
```

While there are several instances in the Suite where the secondary harmonic hexachords between two row forms related by T_5 (e.g., $I_3:I_8$) are clearly articulated, the association of all three row forms ($P_3 \; I_3 \; I_8$) and the delineation of their interlocking secondary harmonic sets is much more frequent.

There is, however, one sketch which unambiguously groups together two row forms ($RI_7 \; RI_2$) which maintain the same relation as I_3 and I_8. It appears in Example 2.20 and reveals one of Schoenberg's typical methods for selecting row pairs. Here, Schoenberg notates the principal permutation and then lists the possible row forms he is considering above and below it. In this instance, the principal permutation is RI_7 and he has begun by considering P_1 and RI_6.

54   Schoenberg's Sketches for the Suite op. 29 (Septett)

Example 2.20   Suite, op. 29, #1184

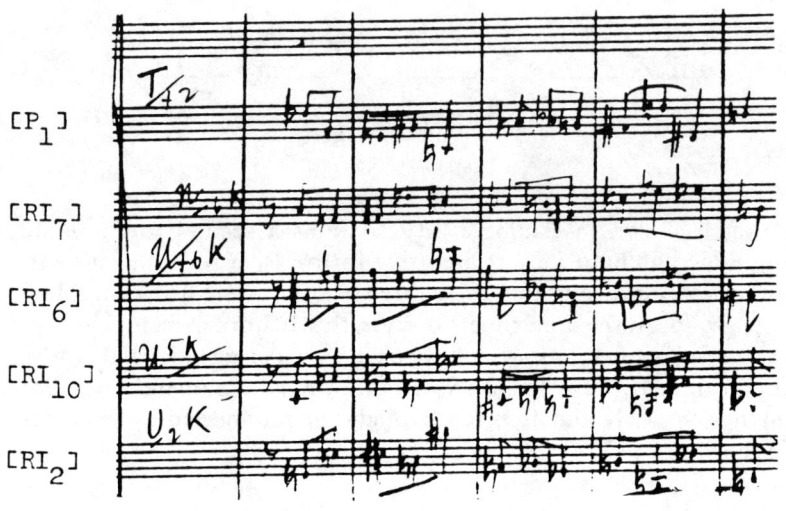

Example 2.21   Suite, op. 29, #1185

He has rejected these along with RI_{10}, as is indicated by the diagonal lines across the row labels. The only row form not crossed out is RI_2. (The formation of secondary harmonic sets between RI_7 and RI_2 is identical to that occurring between I_3 and I_8.) This typical procedure gives us a very good indication of Schoenberg's criteria for associating row forms. Consistently, the possibilities rejected are row forms that, when combined, fail to produce pc sets equivalent to linear segments of the basic set.

Reorderings of the Basic Set

The following section analyzes sketches that involve the internal reordering of P. Reorderings of the basic set, as the sketches indicate, are not merely local events, but often have long range structural importance. These events frequently involve the generation of secondary harmonic sets and the formation of multidimensional harmonic structures. The reordering of P is not *always* explained by the formation of secondary harmonic sets, for in any specific context reorderings may be based on multiple considerations. But certainly one recurring reason Schoenberg reorders P is to generate more than one dimension of harmonic structure derived from the harmonies of P.

Example 2.21 shows the simultaneous unfolding of the tetrachordal partitions of P_3 and P_5. The upper configuration (a) maintains the original ordering of P. In the lower two sketches, (b) and (c), the R operation has been applied to the second tetrachord of each permutation. Each of these configurations produces the secondary harmonic sets 9-3 and 3-3. Especially revealing is the omission of the two remaining possibilities for similar reorderings of tetrachordal segments, that is, the application of R to the first tetrachord only and to the last tetrachord only. It is significant that neither of these latter two types of configurations produce secondary harmonic sets, for it explains why Schoenberg has excluded them from his sketches as well as from op. 29 itself.

Example 2.22 Suite, op. 29, #1192

56   Schoenberg's Sketches for the Suite op. 29 (Septett)

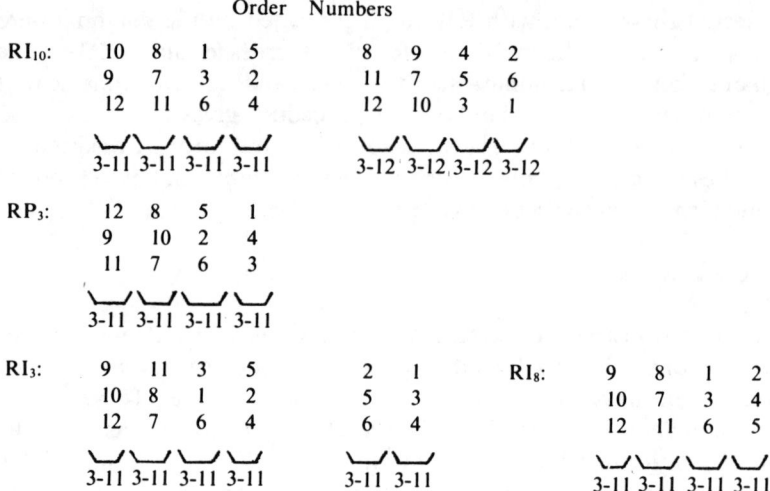

Order Numbers

RI₁₀: 10 8   1   5   8   9   4   2
         9 7   3   2   11   7   5   6
        12 11   6   4   12 10   3   1
        ⌣ ⌣ ⌣ ⌣   ⌣   ⌣   ⌣   ⌣
       3-11 3-11 3-11 3-11   3-12 3-12 3-12 3-12

RP₃: 12 8   5   1
         9 10   2   4
        11 7   6   3
        ⌣ ⌣ ⌣ ⌣
       3-11 3-11 3-11 3-11

RI₃: 9 11   3   5   2   1   RI₈: 9   8   1   2
        10 8   1   2   5   3   10   7   3   4
        12 7   6   4   6   4   12 11   6   5
        ⌣ ⌣ ⌣ ⌣   ⌣   ⌣   ⌣   ⌣   ⌣   ⌣
       3-11 3-11 3-11 3-11 3-11 3-11   3-11 3-11 3-11 3-11

Example 2.23   Suite, op. 29, #1195

Order Numbers

P_{11}: I_4:

	4	5	6					6	5	4	6	5	4
1	2	3	1	2	3			10	11	12	10	11	12
	9	8	7						7	8	9	7	8	9

```
                       ┌──── 4-10 ────┐
P₁₁:    B   E♭  D   F#  B♭  G   A♭  F   E   C   D♭  A
I₄:     E   C   D♭  A   F   A♭  G   B♭  B   E♭  D   F#
                       └──── 4-10 ────┘
```

In op. 29 Schoenberg frequently reorders P in order to create an additional harmonic dimension which emphasizes the derivational property of the principal hexachord 6-20. In some instances the reordering is so extensive that it is impossible to identify the original permutation. Example 2.22 contains a sketch showing Schoenberg's derivation of four permutations (RI_{10}, RP_3, RI_3, RI_8) by pc set 3-11 and the derivation of one permutation (RI_{10}) by pc set 3-12. Within each row form successive trichords (pc sets 3-3) are divided between two successive vertical trichords and each of these vertical trichords represents pc set 3-11 (RI_{10}, RP_3, RI_3, RI_8) or pc set 3-12 (RI_{10}). As the order numbers in Example 2.22 indicate, the repeated formation of the derivational trichords 3-11 and 3-12 as a vertical harmony has required the reordering of one or two trichords within each permutation. In this instance, the reorderings allow the formation of a secondary harmonic dimension based on the secondary harmonic trichords 3-11 and 3-12.

As mentioned at the beginning of this section, the reordering of P can be motivated by various considerations that depend on the specific musical context and the invariant relations between associated row forms. The sketch displayed in Example 2.23 contains a reordering of P which functions not only to generate an additional harmonic dimension, but also to emphasize an invariant relation between P_{11} and I_4. Example 2.23 represents an early version of m.120 of the Gigue and includes two row forms which share three invariant tetrachords. In the upper portion of the sketch Schoenberg has notated P_{11} and I_4 (probably to aid his memory) and sketched the configuration below. One trichord from each row form is missing and appears in the final version as a sustained chord which is texturally separated from the configuration appearing in the sketch. In P_{11} the R operation has been applied to the third partitioned trichord (order numbers 7, 8, 9) and in I_4 a similar reordering affects the second partitioned trichord (order numbers 4, 5, 6). These reorderings create two forms of the secondary harmonic tetrachord 4-10 which link together the upper and lower voices in both row forms. Notice that Schoenberg does not reorder the middle voice since it is already connected by the secondary harmonic tetrachord 4-17. (Because Schoenberg's sketch separates the row forms, one might suspect that he did not intend to join them; but this reading is incorrect since this exact passage appears in the final version.)

In addition to interrelating the nonlinear harmonic segments linking the upper and lower voices, these reorderings emphasize the invariant tetrachordal relation between P_{11} and I_4 by duplicating the ordering of pcs within the middle invariant tetrachordal segments. That is, the middle tetrachord of P_{11} is (B♭ G A♭ F) and the corresponding tetrachord in I_4 is (F A♭ G B♭). The reordering projects these two tetrachords, (B♭ G A♭ F) and (F A♭ G B♭), as the secondary harmonic tetrachords (4-10) that link together both row forms. Thus, in addition to forming an interrelated harmonic dimension, these reorderings also emphasize an invariant relation between P_{11} and I_4, a relation that would have been concealed in this particular configuration if P had maintained its original order.

Combinatoriality As Exhibited in the Sketches

The sketches appearing in this section all address the question of to what extent Schoenberg understood the property of combinatoriality. Hexachordal combinatoriality is a specific case of the more general property of combinatoriality, for combinatoriality can occur with all possible partitionings of the row and is not limited to hexachordal partitioning. It is not, then, limited to the segmentation of aggregates into two, three, four, or six equal size parts, a restriction that would necessarily limit the number of rows which possess this property. Combinatoriality is a more inclusive property, pertaining to *all* rows and not just to some of them.[9] Because of Schoenberg's public statements, theorists have assumed that in his early works he used only hexachordal inversional combinatoriality. But Schoenberg's statements again prove less than complete, for the sketches and music show that he was aware of the all-combinatorial property and also experimented with constructing aggregates using trichordal and tetrachordal segments.

Two sketches demonstrate that Schoenberg knew of all the T, RT, I and RI combinatorial properties of P. In the sketch appearing in Example 2.16 he lists all twelve T, RT, I, and RI combinatorially related row forms; while he has not listed the second twelve-tone group, it is unlikely that he was not aware of their similar combinatorial properties. Each row label appears with the initial pitch of its prograde permutation for reasons which have been discussed (see explanation of Example 2.16). Notice, however, that the R operation is applied to six row forms in order to ensure all the possible aggregate formations.

A second sketch appearing in Example 2.24 shows that Schoenberg has considered the use of each type of combinatorial relation within the composition. The sketch contains a list of nine combinatorially related row forms. The top row form (P_3) presents a theme and each of the remaining row forms presents the accompaniment. While most of the accompaniments have been rejected (see the diagonal lines across the row labels), Schoenberg has considered using all four types (T, RT, I, RI) of combinatorial relations.

Example 2.24 Suite, op. 29, #1184

60   Schoenberg's Sketches for the Suite op. 29 (Septett)

One of several sketches for op. 29 that suggests Schoenberg was interested in the use of tetrachordal combinatoriality appears in Example 2.25. Schoenberg here groups together three row forms: RP_7, RP_{11} and RP_3. Notice that he has used a bracket and diagonal lines to mark the two occurrences of pc set 6-20 that are formed by the association of the third dyad from each row form and by the association of the fourth dyad from each row form. The combined pc content of both forms of pc set 6-20 contains the universal set and thus represents an example of an aggregate formed by tetrachordal segments.

Example 2.25   Suite, op. 29, #1184

							12-1				
RP_7:	F	A	A♭	C	D♭	E	E♭	F♯	D	B♭	B	G
RP_{11}:	A	D♭	C	E	F	A♭	G	B♭	F♯	D	E♭	B
RP_3:	D♭	F	E	A♭	A	C	B	D	B♭	F♯	G	E♭
					6-20		6-20				

3

Harmonic Organization in Music from the Suite op. 29

The analyses of the sketch material for the Suite op. 29 strongly imply that Schoenberg's concept of harmonic structure was multidimensional, that he interrelated these dimensions by limiting the harmonic sets to those that occur as linear segments of P, and that his method of organizing harmonic structure was fundamentally the same with or without the combinatorial property.

The sketches are frequently incomplete, however, sometimes consisting only of lists of associated row forms without their compositional setting, or of preliminary sketches whose subsequent revisions appear only in the completed composition. Consequently, it is necessary to confirm the sketch analyses by showing how the structural relations sometimes only hinted at in the sketches are developed in the finished piece. The examples in this chapter, mostly drawn from the Overture, not only clarify how Schoenberg creates multidimensional harmonic structures, but also the role of surface features such as register, rhythm and orchestration.

As discussed in Chapter 2, the Suite is particularly well-suited for analyzing Schoenberg's method of organizing harmony in both the combinatorial and noncombinatorial situations. Even though its row is all-combinatorial, there are many sections where the combinatorial property is not used. Thus, while one level of harmonic structure is frequently controlled by combinatoriality, there are enough noncombinatorial sections to provide a useful model for comparing Schoenberg's techniques for organizing harmonic structure in both types of situations.

In determining the secondary harmonic segments in the following examples, I adhere to Schoenberg's conception of a twelve-tone harmony (see Chapter 1): that it consists of at least two successive intervals of the basic set; that it is identified primarily by its total intervallic content so that the ordering of its intervals need not duplicate the ordering of the basic set; that it can occur in either the vertical or horizontal dimension; that it is determined by rhythmic or registral association, or by functional similarity (melody or accompaniment); that it overlaps and occurs simultaneously with other harmonic events; and that it is not restricted to a fixed pitch-class content.

Schoenberg asserts that all elements of a single harmonic event occupy, in his words, the same spatial continuum. The types of configurations he uses to project ordered segments of the row give a good indication of what he views as the same spatial continuum. As in Chapters 1 and 2, in order to reconstruct Schoenberg's harmonic structures, I mark as discrete harmonic dimensions only those configurations which Schoenberg might use to display ordered segments of the basic set. In the following examples, then, one criterion for isolating an harmonic dimension is that the configuration could be used to project an ordered segment of the row.

It may be helpful to review briefly some of the more important definitions of terms. There are two general types of harmonic dimension. The first, provided by the original ordering of P, controls the harmonic structure of a single dimension and is called the "primary dimension" of harmonic structure. The second, based on pc sets equivalent to those formed by the linear segments of P and comprised of noncontiguous elements drawn from one or more row forms, is called the "secondary dimension" of harmonic structure. The terms "primary" and "secondary" are not intended to imply relative importance; "primary" indicates only that the harmonic event represents a linear segment and "secondary" indicates a nonlinear segment. It is worth emphasizing that I use "linear segment" and "harmony of P" synonymously; but since the harmonies of P represent all segments composed of three to nine contiguous order numbers *and their complements,* a "linear segment" may sometimes contain, for example, the final and initial segments of the basic set. To call such a segment "linear" may seem confusing if one does not clearly understand Schoenberg's definition of a basic set. The reasons for including complements as harmonies of the basic set are given in Chapter 1, but it is useful in studying the following analyses to keep in mind the notational similarity between the labelling of sets that are complementary.[1]

Unless otherwise noted, all of the following musical examples maintain the original ordering of the basic set. Because their primary dimensions of harmonic structure are thus on one level identical—even though they may unfold with a variety of partitions and configurations—I have marked *only those sets which represent secondary dimensions of harmonic structure.* In other words, all of the indicated pc sets represent non-linear harmonic segments, but project sets equivalent to linear segments of P. Below each musical example I indicate where these equivalent sets occur as linear segments of P. As in Chapter 2, a "secondary harmonic set" is one which occurs *simultaneously* in a primary and secondary harmonic dimension. Its chief function is to relate two or more dimensions of harmonic structure to a single source, the basic set. Since all of the marked harmonic sets unfold secondary harmonic dimensions, they all represent secondary harmonic sets. (See Example 2.3 for the most important secondary harmonic sets.)

My discussion is divided into four sections. The first analyzes Schoenberg's method of organizing harmonic structure within single row forms. The second concentrates on his techniques of combining two or more row forms. Dealing first with noncombinatorial and then with combinatorial related row forms, I demonstrate that an important consideration in the pairing or grouping of rows is their potential for forming interlocking harmonic sets which duplicate sets occurring as linear segments of P, and that Schoenberg realizes this potential through manipulation of surface features such as rhythm, dynamics, register and orchestration.

The third section clarifies the extent to which Schoenberg uses the combinatorial property. Musical examples illustrate how the diverse methods of aggregate formation only hinted at in the sketch material are realized in the completed composition. The fourth section deals with the internal reordering of P. I show that reorderings are not merely local occurrences with no structural significance, but are often required in order to generate secondary harmonies involving more than one dimension.

A topic crucial to each of the above sections is the role invariants play in the organization of multidimensional harmonic structures. As discussed in Section 3.2, twelve-tone theorists typically imply that row succession or pairing is controlled primarily by the association of invariant segments. Both the sketches and op. 29 itself show, however, that equally and perhaps more important is the potential of two rows to form sets equivalent to linear segments of P. Moreover, it appears that invariant pitches or segments serve primarily to *limit* the number of pitch-classes within secondary harmonic sets that contain duplicated pitch-classes.

The Harmonic Organization of Individual Row Forms

The sketches for op. 29 contain many incomplete or simplified models for individual row configurations. Often they consist only of a series of chords with little or no rhythmic differentiation and offer more than one possible interpretation for the segmentation of secondary harmonic dimensions. The harmonic dimensions Schoenberg intended become clear, however, within the context of the composition. We find that a simplified model in the sketches frequently serves as the basis for many varied configurations, all sharing a similar multidimensional harmonic structure. Comparison of these related configurations clarifies the function of surface features in the delineation of secondary harmonic dimensions.

A sketch discussed in Chapter 2 (Example 3.1) which displays the simultaneous unfolding of the four trichordal segments of P_3 offers an

Example 3.1 Suite, op. 29, #1185

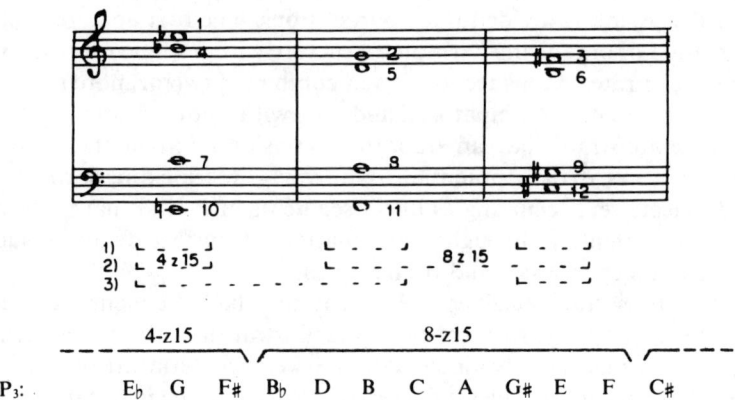

excellent example of how Schoenberg elaborates a simple harmonic model within the composition.[2] While the original ordering of P controls the horizontal primary harmonic dimension, there is no indication as to which segments constitute the vertical secondary harmonic dimension. As shown in Example 3.1, there are three possibilities: 1) three harmonic segments, each containing one vertical chord, 2) two harmonic segments, the first containing the first chord and the second containing the final two chords and 3) two harmonic segments, the first containing the first two chords and the second containing the final chord. The rhythmic structure of the sketch favors each possibility equally, but only the second segmentation projects pc sets equivalent to linear segments of P, the complementary sets 4-z15 and 8-z15.

Example 3.2 Suite, op. 29, Overture

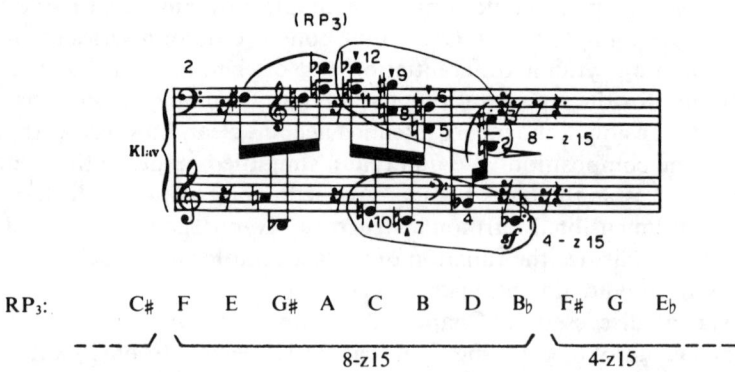

When Schoenberg uses this model in op. 29 he clearly delineates the secondary harmonic sets 4-z15 and 8-z15. In Example 3.2, rhythm and register clearly indicate the structure of the secondary harmonic dimension. Notice how different this configuration is from the sketched model; while both contain identical primary and secondary harmonic dimensions, their vertical and horizontal pc sets have been switched.

Example 3.3 Suite, op. 29, Overture

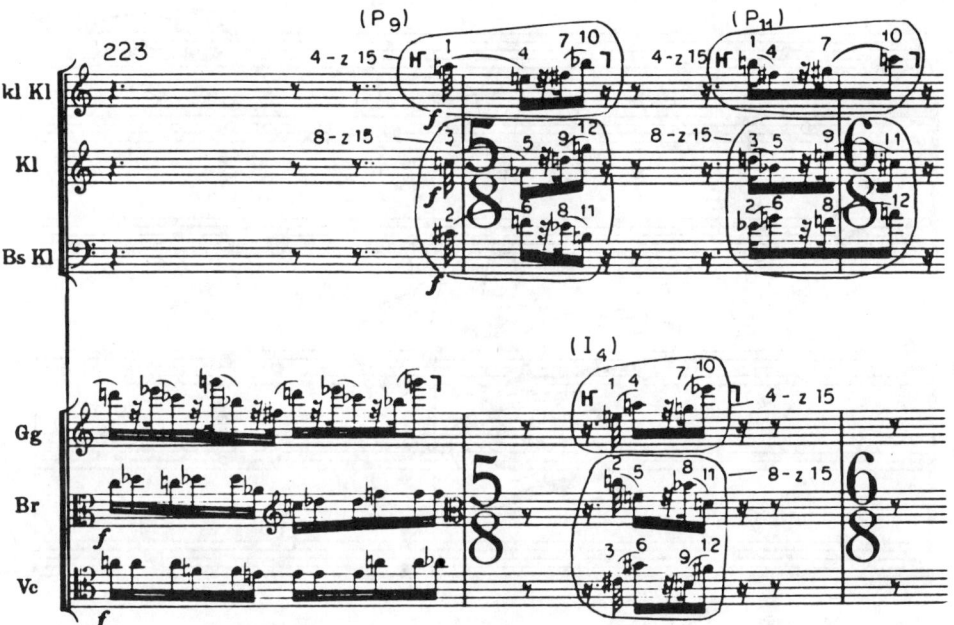

Another configuration based on this same model appears in Example 3.3. In this instance Schoenberg indicates the secondary harmonic dimension not by rhythm or register, but by designating the principal melodic line (H⁻). He thus effectively divides the configuration into two horizontal harmonic segments that are determined by textural function (melody and accompaniment) and that project the secondary harmonic sets 4-z15 and 8-z15. In the absence of rhythmic and registral differentiation, then, we find that Schoenberg often adds the H⁻ marking to insure the appropriate segmentation of the secondary harmonic dimension.

The inclusion of H⁻ and N⁻ markings serves to separate the principal melodic voices from the accompaniment. Schoenberg typically includes a single H⁻ marking; however there are many instances where none occurs, or where various combinations of two or more H⁻ and N⁻ markings occur simultaneously. As indicated by Example 3.3, one reason for including the H⁻ marking, then, is to clarify the division of the texture into theme and accompaniment and in so doing to delineate the simultaneous secondary harmonic dimensions. The inclusion of a second N⁻ or H⁻ marking appears to be motivated by similar, but slightly different, considerations.

Example 3.4 Suite, op. 29, Overture

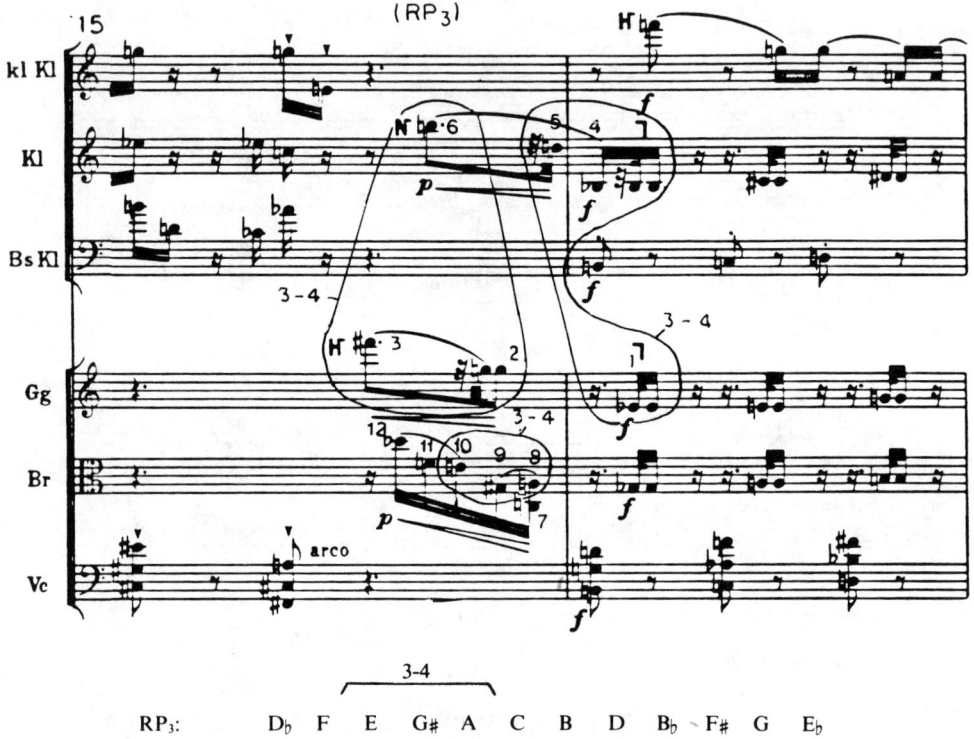

Example 3.4 contains the final version of the sketch appearing in Example 2.5. The combined upper voices project vertically two forms of pc set 3-4; both contain noncontiguous elements and represent a secondary harmonic dimension. Two revisions are made in the final configuration. The first involves the addition of the H⁻ and N⁻ markings; notice that without them the final pitch of pc sets 3-4 (Cl., Vln.) would not be differentiated from the additional voices entering on the first and second beats of m.16. The second involves the simultaneous statement of the dyad occurring on order numbers 7 and 8 (dyad C A). By placing the pitch represented by order number 7 below that of order number 8, Schoenberg makes more prominent the single linear

occurrence of pc set 3-4 in the basic set and thus effectively reinforces or complements the equivalent forms of pc set 3-4 that structure the secondary harmonic dimension. Similar to Example 3.3, the H⁻ and N⁻ markings in Example 3.4 clarify the structure of secondary harmonic dimensions; in this instance they indicate the specific melodic voices whose interaction projects a discrete harmonic dimension. As this example shows, the inclusion of more than one melodic voice (H⁻ or N⁻) indicates not only that each voice contains a separate harmonic segment (in this instance an ordered segment), but that the voices *together* are separated from the accompaniment and project a single harmonic dimension.

Example 3.5 Suite, op. 29, Overture

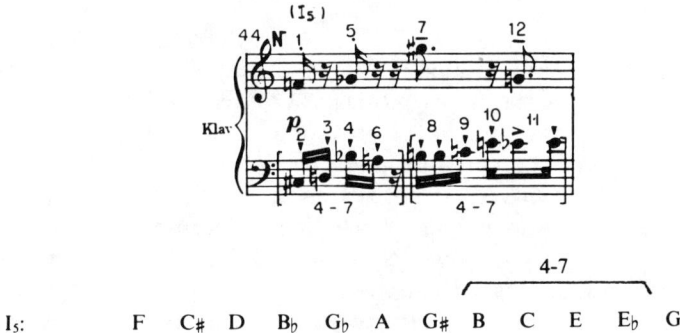

Schoenberg frequently uses a secondary harmonic dimension to duplicate sets that appear in the piece itself as partitioned segments of the primary harmonic dimension. In Example 3.4, for instance, both secondary harmonic segments contain pc set 3-4 and the simultaneous primary dimension literally projects pc set 3-4 as an ordered segment (viola). A less complex, but perhaps clearer use of this technique appears in Example 3.5. Notice that the lower voice of the piano consists of two rhythmically partitioned segments, each projecting pc set 4-7; the first occurrence represents a nonlinear segment, and the second represents a partitioned linear segment. The secondary harmonic dimension, then, sometimes duplicates or reiterates pc sets appearing as partitioned ordered segments in the primary harmonic dimension, a technique which effectively limits the number of different harmonic sets and saturates the primary and secondary harmonic dimensions with equivalent forms of the same sets.

The discussion of Example 1.11 clarified the conditions under which Schoenberg rotates partitioned segments of the row. (In Example 1.11, the rotation of a hexachordal segment maintained a tetrachordal pattern that spanned the linear statement of the original basic set.) Similarly, in op. 29

Example 3.6 Suite, op. 29, Overture

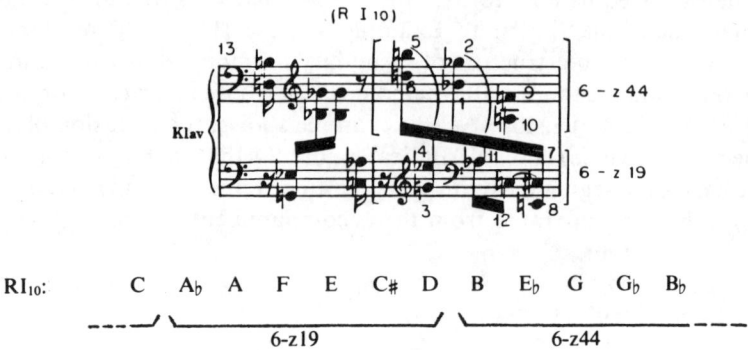

RI₁₀: C   A♭   A   F   E   C♯   D   B   E♭   G   G♭   B♭
    ---⏝_____/_____/---
              6-z19   6-z44

when a segment is cyclically rotated it usually preserves a specific structural pattern that spans the basic set. Often this pattern derives not from a simple linear statement of the row, but from some other more complicated configuration. Example 3.6 contains a configuration of RI₁₀ similar to the sketch appearing in Example 2.7. In both examples the registral association of alternating dyads creates a secondary harmonic dimension that projects the complementary, secondary harmonic sets 6-z19 and 6-z44; however, unlike Example 2.7, Example 3.6 uses a rotated hexachordal segment (C, A♭, A, F, E, C♯). If Schoenberg had applied this specific configuration to a row form whose rotated segment contained an odd number of pitches (1, 3, or 5 pcs), then the registral association of alternating dyads would not have produced hexachords equivalent to harmonies of the basic set. Only by rotating a segment containing an even number of pitches (2, 4, or 6 pcs) could Schoenberg reproduce the same harmonic dimension that is formed when this configuration unfolds the original form of P (that is, P without cyclical rotation). Thus, the specific structural pattern of the basic set which is duplicated by rotation does not necessarily appear in the linear statement of the row, but can be a pattern projected when the row appears in a specific configuration. In this example, the configuration when applied to the basic set *and* its rotated form produces an identical secondary dimension of harmonic structure.

As shown by Example 2.7, the display of vertical partitioned tetrachords often projects a horizontal harmonic dimension composed of secondary harmonic hexachords. Example 3.7 shows Schoenberg applying this technique to four successive row forms and creating a secondary harmonic dimension containing the complementary hexachords 6-z19/6-z44 and 6-z24/6-z46.[3] Pc sets 6-z19/6-z44 are extracted in two different ways: the first (I_{11}), similar to Example 2.7, associates alternating dyads 1, 3, 5 and 2, 4, 6,

Example 3.7 Suite, op. 29, Overture

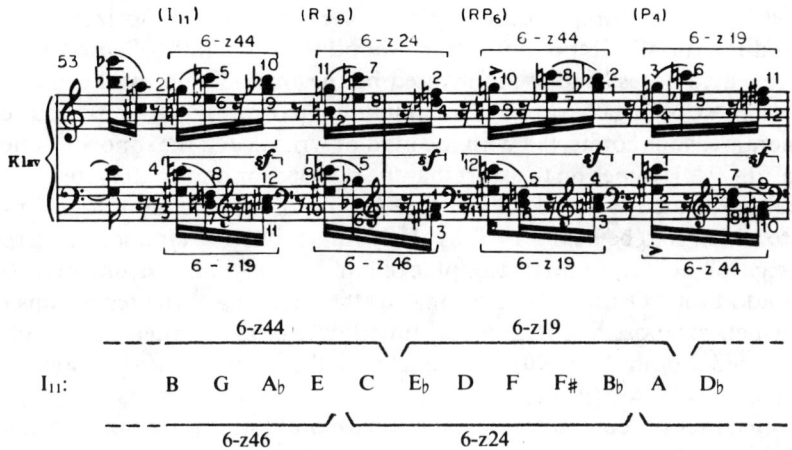

and the second (RP$_6$, P$_4$) associates dyads 1, 4, 5 and 2, 3, 6. Notice that the use of different dyadic patterns in I$_{11}$ and RP$_6$ (that is, dyads 1, 3, 5/2, 4, 6 and dyads 1, 4, 5/2,3,6) results in the extraction of identical forms of 6-z19/6-z44. The formation of 6-z24/6-z46 is more complicated; it requires the splitting of dyads and the association of pitch classes represented by order numbers 2, 4, 7, 8, 11, 12 and 1, 3, 5, 6, 9, 10. In this example, four successive row forms are grouped together by a repeating configuration and by a secondary harmonic dimension which displays secondary harmonic hexachords. We thus find that Schoenberg constructs a model configuration to display not just a specific secondary set (that is, hexachord), but various secondary sets of the same cardinality, all of which produce sets equivalent to the linear harmonies of P.

Pitch Repetitions and Doublings

In "Composition with Twelve Tones" Schoenberg prohibits the repetition of any pitch in the basic set outside of its normal order position. Such a procedure would disturb the intervallic progression of the set and give unequal emphasis to the repeated pitch. Unequal emphasis also arises from octave doubling and, according to Schoenberg, should be avoided, for it might create undesired tonal effects. These restrictions do not apply, however, to the immediate repetition of pitches or to their doubling within the same register. Both represent techniques for pitch repetition which Schoenberg frequently uses.

Twelve-tone theorists say little about Schoenberg's use of pitch repetitions and doublings, and none discuss how they effect harmonic structure.

Josef Rufer, who as a student of Schoenberg is viewed as a reliable source for his twelve-tone procedures, claims that repetitions increase the flexibility of a basic set "from the compositional point of view in both the horizontal and vertical dimension."[4] Repetitions "correspond to a held note of equal length to the repeated notes" and are motivated by the "melodic line of the musical conception, or by the character of an individual part or figure, or as required for general reasons connected with the kind of writing and the sonority aimed at" (pp. 70-71). He goes on to assert that the reasons for immediate repetitions are often associated "with instrumental technique or on grounds of sonority—if a note which is to be held for a fairly long time is liable to stop sounding too soon (e.g., piano, string pizzicato, plucked and percussion instruments)" (p. 87). In addition: "Ostinato also belongs to the category of the repetitions of notes which are possible; its musical function can be regarded as that of a 'melodic pedal-point'" (p. 90). He concludes that "the inspiration alone is decisive in each case" (p. 71).

Notice that his comments deal more with orchestration techniques than with the nature of repetition as a compositional procedure. To continue his analogy with tonal music, pedal points are important because of their harmonic function, and to describe a related technique in twelve-tone composition without clarifying its harmonic implications is not very useful. Moreover, his assertion that "inspiration alone is decisive in each case" suggests that different considerations govern every case and consequently no general description would be particularly informative. As shown by the following examples, repetitions and doublings do have specific harmonic implications and most often are required to generate multidimensional harmonic structures.

Example 3.8 contains the opening measures of the Overture and shows three successive row forms set forth by similar configurations (P_3, I_8, I_{10}). The primary harmonic dimension is controlled by the regular ordering of P. The winds and strings, however, articulate simultaneously a secondary harmonic dimension. The first hexachord of each permutation contains six repeated pitch-classes which function to generate four nonlinear and nonidentical forms of pc set 3-11; the cello, violin, viola, and woodwinds each project one occurrence of pc set 3-11. As discussed in Chapter 2, pc set 6-20 is the only hexachord which can be derived in three different ways by the trichord 3-11. The formation of four different forms of 3-11 thus emphasizes the derivational property of 6-20. The second hexachord of each permutation (piano) similarly displays a secondary harmonic dimension based on pc set 3-11; in each row form register delineates a single derivation of 6-20 by 3-11.[5] Thus in Example 3.8, pitch doublings, along with register, generate a secondary harmonic dimension based on the unique derivational property of the principal hexachord of P.

Harmonic Organization in Music from the Suite op. 29   71

Example 3.8   Suite, op. 29, Overture

72 Harmonic Organization in Music from the Suite op. 29

Example 3.9 Suite, op. 29, Overture

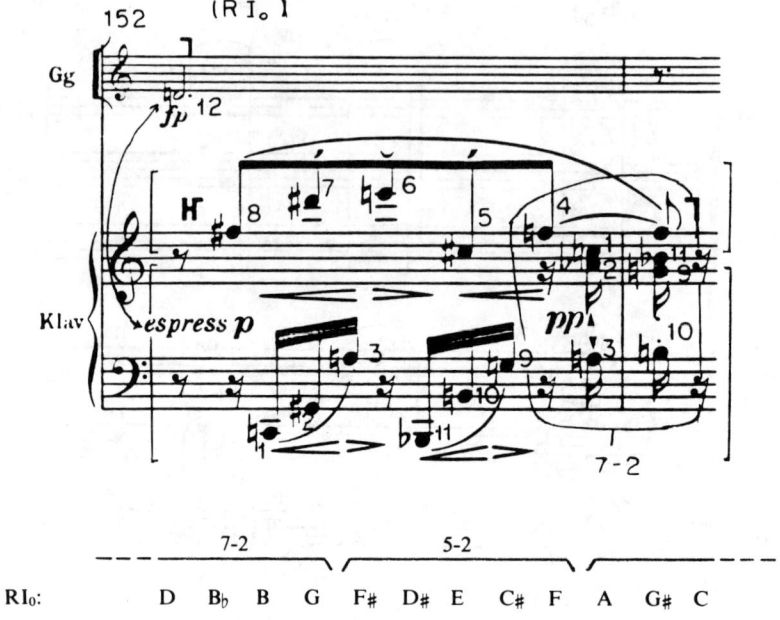

In configurations for single row forms Schoenberg frequently repeats partitioned segments, for in his view, if the ordering of P is maintained by the original segment, then its repetition does not constitute a reordering. As shown by Example 3.9, these repetitions frequently articulate an added secondary harmonic dimension. In Example 3.9, the H⁻ marking distinguishes the melodic line (pc set 5-2) from the accompaniment (pc set 7-2); both represent linear segments of RI_0, as indicated.[6] The accompaniment consists of one sustained pitch (violin) and two trichords (piano); the immediate repetition of both trichords is rhythmically associated with the final sustained pitch of the melodic line (F) and creates an equivalent form of pc set 7-2. This example is particularly interesting, for not only does the repetition create a secondary harmonic dimension, but it duplicates a set emphasized by the original partitioning of the basic set. The repeating trichords thus serve to saturate both dimensions of harmonic structure with equivalent forms of the same set, 7-2. The function of the repetition also explains why one pitch (D) of the accompaniment is texturally isolated from the remaining accompaniment figure: if the D had been repeated with the remaining accompaniment, the secondary set 7-2 would not have been formed and the primary and secondary dimensions consequently would not have projected equivalent sets.

Example 3.10 Suite, op. 29, Overture

The immediate repetition of partitioned row segments often functions to complete a rhythmic design or a secondary harmonic dimension. An instance of the latter case appears in Example 3.10 where there appears what one might mistakenly interpret to be a haphazard repetition of partitioned trichords.

The H⁻ voice (violin) projects an ordered horizontal statement of P_7 and is accompanied by successive repetitions of partitioned trichords.[7] If the successive trichords are numbered 1, 2, 3 and 4 in the prograde permutation, their registral pattern in the first configuration is:

```
        Woodwinds:  2
        (H⁻) Violin: 1
            Piano:  3 4
```

One might expect similar patterns in the remaining configurations, that is:

```
        Woodwinds:  2    1    4    3
        (H⁻) Violin: 1    2    3    4
            Piano:  3 4  3 4  1 2  1 2
```

This produces a symmetrical pattern, tightly organized by three horizontal aggregates, which maximizes the juxtaposition of contiguous trichords within each configuration. Instead, the following pattern occurs:

```
        Woodwinds:  2    3    4    1
        (H⁻) Violin: 1    2    3    4
            Piano:  3 4  4 1  1 2  2 3
```

This design, while producing the same horizontal aggregates, is less symmetrical and creates irregular ordering implications, especially in the second configuration.

The reason for this specific succession of trichords becomes apparent if one considers the successive vertical simultaneities between the violin (H⁻) and winds. Each of the vertical harmonies, most of which contain noncontiguous pitches in the basic set, represents a tetrachord equivalent to a linear segment of P. No other grouping of trichords will produce an uninterrupted succession of secondary harmonic tetrachords. Thus, a texture which seems to be dominated by repeating, partitioned and arbitrarily grouped trichords is controlled by a secondary harmonic dimension derived by associating vertically noncontiguous elements of P.

The Harmonic Organization of Two or More Row Forms

Twelve-tone theorists traditionally describe two general methods for organizing harmonic structure between successive or simultaneous row permutations. The first relies on the association of row forms through invariant segments, and the second prescribes the use of the combinatorial property to form aggregates. Rufer describes the first method by noting that the "three chief means of joining two series together in a linear manner are the note, the motive and the chord" (p. 132). He compares the note technique to the classical procedure where "the consequent of a theme begins with the last note of the antecedent and continues the former in a fluent manner" (p. 132). When applied to twelve-tone composition, this method creates continuity by overlapping the final pitch of one row form with an invariant first pitch of the following row form. He describes motive technique as when "two phrases or sections of themes are joined together by a subsidiary part which goes across the join" (p. 133).

The third technique, similar to the first, deals with invariant segments: "the chord can make a convincing connection between two series, especially when these contain the same chords as one another, either partly—e.g. in certain note groups—or as wholes" (p. 133). In this instance, the invariant chords represent either internal or overlapping end segments whose connecting effect "depends on their dual meaning" (p. 133). Rufer's view—that the association of row forms through invariant segments represents a principal method of creating harmonic structure—recurs in most theoretical writings on twelve-tone music.

The second method of organizing harmonic structure between two row forms relies on the use of the combinatorial property to form aggregates. In "Composition with Twelve Tones" Schoenberg confirms this technique and gives the following description:

> Later, especially in larger works, I changed my original idea [that is, basic set], if necessary, to fit the following conditions: the inversion a fifth below of the first six tones, the antecedent, should not produce a repetition of one of these six tones, but should bring forth the hitherto unused six tones of the chromatic scale. Thus, the consequent of the basic set, the tones 7 to 12, comprises the tones of this inversion, but, of course, in a different order.[8]

As discussed in Chapter 1, Schoenberg's emphasis on inversional combinatoriality at the lower fifth has given rise to the common view that not only did he prefer this type of combinatoriality, but that it was the only type he used.[9] It also has led to the opinion that his early twelve-tone compositions are exploratory and important largely because they lead to the mature combinatorial pieces.

Even though analysis of his early works dispels both opinions, it is generally assumed that the combinatorial property more fully integrates harmonic structure. It is this assumption which leads Perle, for example, to assert that "combinatoriality is the only general principle for the simultaneous alignment of different set-forms that has so far been employed."[10]

Without question, Schoenberg frequently uses invariant segments and combinatoriality to organize harmonic structure between discrete row forms. But in addition to these techniques, as the following examples show, he devises other, perhaps more important methods. As the sketches reveal, one important technique for the pairing or grouping of rows is the formation of interlocking harmonic sets which duplicate sets occurring as linear segments of P. While this method in some instances is dependent on invariant segments, Schoenberg's use of invariant segments is much more complex than the "linking" or "overlapping chords" described by Rufer.

I begin by reviewing briefly the important combinatorial properties of the basic set. The Suite's all-combinatorial row maintains combinatorial relations at three transpositional levels for I, T, RI and RT. This means that out of twenty-four possible permutations, there will be two groups, each consisting of twelve row forms whose hexachords contain the same pitch classes. With the use of the retrograde operation, all can be made combinatorially related to each other.[11] As described in Chapter 2, the structure of the principal hexachord (6-20) accounts for the high density of combinatorial relations. Since there are only four possible unordered forms of this hexachord, only two rows with nonidentical hexachords can be constructed. Thus, among the twenty-four permutations of P, each permutation is combinatorially related to eleven other permutations. Despite the frequent pairing of combinatorially related row forms, the Suite contains many instances where noncombinatorially related row forms are joined. This clearly suggests that while Schoenberg was aware of the combinatorial property, he did not regard it as the only effective means of harmonic organization.

As discussed in Chapter 2, the hexachord 6-20 has the unique property of derivation by each of its four trichords (3-3, 3-4, 3-11, 3-12). Among these four trichords, only 3-11 does not occur as a linear segment of P. (Its inclusion would have prohibited the symmetrical occurrences of pc sets 3-3 and 4-17.) Schoenberg does, however, use pc set 3-11 consistently to structure secondary harmonic dimensions (see Example 3.8). In such a context, it integrates primary and secondary harmonic dimensions by emphasizing the unique derivational property of the principal hexachord. Pc set 3-11 is thus the only set I refer to as a secondary harmonic set which does not occur as a linear segment of P.

The invariant segment between any two hexachords from noncombinatorially related row forms (that is, between row forms whose hexachords do not contain the same pitches) is always pc set 3-12, a feature determined by the limited number of unique forms of 6-20. It is significant that Schoenberg includes pc set 3-12 as a linear segment of P (order numbers 3-5), for whenever the hexachords from two noncombinatorially related row forms are associated, the invariant trichord 3-12 functions to integrate both their primary and secondary harmonic dimensions. If pc set 3-12 had not been included as a linear segment, then the absence of the combinatorial property could have resulted in less integrated harmonic structures.

Harmonic Organization in Music from the Suite op. 29   77

The first group of examples deals with harmonic structure between row forms that are not combinatorially related. As in the previous sections, *all* pc sets marked on the musical examples contain noncontiguous elements of one or more row forms and represent secondary harmonic dimensions derived from the linear set structure of P.

Example 3.11   Suite, op. 29, Overture

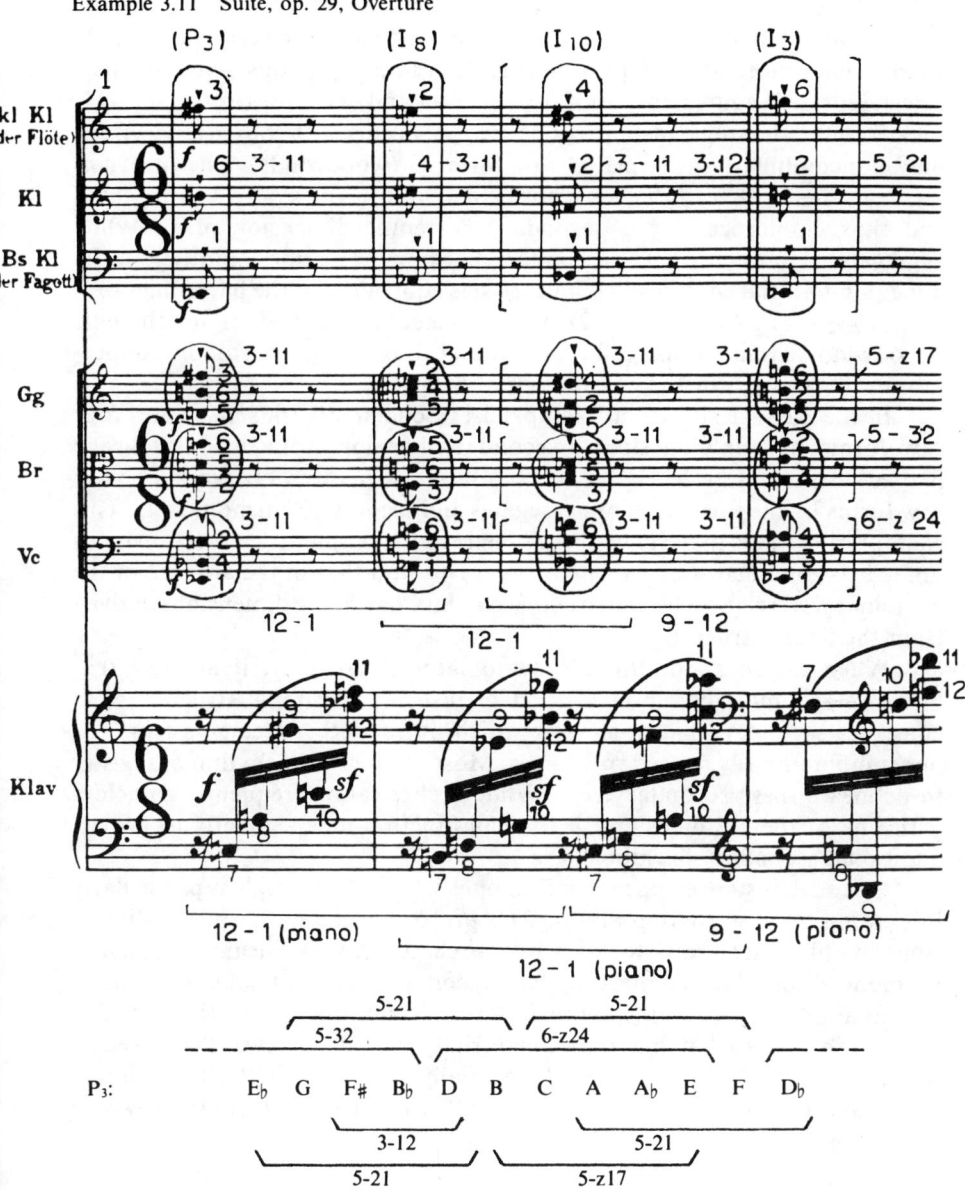

Noncombinatorially Related Row Forms

The introduction to the Overture presents the row succession $P_3:I_8:I_{10}:I_3$. The combinatorial property structures $P_3:I_8:I_{10}$, but does not associate I_3. Secondary harmonic dimensions within each row form exploit the derivational property of pc set 6-20 by 3-11. (See the discussion of Example 3.8.) Schoenberg's awareness of the special significance of pc set 3-12 (see p. 76) is dramatically illustrated with the entrance of I_3. In all four permutations, the winds, cello, viola and violin project sixteen noncontiguous simultaneities; fifteen represent equivalent forms of pc set 3-11 and one represents pc set 3-12. Significantly, the single instance of pc set 3-12 occurs with the entrance of the only noncombinatorially related row form, I_3 (woodwinds). The invariant segment, then, between the hexachords of I_3 and I_{10} (pc set 3-12) is repeated and thus emphasized by a secondary harmonic dimension of I_3. While aggregates connect $P_3:I_8:I_{10}$, secondary harmonic sets horizontally join the noncombinatorial row forms I_3 and I_{10}; sets equivalent to the harmonies of P (5-21, 5-z18, 5-32, 6-z24, 9-12) are projected by individual instruments (woodwinds, violin, viola, cello, piano) and thus provide harmonic connection in the absence of the combinatorial property.

In the passage shown in Example 3.11 Schoenberg thus associates four row forms by applying similar secondary harmonic dimensions to each individual permutation. He creates harmonic structure *between* successive row forms by the formation of aggregates and secondary harmonic sets. This example illustrates that Schoenberg's concern for harmonic connection is not limited to combinatorially related row forms and that in the absence of the combinatorial relation he constructs secondary harmonic dimensions derived from the linear structure of P.

When he does not use the combinatorial property, it appears that Schoenberg's most common method of insuring harmonic structure is to construct secondary harmonic sets which link together elements from the noncombinatorially related row forms. Most often he uses rhythm or register to delineate these secondary sets. While orchestration frequently coincides with one of these dimensions, it too can function independently to project additional secondary harmonic sets.

One such instance appears in Example 3.12. This example is particularly interesting because rhythm and register project secondary harmonic dimensions within each row form, while orchestration delineates secondary harmonic dimensions connecting the noncombinatorially related row forms.

Example 3.12 contains two pairs of associated row forms ($P_8:I_5$, $I_0:P_7$). The members of each pair are combinatorially related; however, as marked by the dotted line, $P_8:I_5$ is not combinatorially related to $I_0:P_7$. The internal secondary harmonic structure of P_8 and I_0 is identical to that shown in

Example 3.12 Suite, op. 29, Overture

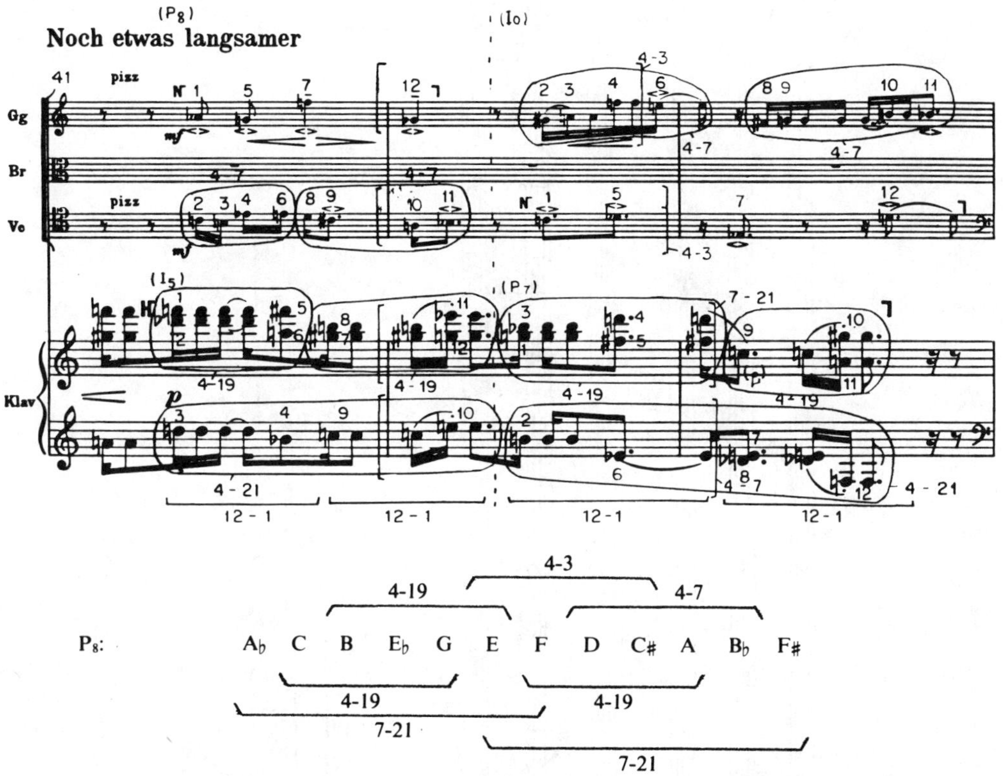

Example 3.5; their primary and secondary harmonic dimensions both project pc set 4-7. Similarly, I_5 and P_7 share identical secondary harmonic dimensions comprised of two occurrences of pc set 4-21 and four repetitions of pc set 4-19.[12] Thus, in each *individual* row form, rhythm and register project secondary harmonic dimensions and aggregate formation controls the vertical harmonic structure between combinatorially related row forms (indicated by pc set 12-1). But in addition Schoenberg uses the instrumentation to generate the secondary harmonic sets (4-3, 4-7, 7-21) that link together the noncombinatorially related row forms. All of these sets represent harmonies of P and their formation is dependent on instrumentation alone.

Throughout the Suite the principal voices of independent phrases typically display a uniform type of partitioning, that is, they all exhibit, for example, either trichordal, tetrachordal, or hexachordal partitioned segments. When Schoenberg interrupts such a pattern, most often it is required for the generation of a secondary harmonic dimension, as for example in the phrase shown in Example 3.13.

Example 3.13 Suite, op. 29, Overture

Example 3.13 contains the principal voices of a complete phrase ($I_3:I_{10}:RP_3$). Although I_{10} and RP_3 are combinatorially related, they are not connected by aggregates; I_3 is not combinatorially related to either I_{10} or RP_3 (marked by dotted line). The first two permutations (I_3, I_{10}) display overlapping trichordal partitions which create two equivalent vertical forms of 3-11 between each pair of partitions; in each case 3-11 is formed by noncontiguous elements and thus represents a secondary harmonic dimension. Schoenberg creates an additional secondary harmonic dimension by the inclusion of RP_3 in m.20; but notice that its tetrachordal partitioning marks an abrupt change from the preceding texture. With the completion of RP_3 each individual instrument projects a secondary harmonic set containing pcs from two or three row permutations. (The bass clarinet, which contains only one trichord from I_{10}, marks the only exception; but since it contains only contiguous pitches from one row form, it requires no secondary harmonic structures.) If Schoenberg had maintained the preceding textural design and partitioned RP_3 into trichords, a horizontal secondary harmonic dimension connecting all three row forms could not have been formed. In this example, it is this horizontal dimension which gives harmonic coherence to a complete phrase in the absence of the combinatorial property.

Similar to the sets that structure secondary harmonic dimensions in single row forms, those that structure several row forms are often either equivalent or complement-related. Example 3.14 is particularly complex, for it not only uses both equivalent and complement-related sets to structure numerous secondary dimensions, but also employs simultaneously four methods of delineating secondary harmonic sets: rhythm, register, orchestration and textural function. This passage represents the concluding phrase of the first large section of the Overture (mm.1-29). Its four successive row forms, $I_2:I_0:I_7:I_0$, contain one noncombinatorially related row, I_7. Similar to the beginning of this section (see Example 3.11), secondary harmonic sets are formed which emphasize the derivational property of pc set 6-20; within each permutation the instrumentation delineates two occurrences of pc set 3-11 (viola and cello), and registral association projects two occurrences of pc set 3-4 (piano).

As is frequently the case, textural function distinguishes additional secondary harmonic dimensions that serve to connect successive permutations. The H⁻ voice, containing one pc from each of the first three permutations, projects pc set 3-11 and functions not only to join noncombinatorially related row forms harmonically, but also to repeat through equivalent sets a secondary harmonic dimension in each individual row form. The accompaniment in Example 3.14 contains two contrasting textural patterns (viola: cello, piano) that delineate two seperate harmonic dimensions. The piano forms four occurrences of pc set 4-19, each containing contiguous

Example 3.14 Suite, op. 29, Overture

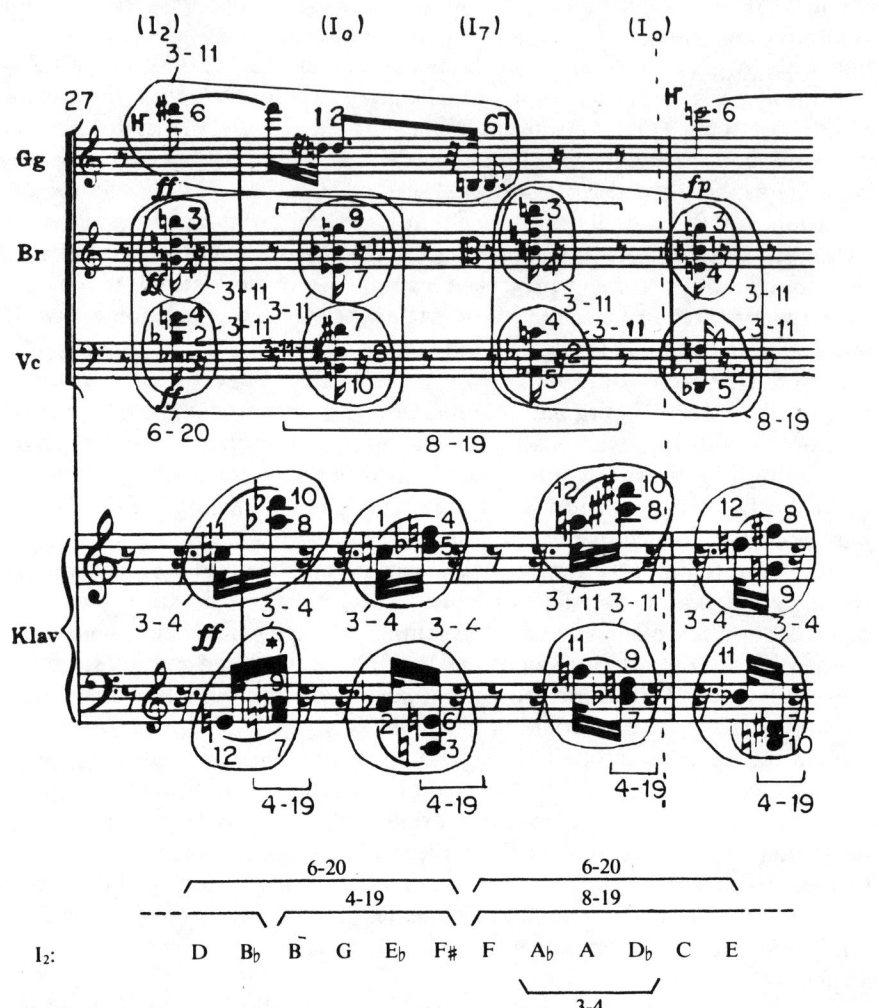

elements from one row form and thus representing the primary harmonic dimension. Simultaneously, the strings join each successive row form through the formation of the complement-related set 8-19 (two occurrences) and 6-20. Thus, within this example each permutation contains two secondary harmonic dimensions (3-11, 3-4), and one partitioned primary dimension (4-19). Successive permutations are harmonically joined by two additional secondary dimensions comprised of pc sets 8-19 and 3-11; in the first, 8-19 represents the complement of the primary harmonic set, 4-19, and in the second, the trichord

3-11 duplicates the secondary trichord that structures individual row forms in the cello and viola. The density of harmonic segments requires the independent use of orchestration, rhythm, register, and texture for the delineation of discrete harmonic dimensions. In this example, Schoenberg creates a totally integrated harmonic structure by using secondary harmonic sets to join noncontiguous elements from two or more row forms. This technique allows Schoenberg to associate noncombinatorially related row forms, but still derive harmonic structure from a single basic set.

Combinatorially Related Row Forms

In "Composition with Twelve Tones" Schoenberg includes only a limited number of examples showing how he used the combinatorial property. These examples generally display aggregates that contain hexachords from two combinatorially related row forms and consist of exactly twelve elements. In the Suite, however, there are many passages that exhibit a more complicated use of this property. If we examine the passages derived solely from combinatorially related row forms, we find that Schoenberg does not use the combinatorial property in a uniform manner, for he frequently does not exploit its potential for aggregate formation and uses instead other methods for organizing harmonic structure. Moreover, when aggregates do occur, they often involve more than two permutations or contain more than twelve elements. The latter instance suggests that to define the function of aggregates merely as a means of ensuring equal pitch-class distribution is somewhat incomplete, as will be discussed below.[13]

In the following discussion I describe three general ways in which Schoenberg uses the combinatorial property. The first involves the formation of aggregates which contain exactly twelve elements; similar to the harmonic structure of noncombinatorially related row forms, these examples often display secondary harmonic dimensions. The second includes examples of aggregates containing more than twelve elements. It will be shown that in such aggregates the duplicated pitches always are required to generate secondary dimensions of harmonic structure. The third method involves the association of combinatorially related row forms in which *no* aggregate formation occurs. In these examples, the structure of secondary harmonic dimensions suggests that the primary function of the combinatorial property is to provide a high density of invariant pitches. Between these three uses of the combinatorial property, Schoenberg's method of organizing harmonic structure does not significantly change. In a way resembling his method of connecting noncombinatorially related row forms, he consistently connects combinatorially related row forms by constructing multiple secondary harmonic dimensions derived from the internal structure of P.

Example 3.15 Suite, op. 29, Overture

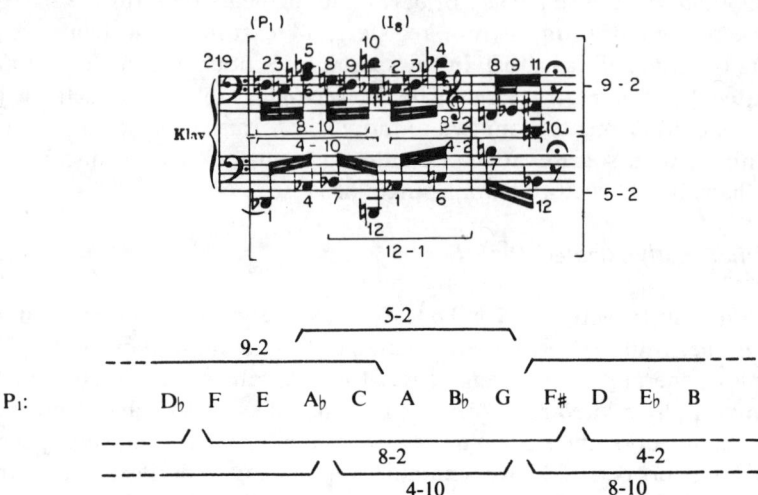

Aggregates containing exactly twelve elements. The least complicated use of the combinatorial property requires the association of hexachords from two combinatorially related row forms and the formation of an aggregate containing exactly twelve elements. In the Suite, aggregates of this type rarely occur independently of other secondary harmonic dimensions. As Example 3.15 shows, aggregate formation alone often does not adequately describe how Schoenberg organizes harmonic structure. In Example 3.15, the successive statements of P_1 and I_8 create an aggregate between the final hexachord of P_1 and the initial hexachord of I_8. In addition, Schoenberg composes secondary harmonic dimensions which link together noncontiguous elements in both voices. Each individual permutation contains two secondary harmonic dimensions; noncontiguous elements in the upper voice of P_1 and I_8 project pc sets 8-10 and 8-2 respectively, and the lower voice similarly projects the complements of these sets, 4-10 and 4-2. All of these sets are equivalent to linear segments of P and thus represent secondary harmonic dimensions.

Another secondary harmonic dimension *joins* both row forms; the complete upper voice contains pc set 9-2, and the lower voice represents pc set 5-2. Both sets again represent linear segments of P. P_1 and P_8 are joined then, by two harmonic segments; the first contains an aggregate, and the second represents a secondary harmonic dimension. Thus, even in the least complicated use of the combinatorial property, Schoenberg employs additional secondary harmonic dimensions to create a totally integrated harmonic structure that is derived from a single basic set.

Example 3.16 Suite, op. 29, Overture

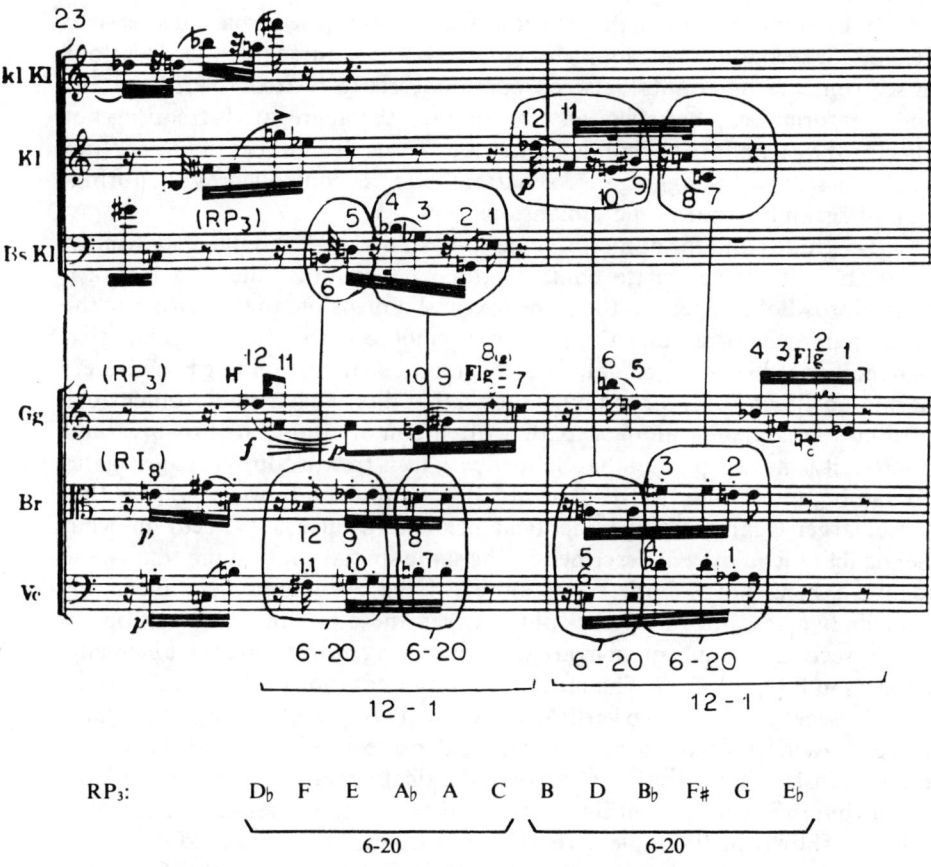

Aggregates containing more than twelve elements. A second use of the combinatorial property involves the formation of aggregates which contain more than twelve elements. In such cases, the aggregate most often represents a vertical formation consisting of three hexachords from two combinatorially related permutations. Example 3.16 contains the simultaneous unfolding of RI_8 (viola:cello) and two occurrences of RP_3 (clarinets). Two vertical aggregates occur, each containing one hexachord from RI_8 and two hexachords from RP_3 (marked by pc set 12-1). Notice that the two identical hexachords appear in the accompaniment and are thus associated by the same textural function. They also display a vertical secondary harmonic dimension which maximizes the number of occurrences of pc set 6-20, the principal hexachord of P. Pc set 6-20 appears four times and each time is formed by segments of unequal size from RP_3 and RI_8; if Schoenberg had associated segments of equal size, pc set 6-20 would not have occurred once.

In Example 3.16 pitch duplications within aggregate formations serve to generate a secondary harmonic dimension. Because these pitch duplications arise from the invariants between combinatorially related row forms, the combinatorial property accounts not only for the aggregate formation, but also for the secondary harmonic dimension. Thus, the number of *pitches* (not pitch-classes) within aggregate formations often is controlled by the formation of secondary harmonic dimensions.

The Suite contains numerous examples similar to Example 3.16. Almost invariably, if an aggregate contains three hexachords, the two identical hexachords both appear in the same textural dimension, that is, either in the accompaniment or among the principal melodic voices. This suggests that Schoenberg views the aggregate as an harmonic structure joining two discrete harmonic dimensions. Since I have shown that discrete harmonic dimensions project secondary harmonic sets that often contain duplicated or invariant pitches, it is not surprising that Schoenberg feels free to construct aggregates containing more than twelve elements. It is significant, however, that within these larger aggregates the identical hexachords ususally occur in what Schoenberg would have described as the same spatial continuum; that is, the identical hexachords both occur either in the accompaniment or in the principal voices, but rarely are split between these two basic dimensions.

A second example of an aggregate containing more than twelve elements appears in Example 3.17. The simultaneous presentation of RI_8 and RP_3 (RP_3 occurs twice) produces two vertical aggregates (12-1); each aggregate contains three hexachords (two are identical) and projects a secondary harmonic dimension that links together the two identical hexachords. Except for the slight rhythmic changes within the first aggregate, this passage is identical to the one shown in Example 3.16. These changes, however, produce a new secondary harmonic dimension. Whereas in Example 3.16, the secondary harmonic dimension within the first aggregate projected pc set 6-20, the rhythmic changes in Example 3.17 produce pc sets 4-17 (two occurrences) and 4-19; both represent linear segments of P.[14] It is significant that in both examples the duplicated pcs within the aggregates occur within the same textural dimension (that is, the accompaniment) and function to generate an additional secondary harmonic dimension.

If we consider the previous two examples, it seems clear that an accurate description of their harmonic structures must include a description of their secondary harmonic dimensions. To assert merely that their harmonic structure is organized by an aggregate is less than adequate. Such a description not only fails to clarify what type of aggregate is formed, but also does not distinguish the unique aspects of the secondary harmonic dimensions within these aggregates.

Harmonic Organization in Music from the Suite op. 29

Example 3.17 Suite, op. 29, Overture

Example 3.18 Suite, op. 29, Overture

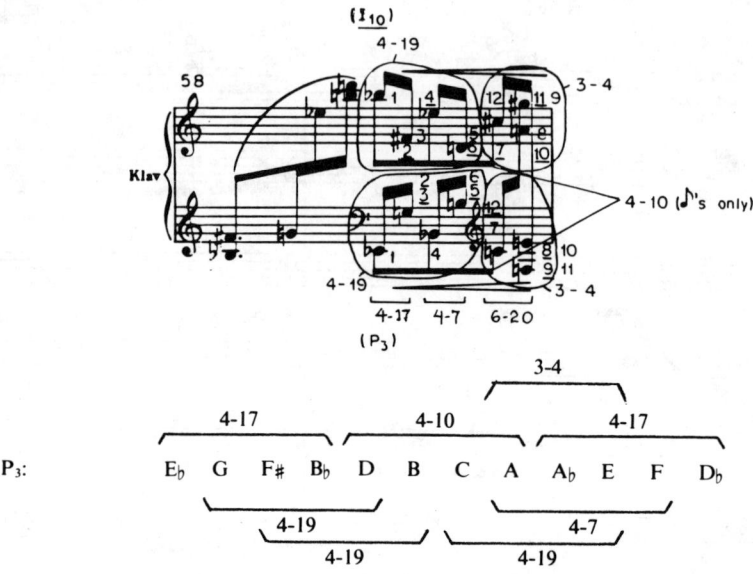

Absence of aggregate formation. Schoenberg frequently uses combinatorially related row forms without exploiting their potential for aggregate formation. When aggregates do not occur, he typically insures harmonic structure by constructing multiple secondary harmonic dimensions. Example 3.18 contains the simultaneous statement of P_3 and I_{10}; while both permutations are combinatorially related, this particular configuration obviates the possibility of aggregate formation. (The order numbers for I_{10} are underlined.) In place of the aggregate, Schoenberg creates three secondary harmonic dimensions by associating segments from both permutations that contain identical order positions.[15] The association of corresponding trichordal segments from I_{10} and P_3 results in the following succession of secondary harmonic sets: 4-17, 4-7, 6-20, 6-20.

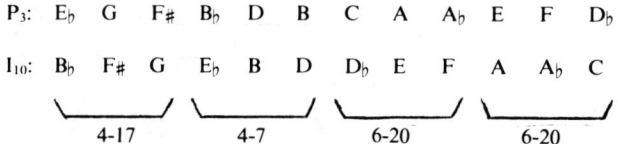

No other association of segments containing the same order numbers produces an uninterrupted succession of secondary harmonic sets. Notice that in Example 3.18 Schoenberg creates the set succession shown above by associating and overlapping pitches occupying identical or contiguous order positions. A unique feature of this example is its use of pitches that simultaneously represent elements from both row forms. In each permutation, four overlapping pitches appear in the first hexachord and six occur in the second. If this distribution had been different, a new set succession would have occurred, one which would not reflect this unique secondary dimension that arises between I_{10} and P_3.

Schoenberg moreover uses rhythm and register to project two additional seondary harmonic dimensions in Example 3.18. Each of these dimensions contains elements from both row forms and projects sets equivalent to linear segments of P. The first, delineated by registral partitioning, contains two occurrences of 4-19 and 3-4. The second, indicated notationally by the double stemming of alternate pitches projects pc set 4-10 (eighth notes only). Notice that this second dimension serves to connect the entire configuration harmonically. Each of these secondary harmonic dimensions depends on the frequent occurrence of invariant pitches, as revealed by comparison of the cardinality of the set with the number of order numbers it contains. The combinatorial property thus affects harmonic structure not by aggregate formation, but by providing invariant pitches or segments.

In this example, the economical use of pitches and the complexity of harmonic design creates a totally unified harmonic structure. Any possible association of noncontiguous elements, either from one or both row forms, produces sets equivalent to linear segments of P. The special care Schoenberg lavishes on this single configuration complements its important position within the formal design of the movement. This measure marks the end of an extended section (mm.29-58) which reappears at the end of the movement in an inverted form (mm.141-70). (In *Skizzenbuch V* this measure is the only one circled by Schoenberg in the entire composition.) Considering the important formal position of this measure, it is significant that Schoenberg does not feel compelled to use aggregates to link together both row forms. One must conclude that he believed the formation of secondary harmonic dimensions to be an equally effective means of organizing harmonic structure.

Schoenberg's sketches indicate that he frequently associates row forms on the basis of their potential for forming interlocking sets equivalent to linear segments of P, and that often these sets are formed by segments occupying identical positions in both permutations. It is not unusual, however, that this technique is applied simultaneously with the technique of associating noncontiguous segments within individual row forms. Occasionally, Schoenberg uses the pc sets arising from both procedures to further integrate harmonic structure between discrete row forms. An example of this procedure appears in Example 3.19.

Example 3.19   Suite, op. 29, Overture

Example 3.19 contains two combinatorially related row forms, RP_5 and I_8, which are not joined by an aggregate. The piano, by associating the initial dyads and the third dyads from both row forms, projects the secondary harmonic sets 4-7 and 4-10. (Notice that the piano contains a repetition of the dyads in RP_5.) At the same time, both dyads from each row form are associated to create the secondary harmonic set 4-19. Thus, the piano projects two secondary harmonic dimensions; the first horizontally connects both row forms by pc sets 4-7 and 4-10, and the second involves the vertical nonlinear occurrences of 4-19.[16]

If we compare the pc content of the nonlinear statements of 4-19, we find that both represent invariant segments in the corresponding row form.

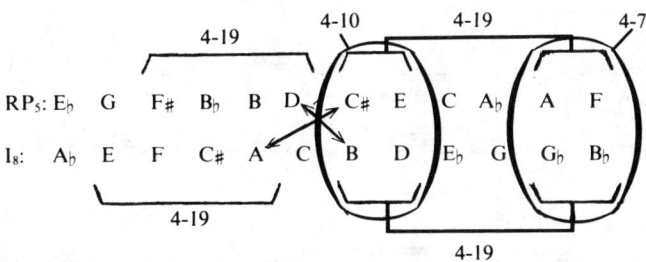

For example, the noncontiguous pcs associated in RP$_5$ (C♯ E A F) represent a linear segment (unordered) of I$_8$; the same relation occurs if the row forms are switched. Thus, Schoenberg not only employs simultaneously two independent harmonic dimensions, but also controls their interaction to create further structural relations. It is the simultaneous use of these types of procedures which allows him to maintain harmonic structure in the absence of aggregate formation.

Example 3.20 offers an excellent example of how Schoenberg harmonically integrates a complete phrase by using invariants to limit the size of secondary harmonic sets. This passage contains two equivalent row cycles: P$_6$, P$_8$, I$_1$, I$_{11}$ and P$_4$, P$_6$, I$_9$, I$_{11}$. While all row forms are combinatorially related, the formation of aggregates is obviated by the presentation of both hexachords from each row form simultaneously. The four permutations in each cycle are associated by an invariant tetrachord (B, G, A♭, E) which appears at the beginning of each permutation.

Schoenberg integrates harmonic structure by constructing three secondary harmonic dimensions. The first involves each individual permutation; each instrumental line contains noncontiguous pcs from discrete row forms that project sets equivalent to linear segments of P (3-3, 3-4, 3-11, 6-z19/6-z44, 6-z24/6-z46). The second dimension comprises the complete pc content of each instrumental line. The violin contains an aggregate derived from four permutations. Each remaining instrumental line represents a secondary harmonic set (4-7, 5-21, 8-19).

What is remarkable about this second dimension is that no individual line projects pc set 6-20; notice that even though each line consists of at least twelve pitches drawn from *identical* hexachords, each contains only four or five pitch-classes. (The piano is excluded from this pattern since its independent lines contain pitches from both hexachords.) Schoenberg thus uses pitch doublings to preserve the identity of specific horizontal sets; without these doublings, the sets would contain a greater number of pitch classes and would

92 *Harmonic Organization in Music from the Suite op. 29*

Example 3.20 Suite, op. 29, Overture

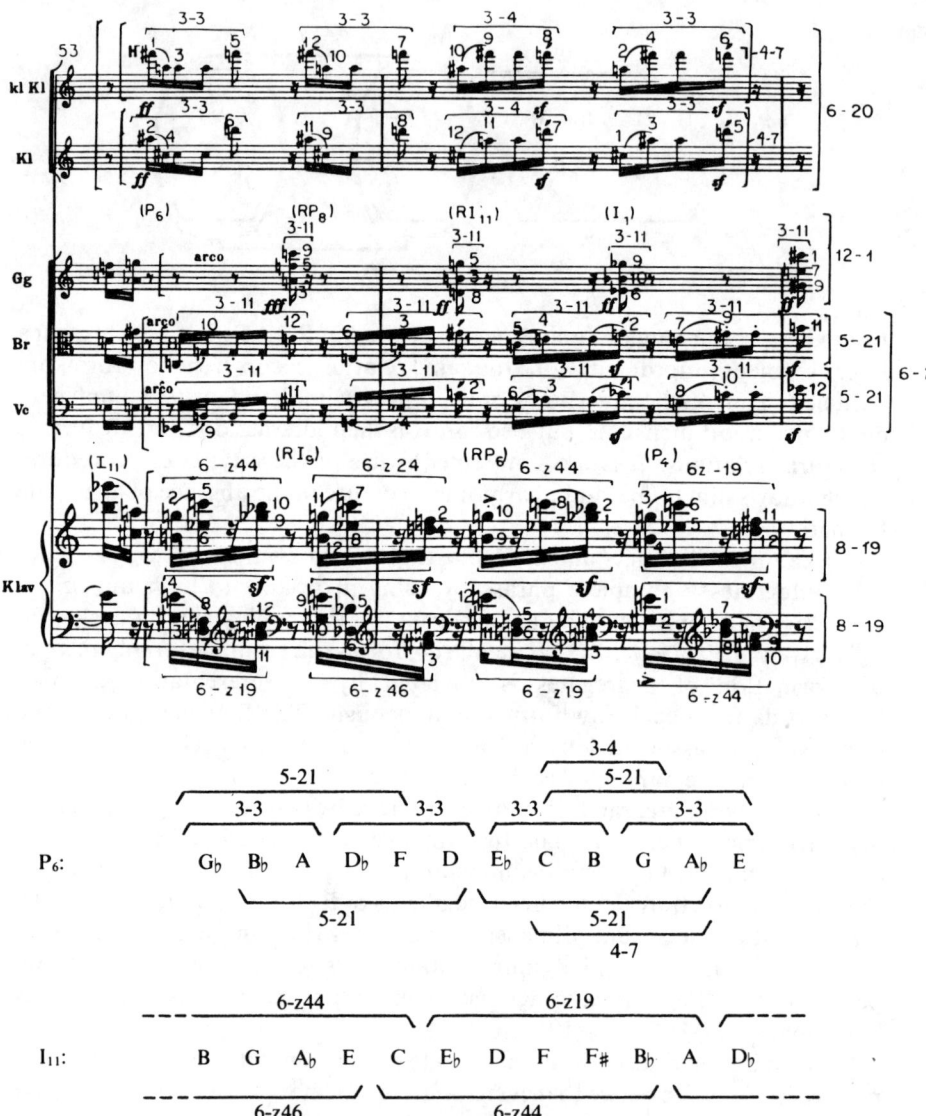

all become pc set 6-20. Pitch doublings (that is, invariants) consequently function here to maintain or limit the size of the horizontal harmonic sets. In this example, by avoiding the formation of pc set 6-20 by individual instrumental lines, Schoenberg creates a third harmonic dimension which projects pc set 6-20 through the composite pc content of paired instrumental groups (woodwinds; viola and cello).

This example demonstrates Schoenberg's use of secondary harmonic dimensions to organize harmonic structure between combinatorially related row forms. The combinatorial property here is not used to form aggregates, but functions instead to provide invariants. Schoenberg depends on these invariants to form secondary harmonic dimensions and to limit the size of their nonlinear harmonic sets.

Schoenberg's Use of the Combinatorial Property

Most theoretical writings on Schoenberg's twelve-tone composition do not adequately describe the extent to which Schoenberg employed the combinatorial property. Typically, as pointed out above, theorists assert not only that Schoenberg used only hexachordal inversional combinatoriality, but that he was unaware of other types. Even though theorists have pointed out that in op. 29 Schoenberg uses an all-combinatorial row, the usual view is that he uses it as if it were merely semicombinatorial and thus was unaware during his early period of twelve-tone composition of the total combinatorial resources of the all-combinatorial row. Schoenberg's sketches for op. 29, and the composition itself, refute both of these assertions. As the following examples show, Schoenberg uses all types of combinatorial relations (I, RI, T, RT) and thus understands fully the all-combinatorial property of his basic set.

As discussed in Chapter 2, combinatoriality can occur with all possible partitionings of the row and is not limited to hexachordal partitioning; neither is it limited to the partitioning of aggregates into two, three, four or six equal size parts, a restriction which would necessarily limit the number of rows which possess this property. Combinatoriality is a more inclusive property, pertaining to all rows and not just a subuniverse of them. The sketches, and the Suite itself, show that not only does Schoenberg construct aggregates using trichordal and tetrachordal segments, but that he was aware of the possibility of building aggregates from unequal row segments. While such formations are relatively infrequent, they indicate that even with his earliest twelve-tone compositions he understood this inclusive aspect of the combinatorial property.

The following section gives examples showing Schoenberg's use of I, RI, T and RT hexachordal combinatoriality and of aggregate formation involving trichordal and tetrachordal segments and segments of unequal size.

94   Harmonic Organization in Music from the Suite op. 29

I, RI, T, and RT Hexachordal Combinatoriality

The sketches appearing in Examples 2.19 and 2.31 indicate that Schoenberg knew all the hexachordal I, RI, T, and RT combinatorial properties of P. In the Suite itself the formation of aggregates is not limited to inversional combinatoriality; on the contrary, horizontal and vertical aggregates occur frequently between T, RT, and RI related permutations.

Example 3.21   Suite, op. 29, Overture

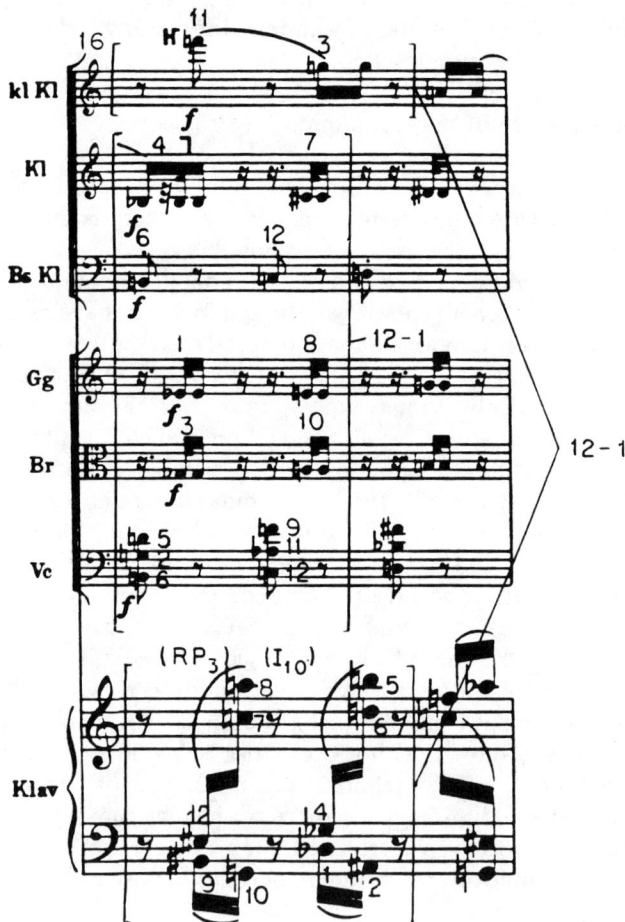

The introduction (Example 3.11), for instance, exploits two types of combinatorial relations; inversional combinatoriality (I_5) creates two horizontal aggregates between P_3 and I_8, and transpositional combinatoriality projects similar formations between I_8 and I_{10}. While inversional combinatoriality at the lower fifth appears most often, other inversionally related transpositions are not infrequent. For instance, the passage displayed in Example 3.12 shows two horizontal aggregates between row forms related by I_9 (P_8:I_5). An instance of aggregate formation between row forms related by retrograde inversion (RP_3:I_{10}) appears in Example 3.21. The final example (Example 3.22) shows the use of hexachordal combinatoriality between two row forms related by retrograde transposition (RI_5:I_9). In this instance, the permutations are displayed successively and the formation of a horizontal aggregate requires the retrograde permutation of I_9 (RI_5:RI_9).

Example 3.22 Suite, op. 29, Overture

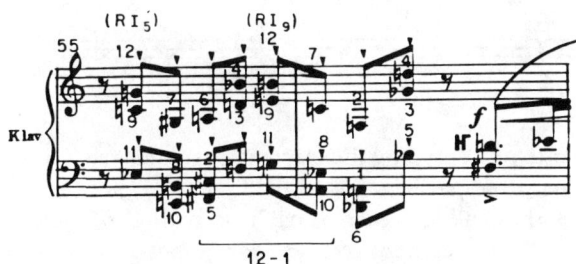

Trichordal and Tetrachordal Aggregates

Schoenberg clearly understood that aggregate formation was not limited to hexachordal segments, but could occur with different kinds of row partitioning. For instance, the sketches appearing in Examples 2.18 and 2.25 show Schoenberg deriving aggregates formed by tetrachordal segments between P_3:I_4:I_0 and P_3:P_7:P_{11}. Within the composition, moreover, several examples of aggregates formed by trichordal segments occur. One instance, appearing in Example 3.20, has already been mentioned; in this passage an aggregate containing four trichordal segments gives harmonic structure to a single line of the accompaniment (violin).

Example 3.23 contains an exceptionally complex instance of trichordal combinatoriality. Two aggregates, one hexachordal and the second trichordal, simultaneously integrate four successive permutations. Both are delineated by individual instrumental lines; the clarinet contains two hexachordal

96 Harmonic Organization in Music from the Suite op. 29

segments from P_3 and I_0, and the lower voice of the piano consists of four trichordal segments from $P_3:I_2:I_0:P_1$. (Schoenberg probably intended the final trichord of I_2 to be D♭, C, E, and not G, F♯, E♭; this error, however, does not affect the two aggregate formations.)

Example 3.23 Suite, op. 29, Overture

The aggregate presented by the clarinet is particularly interesting, for it is based not on the principal hexachord of P, but on an internal hexachordal segment. Notice that the H⁻ voice of each individual row form presents the hexachord 6-2, a linear segment of P appearing between order numbers 4-9. The clarinet contains the H⁻ voices from P_3 and I_0 which share no invariants. Thus, even when Schoenberg uses hexachordal combinatoriality, the aggregates are not restricted to the principal hexachords of P. In this example, he creates harmonic structure between two internal combinatorial hexachords. The second aggregate, which represents an example of a trichordal aggregate, contains one trichord from each of the four row permutations (piano). Notice that Schoenberg has delineated this aggregate by placing accents ('sf') and individual chord articulations ({) on each participating trichord.

Aggregates Displaying Unequal Row Partitioning

The final example (Example 3.24) shows the formation of an aggregate by row segments of unequal size. This important passage, which presents the first linear statement of P in the Overture, introduces much of the thematic material for the entire movement. Three aggregates appear between the simultaneous linear statements of P_3, I_8 and I_{10}. The first, containing more than twelve elements, consists of one hexachordal segment from each row

Example 3.24   Suite, op. 29, Overture

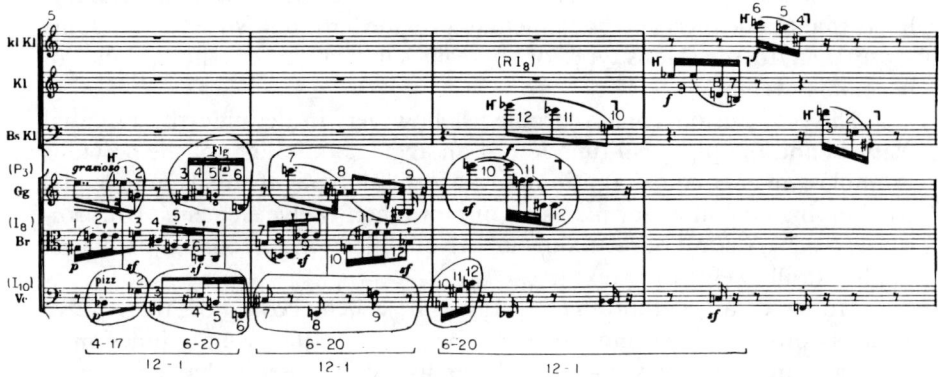

form. The second and third, containing exactly twelve elements, consist of one trichordal segment from both P_3 and I_{10}, and one hexachordal segment from I_8. Within the first aggregate, similar to those appearing in Examples 3.16 and 3.17, an additional secondary harmonic dimension is projected by the specific rhythmic design that associates hexachords containing the same pitch classes. In this instance, the identical hexachords from P_3 and I_{10} are vertically aligned to project pc sets 4-17 and 6-20. The second and third aggregates, which continue this secondary dimension between P_3 and I_{10}, rhythmically group trichordal segments and project two additional statements of pc set 6-20. The set succession between P_3 and I_{10} (4-17, 6-20, 6-20, 6-20) contains the maximum number of possible occurrences of 6-20. If Schoenberg had associated trichordal segments within the first aggregate, similar to the second and third, pc set 6-20 would not have occurred.

We might suspect that the formation of the second aggregate by unequal segments was an unintentional consequence of this secondary harmonic dimension were it not for the way the phrase is completed; Schoenberg does not leave the final two trichords of P_3 and I_{10} dangling, but associates them with a repetition of RI_8 and thus forms a second, "complementary" aggregate containing the same kind of unequal row segments from the same three row forms.

Definition of an Aggregate

The aggregates in Example 3.24 are particularly interesting, for not only do they represent atypical formations (that is, they contain either segments of unequal length or more than twelve elements), but they are also juxtaposed within a single phrase. If this phrase were a transitional passage, or perhaps less clearly defined, we might suspect that its aggregates were unintentional. But because this phrase is one of the most important in the movement, it seems likely that Schoenberg intended them to provide harmonic structure. In some sense, then, these various types of aggregates must represent similar kinds of harmonic events.

This conclusion creates problems, however, in defining the essential features and the principal function of an aggregate. In light of the previous examples, an adequate definition must accept all types of equal and unequal partitioning *and* allow for inclusion of more than twelve elements. Unfortunately, such a definition, without further qualification, pertains equally well to almost all twelve-tone textures.

Moreover, any definition of an aggregate which allows more than twelve elements prohibits what most theorists believe to be the primary function of an aggregate. Theorists such as Rufer and Perle assert that aggregates function primarily to insure equal pitch-class distribution and thus must consist of exactly twelve elements. This position is most clearly articulated by Starr and Morris:

> The concept of combinatoriality originated in Schoenberg's row compositions and was subsequently generalized as a compositional technique by Babbitt and others during the 1950s. It is a scheme for the contrapuntal combination of rows that is consistent with the more fundamental concept of pitch-class saturation.... Though the row was invented at first for this very purpose, the mere usage of rows is not sufficient to guarantee saturation when several rows at a time are used in counterpoint. Combinatoriality fills this gap in row technique.[17]

If we believe that Schoenberg uses twelve-element aggregates to insure equal pitch-class distribution, then the structures appearing in Examples 3.16, 3.17 and 3.24 cannot be described as aggregates. But to exclude such structures, I believe, is to misunderstand Schoenberg's procedures for organizing twelve-tone harmony.

If we reexamine Schoenberg's description of combinatoriality in "Composition with Twelve Tones" (see p. 75), it is easy to understand why theorists go astray. All his examples of aggregates contain twelve elements and project the universal set, and they consequently provide equal pitch-class distribution. Moreover, Schoenberg repeatedly stresses that unequal pitch emphasis caused by doubling or repetition must be avoided. His description, however, contains one important ambiguity that needs to be clarified. He states that he constructs the first hexachord of the basic set so that the first hexachord of the row form related by I_5 "would not produce a repetition... but should bring forth the hitherto unused six tones of the basic set." In other words, he implies that repetitions are avoided by employing the universal set, rather than that repetitions are avoided in order to produce the universal set. While each condition in certain contexts may imply the other, within the context of the Suite, they lead to contradictory estimates of what constitutes an aggregate.

A letter Schoenberg wrote to Rufer, dated April 8, 1950, partially resolves the problem. He describes the advantage of using the combinatorial set:

> Personally I endeavour to keep the series such that the inversion of the first six tones a fifth lower gives the remaining six tones. The consequent, the seventh to twelfth tones, is a different sequence of these second six tones. This has the advantage that one can accompany melodic phrases made from the first six tones with harmonies made from the second six tones, without getting doublings.[18]

Here he stresses two new aspects; first, that the combinatorial property primarily involves melody and accompaniment, and second, that these separate dimensions contain all *harmonies* of the basic set, rather than all of its pitches.

As I argue in Chapter 1, Schoenberg refers to the basic set as a group of specific harmonies, rather than as a group of twelve ordered pitch-classes. It should not be surprising, then, that when he discusses the relation between the aggregate and the basic set, he says that they contain the same harmonies, rather than that they both project all twelve pitch-classes. The importance Schoenberg placed upon avoiding repetitions now appears in a different light. Because repetitions within the basic set interrupt its intervallic succession and consequently alter its harmonies, repetitions within the aggregate would necessarily have the same effect. Thus, Schoenberg's primary reason for employing the universal set is to avoid repetitions within the aggregate, since they would necessarily disrupt its relation to the basic set.

At the same time, however, Schoenberg asserts that the partitioned segments of the combinatorially related row forms can occupy *different* harmonic dimensions. In "Composition with Twelve Tones" he specifies that pitches have one of two formal functions: either melodic or accompanimental. And, as the previous examples show, textural function is one of the principal ways of distinguishing discrete harmonic dimensions. Thus, for Schoenberg, aggregates contain the harmonies of the basic set, and these harmonies can occur in separate harmonic dimensions.

Because twelve-tone harmonies are defined primarily by their intervallic content, and not by the ordering or identity of their pitches, any repetition of elements already contained in the harmony will not affect its intervallic content and thus will not affect its identity. As I have shown, repetitions and invariants often serve to limit the number of pcs within harmonic sets. Thus, it is possible for the discrete harmonic dimensions of an aggregate to contain duplicate pitches without affecting the harmonies of the aggregate itself.

It should now be clear why Schoenberg can include two identical hexachords within one aggregate, and why he consistently interconnects these hexachords by a secondary harmonic dimension. By associating the duplicated pitches (either through rhythm, textural function or register) to project secondary harmonic sets, he ties them to the *same* harmonic dimension and effectively separates them from the remaining harmonies of the aggregate. In each of the examples of aggregates containing three hexachords, neither of the duplicated hexachords can be associated in any way *primarily* with the nonduplicated hexachord; through the formation of secondary harmonic sets, they associate most strongly with each other.

The best definition of Schoenberg's aggregate is, therefore, that it contains all the harmonies of the basic set contained in its partitioned segments, that its harmonies can occupy more than one harmonic dimension, and that *between dimensions there are no invariant pitches*. This definition allows for all possible row partitioning, requires the occurrence of the universal set and accepts the inclusion of more than twelve elements.

Reorderings of the Basic Set

In "Composition with Twelve Tones" Schoenberg claims that while the harmonies of the basic set cannot be altered, occasionally its elements appear in a different order. It will be recalled that he gives one example from op. 25 in which the final tetrachord of P appears before the completion of the middle tetrachord. In this instance, reordering is permitted for two reasons; first, it does not occur until the basic set has already become familiar, and second, the original ordering within each partitioned tetrachord allows them, in Schoenberg's terms, to be treated as independent small sets. He adds further that "this treatment is supported" by the presence of an invariant interval between the first and second tetrachords, and that "this similarity, functioning as a relationship, makes the groups interchangeable."[19]

As shown by Examples 1.7 and 1.9, the relationship Schoenberg refers to is not the mere occurrence of an invariant interval, but the formation of interlocking sets between the second and third tetrachords that are equivalent to those projected individually by the first and second. Unfortunately, theorists such as Perle and Rufer misunderstand what relationship Schoenberg intends and assert that the occurrence of the invariant interval alone permits the reordering of the basic set. Even if this were an accurate interpretation, it is not at all clear why an invariant interval between the first and second tetrachords should allow the third to be reordered.

In his earlier version of "Composition with Twelve Tones," Schoenberg mentions the possibility of reordering elements *within* partitioned segments. He asserts that "in the course of a piece, and if the basing [sic] set is already known, it happens sometime[s] that inside of such a group the succession of tones is a little changed."[20] While twelve-tone theorists frequently describe reorderings of this type, they seldom explain the specific reasons for their occurrence. Most often they are interpreted as local events with no significant structural implications. Brian Fennelly, for example, discusses reorderings in op. 25 and gives the following explanations:

> Of special note is the exchange of order of some dyads within tetrachords and the reordering within dyads for specifically musical reasons, a not uncommon device of Schoenberg at this point in a piece, pointing to the flexibility with which he regarded set order.
> More sophisticated [reordering] devices... appear in the Prelude of this *Suite*, but in an isolated fashion that affects local detail and does not contribute to long range structure.[21]

From this description we learn only that musical reasons motivate reorderings and that they have no long range structural significance.

George Perle, while claiming that reorderings serve primarily to create linear variety,[22] asserts they do have significant implications. In discussing the systematic reorderings of hexachords in the String Trio op. 45, he states:

> These reordered formations represent a modification of the traditional twelve-tone precept that only one set should be used in a composition.[23]

Milton Babbit interprets Schoenberg's reorderings of the basic set in yet another way:

> In his later works, his increased preoccupation with the hexachord as an independent unit led to his using it often without regard to fixed ordering, but merely with regard to total content.[24]

Babbitt's description is most informative for it suggests that reorderings occur within independent units (that is, harmonies) that are defined not by the ordering of their elements, but by their total pitch-class and interval-class content.

In the following section, I show that the musical reasons which require reorderings of the basic set often involve formation of secondary harmonic dimensions, that these dimensions do have important long-range significance, and that because reorderings occur within discrete harmonic dimensions, they do not necessarily constitute what Perle would probably describe as a new basic set.

Because harmonies of the basic set are defined by their intervallic content, and not by the ordering of their elements, reordering *within* partitioned segments does not represent a significant change in the basic set.

102 *Harmonic Organization in Music from the Suite op. 29*

Example 3.25 Suite, op. 29, Overture

Harmonic Organization in Music from the Suite op. 29   103

In order to structure nonlinear harmonies, Schoenberg often reorders elements within partitions to project sets equivalent to linear segments of P. Consider, for instance, Example 3.25 where the associated melodic voices designated by N⁻ contain a trichord partitioning of the first hexachord of P_{11} and I_5. In each hexachord the order of the second trichord is reversed (order numbers 4-6). Notice that this enables the associated, but noncontiguous elements within and between each row form to project a tetrachord equivalent to a linear segment of P (pc sets 4-19 and 4-17). If this reordering had not occurred, the overlapping tetrachords would have projected pc sets 4-20 and 4-26, neither of which represent linear segments of P.

Example 3.26   Suite, op. 29, Overture

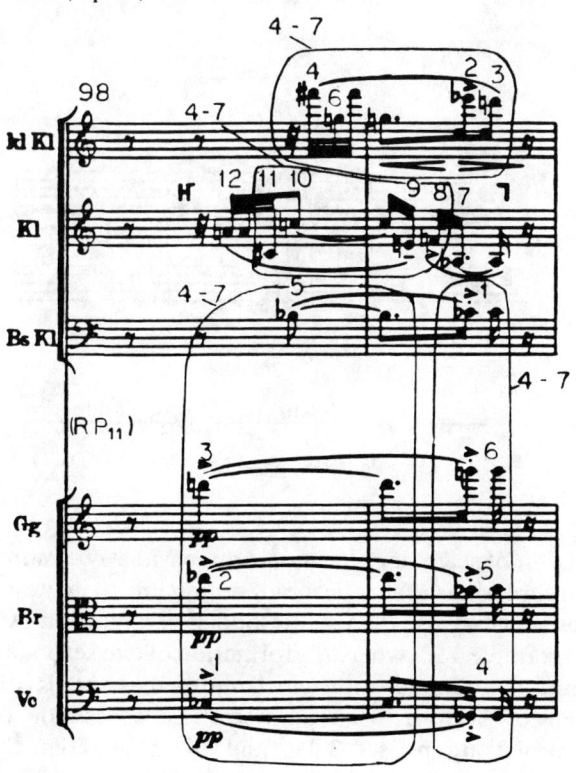

P_{11}:   B   E♭   D   F♯   B♭   G   A♭   F   E   C   D♭   A
                                         _____/
                                                4-7

In the first section of Chapter 3, it was shown that the repetition of pitches or partitioned segments within single row forms often serve to generate secondary harmonic dimensions; similar considerations motivate reorderings of repeated segments. In Example 3.26, for instance, the configuration for P_{11} contains a reordered repetition of the first ordered hexachord that rhythmically imitates the H⁻ voice. Notice that the reordering creates three nonlinear occurrences of the secondary set 4-7, a set that appears as an ordered linear segment of the H⁻ voice. It is important that the imitation within this configuration is not merely rhythmic, but is reflected by the projection of equivalent sets in the primary and secondary harmonic dimensions. If the repeated hexachord had not been reordered, what we might describe as an harmonic imitation would not have occurred.

Example 3.27 Suite, op. 29, Overture

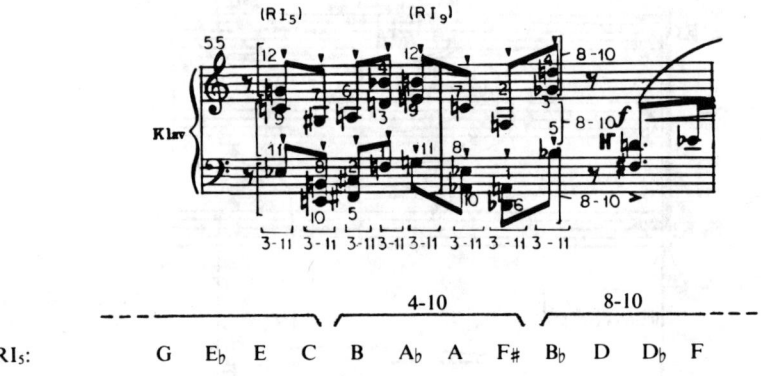

The projection of secondary harmonic dimensions occasionally requires such extensive reorderings that it becomes impossible to identify not just the level of transposition, but also the specific kind of permutation. An instance of this appears in Example 3.27, where the formation of two secondary harmonic dimensions results in a configuration which represents either $RI_5:RI_9$ or $P_0:P_4$. The first dimension comprises an uninterrupted succession of nonlinear simultaneities projecting pc set 3-11, and the second consists of three horizontal formations of pc set 8-10. Each occurrence of pc set 8-10 spans the entire configuration and consists of all the upper, middle or lower pitches from each statement of 3-11. In all these harmonic dimensions, the secondary harmonic sets are composed of noncontiguous elements of P. Notice that the extensive reorderings are caused not by any single secondary dimension, but by the simultaneous interaction of all.

Example 3.28 Suite, op. 29, Overture

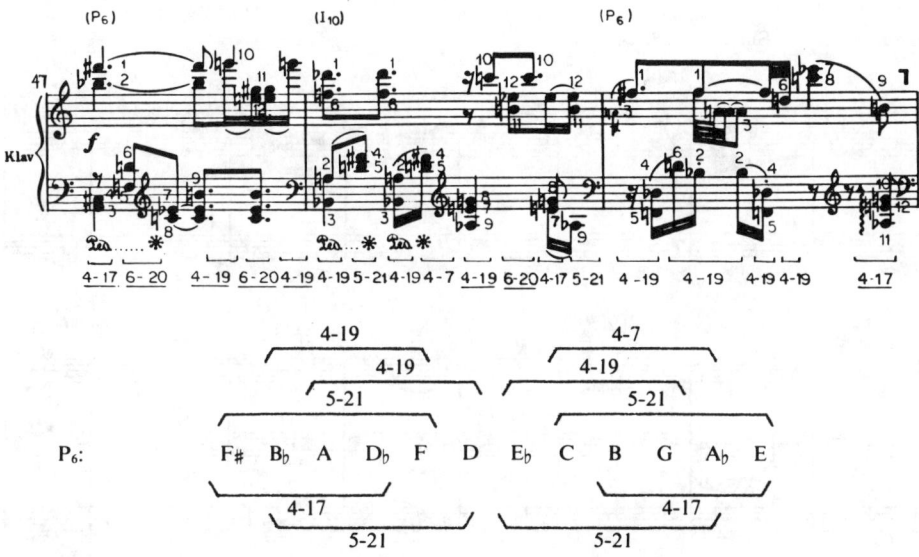

A change in the original ordering of P sometimes is motivated by events not directly associated with the phrase in which the reordering occurs. In *Skizzenbuch V*, for example, above the passage appearing in Example 3.28 Schoenberg writes "(33)" after *wieder breit, wie vorher*. Here, "(33)" refers to measure 33 where *wieder breit* previously occurred. The earlier passage (mm.33-35) displays a homophonic texture consisting entirely of vertical simultaneities projecting linear segments of P. The later passage contains a more polyphonic texture with many nonlinear simultaneities, but these simultaneities nevertheless project tetrachords that are equivalent to those that appeared in the earlier passage.

Example 3.28 contains two reorderings of P; the first displaces the pc designated by order number 6 in I_1 (m.48), and the second reorders two pcs represented by order numbers 2 and 3 in P_6 (m.49). Both reorderings enable Schoenberg to project a greater number of secondary harmonic tetrachords than would have occurred if he had maintained the original ordering of P. (Simultaneities representing linear segments are underlined.) In this example, reorderings of P serve to associate two nonadjacent phrases and thus clearly have long-range structural significance.

In addition to the formation of interlocking harmonic sets, reorderings also serve to emphasize structural features arising from the intersection of two or more row forms. In these instances, the structural feature is not a result of the reorderings, but evolves from the original ordering of P; the reorderings merely serve to indicate more clearly which relation associates the various row forms. One such instance appears in Example 3.29.

Example 3.29 Suite, op. 29, Overture

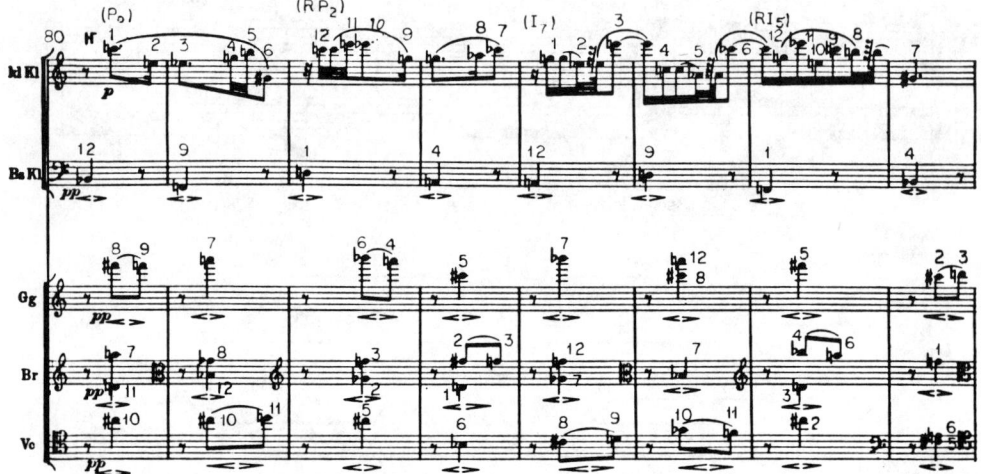

In Example 3.29 the row cycle $P_0:RP_2:I_7:RI_5$ presents the second principal theme of the first movement. In each row form, two types of reorderings occur; the first involves the application of the retrograde operation to only one of the two hexachords, and the second involves the reorderings of the pcs designated by order numbers 4 and 9 in the bass line (bass clarinet). The structural feature explored in this passage (indicated on the sketch appearing in Example 2.17) arises from the simultaneous intersection of all four permutations.

Harmonic Organization in Music from the Suite op. 29   107

An invariant tetrachord occurs at the beginning of each permutation; the upper two are identical and are related to the lower two by the R operation. In Example 3.29 the H⁻ voice accentuates this invariant relation by placing the invariant tetrachord (C, E, E♭, G) at the beginning of each short melodic phrase. In addition to this invariant tetrachord, a similar relation occurs within the final tetrachord of each row form under order numbers 9 and 12. Notice that the ordering of pitch-classes within the first two row forms again is related to those occurring in the final two permutations by the R operation. A similar type of relation thus exists between $P_0:RP_2$ and $RI_5:I_7$ at symmetrical points within the complete four-row cycle.

It now becomes clear what function the reorderings serve in this phrase. The application of the retrograde operation to only one hexachord within each row form articulates the symmetrical relation between the identical patterns of intersection, and the specific reorderings in the bass line define the points of intersection where these patterns occur. The reorderings thus do not merely indicate invariant segments between row forms—a feature controlled by the normal ordering of P—but articulate a relation derived from their simultaneous intersection. This latter relation represents a secondary harmonic dimension involving not just the set structure of a single row form, but the interlocking sets between four row forms.

A repeated reordering of P which is not specifically related to the set structure of P rarely occurs. But it is always necessary to determine if a characteristic configuration is associated with the reordering before its relation to P can be determined.

Example 3.30   Suite, op. 29, Overture

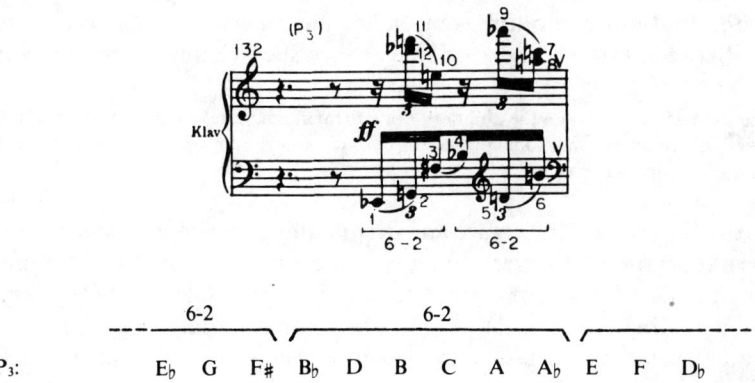

In the middle section of the first movement, for instance, one hexachord from each row form consistently appears in its retrograde form. This implies a new ordering of P designated by the order numbers [1,2,3,4,5,6,12,11,10,9,8,7]; this reordering, however, never occurs as a linear statement of P, but only with the simultaneous presentation of both hexachords. Example 3.30 contains the final row form of the middle section which displays the reordering of P with its characteristic configuration. Notice that the vertical harmonic sets (pc sets 6-2) represent linear segments and that both would have been destroyed had Schoenberg applied the reordering to a linear statement of P. By associating this reordering only with a specific configuration, Schoenberg succeeds in duplicating the harmonies of the basic set. Moreover, if the reordered hexachords in this example had occurred in direct succession, not only would pc set 6-2 not have appeared, but no secondary harmonic set would have linked together the principal hexachords.

Thus, even when P is repeatedly reordered, it does not necessarily represent a "new" basic set; as Example 3.30 demonstrates, a reordering of P must be interpreted with its characteristic configuration. Invariably, Schoenberg associates reorderings with configurations in which the harmonies of the basic set remain unchanged. If this aspect is overlooked in the Overture, then it mistakenly appears that there is no harmonic connection between the two principal sections and that the movement is based on two different basic sets.

One obvious question remains: If Schoenberg knew how he was using the row to structure his harmonies, as his sketches and music together suggest, why didn't he say so? An answer may emerge from a brief consideration of the authority of "Composition with Twelve Tones." The lecture, given in 1934 and again in 1935, 1941 and 1946, is Schoenberg's major public exposition of his system, and it has, since its publication in 1950, been reputed as a kind of manifesto. And not without reason; Schoenberg begins with a conspicuous analogy between himself and God and makes such claims as the following:

> The time will come when the ability to draw thematic material from a basic set of twelve tones will be an unconditional prerequisite for obtaining admission into the composition class of a conservatory.[25]

Yet despite the tone of the lecture and despite this essay's dependence upon it, it seems important not to overestimate its authority. It is less than a manifesto because it fails to make manifest several key principles of Schoenberg's system, including those I have described. That failure may have been deliberate, prompted by a secrecy that after years of hostile criticism had become almost instinctive.

Schoenberg was perhaps secretive by nature. He asked Erwin Stein, to whom he first confided his twelve-tone method, to "keep this a secret and to consider it as my private method," and he later remembered how unwilling had been his first public announcement: "Others had tried similar procedures and if I wanted to escape the danger of being their imitator, I had to unveil my secret."[26] It appears moreover that Schoenberg's secrecy extended even to his students, for as the comments by Rufer cited in this chapter show, he was largely unaware of his teacher's more sophisticated compositional procedures. The unanimity and virulence of the criticism Schoenberg suffered throughout his career could only add to his secretiveness. Some of these reactions are amusing to recall—fistfights after concerts, for example, or reviews appearing in the crime columns of the Vienna press—but some would have been harder to dismiss. The powerful Richard Strauss suggested not quite publicly that Schoenberg might be helped by psychiatry and would, at any rate, be better off shoveling snow than composing music.[27] As Schoenberg told an audience in Denver in 1937, "An artist treated in this way becomes not only suspicious, but even rebellious."[28] The title of the Denver lecture was "How One Becomes Lonely," but might have been "How One Becomes Secretive."

This situation changed somewhat after Schoenberg came to the United States in 1933. In Europe he had been stamped with the trademark "The Twelve-Tone Constructor, the Atonalist" (the phrases are his own). In the United States his works were no longer attacked because they were not performed, but he himself enjoyed—or rather suffered—public attention, as a theoretician rather than as a composer. "When... I came to America," he wrote, "I could not change my trademark. I was the man with 'the system of the chromatic scale.'" "Laymen, musicians, newspapermen and critics whom I met," he went on, "wanted me to write a lecture and give it in several places, though... I was of course only capable to deliver a superficial explanation."[29] The lecture was "Composition with Twelve Tones," and I can only suggest that the man stamped with the trademark "the twelve-tone constructor" may have wished to be superficial, to appear less systematic than he actually was, to disappoint what he called his "inquisitive tormentors" by letting his music, and not his lecture, be the true manifesto.

4

A Theory of Twelve-Tone Meter

In this final chapter I want to set forth a theory of twelve-tone meter, a topic which evolves naturally from my study of the sketch material. As with the sketch material, I am primarily addressing metrical structure within one or between several row forms; most of my examples, then, show how Schoenberg uses harmony and meter to delineate discrete phrases. By expanding my research in this direction, I hope to lay the groundwork for a study of Schoenberg's larger forms. For it seems clear that, even with the help of Schoenberg's sketches, work on larger forms, without prior understanding of harmony and meter on the smallest scale, would be premature.

The Problem of Twelve-Tone Meter

When Schoenberg abandoned tonality he would seem necessarily to have also abandoned the rhythmical structures set off and sustained by tonal harmony. While Schoenberg returned often to tonal forms in his twelve-tone compositions, he had little to say about the rhythmical structures that unfolded them. Theorists have respected his silence; no one, so far as I am aware, has yet ventured any sustained treatment of this difficult issue, except to criticize Schoenberg's forms and rhythms as trivial vestiges of tonality.[1] In this chapter I argue that Schoenberg did not develop nonmetrical means for organizing rhythm in twelve-tone music, but used metrical relations between harmonic and rhythmical structures analogous to those of tonal music. This argument presupposes both an understanding of twelve-tone harmonic structure and a workable concept of meter. Just as a clearer understanding of tonal rhythm required Schenker's formulation of the structural levels of tonal harmony, so an adequate analysis of Schoenberg's rhythm presupposes a formulation of twelve-tone harmony.

Let me begin by posing the problem with an example: the opening phrase of the Minuet from the Suite op. 25 (Example 4.1). Schoenberg himself analyses this phrase in "Composition with Twelve Tones," and points out that the basic set, which he partitions into three tetrachords, is presented in an

Example 4.1 Suite, op. 25, Minuet

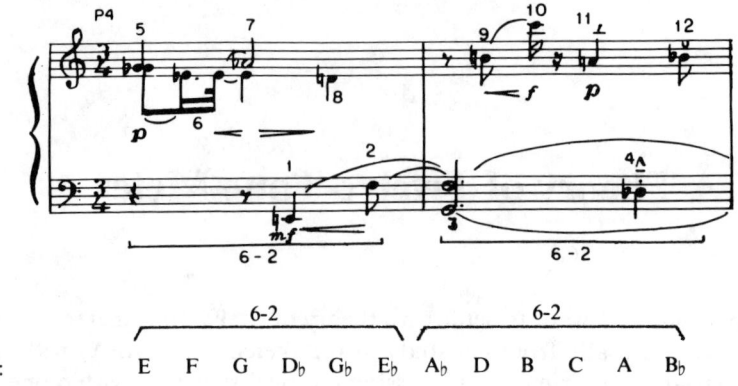

irregular fashion: "The melody begins with the fifth tone, while the accompaniment, much later, begins with the first tone."[2] Schoenberg justifies this irregular presentation in two ways: first, the Minuet represents the fifth movement of the Suite so that the basic set has become sufficiently familiar, and second, each tetrachord maintains the correct ordering of its pitches and consequently can function as an independent small set. But Schoenberg's analysis of this example is hardly complete, for he avoids two important questions: what criteria control *how* these tetrachords are used independently, and how does the rhythmical structure of the movement make it a minuet? As I will show, the answer to the first question provides the answer to the second.

Analysis of the example reveals some of Schoenberg's criteria for using segments of the basic set as independent sets, for it exposes two dimensions of harmonic structure. The first, or primary harmonic dimension, simply reproduces the twelve successive pitches of the basic set. It therefore contains adjacent elements of the basic set and occurs with each of its ordered statements. Here the primary harmonic dimension covers the entire phrase. A secondary harmonic dimension groups pitches which, though nonadjacent in the basic set, are equivalent to one of its linear segments. Here the secondary dimension spans each measure and represents two hexachordal harmonies (marked as pc set 6-2) equivalent to the principal hexachord of the basic set.[3] "Equivalent" here, as before, does not mean identical, but rather related by transposition or inversion or both. This equivalency relates material in the two dimensions even though the hexachords in the secondary dimension do not duplicate the pitches or the ordering of those in the primary dimension.

The two related dimensions in turn shed light on why Schoenberg called this movement a minuet. Notice that the two simultaneous dimensions clearly delineate a two-bar phrase subdivided into two measures of equal length—

each containing three beats. The rhythmic structure of the minuet is not merely a tonal convention arbitrarily imposed, but rather has been recreated through the new resources of twelve-tone techniques. Without an understanding of Schoenberg's harmonic structures, we would be hard pressed to make more than superficial observations about rhythmic structure. Most likely we could make only the true but trivial statement that Schoenberg has notated the movement in a meter typical of tonal minuets, but we could not explain why the movement would not work equally well in the same meter but with the bar lines positioned differently or in a meter of 2/4 or 4/4. This latter point is important, for to argue that Schoenberg's twelve-tone music is metrical will require a theory capable of explaining why one meter works better than another. While such tonal concepts as strong and weak beats will probably need revision in a theory of twelve-tone rhythm, Example 4.1 suggests that in Schoenberg's twelve-tone music, just as in tonal music, meter evolves through multiple levels or dimensions of harmonic structure. Before developing a model for twelve-tone meter, I want to illustrate by way of the following short examples some typical ways in which this mode of rhythmic organization works using a variety of contexts.

First are two examples in which Schoenberg uses a secondary harmonic dimension to establish the basic metrical pulse of the composition. In both examples the accompaniment of a principal theme unfolds partitioned trichords, which are freely ordered and function, in Schoenberg's words, as "independent small sets." Example 4.2 shows a theme from the Overture, Suite op. 29, with a notated meter of 6/8. Freely ordered trichordal segments of the basic set (P_7) accompany the theme (H^-) which sets out an ordered version of the same row form. The reason for this specific succession of trichords becomes apparent when one considers the vertical harmonies formed between the theme (violin) and accompaniment (winds). (For a more complete analysis of this passage see the discussion of Example 3.10.) All of the harmonies, most of which contain pitches nonadjacent in the row, are equivalent to tetrachordal segments of the row. The first vertical harmony, for example, contains pitches with the nonsuccessive order numbers 1, 4, 5, and 6, but represents a transposition of the tetrachord formed by the successive order numbers 8, 9, 10 and 11 (pc set 4-7).[4] As the violin continues, each vertical simultaneity it forms with the winds is equivalent to some linear segment of the row. Example 4.2, then, has two harmonic dimensions derived from a single basic set: the primary dimension contains two statements of P_7, both partitioned into trichords, while the secondary dimension contains accompanying harmonies, each equivalent to tetrachordal segments of the basic set. Schoenberg uses this secondary dimension for two important functions: it connects the vertical harmonies to the basic set and it confirms the basic metrical pulse. Notice that the eighth-note motion of the vertical harmonies

Example 4.2 Suite, op. 29, Overture

confirms the eighth-note pulse indicated by the 6/8 time signature, a specific correspondence of meter and harmony.[5]

The opening theme of the String Quartet no. 4 op. 37 has a similar kind of harmonic structure in which a secondary harmonic dimension again establishes the basic metrical pulse (Example 4.3). As in Example 4.2, the primary dimension derives from a trichordal partitioning of the basic set. The theme

Example 4.3 Fourth String Quartet, op. 37, Allegro

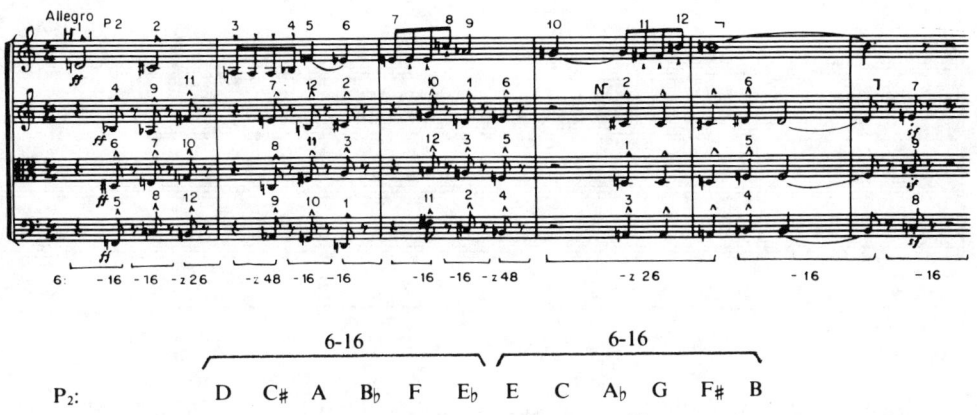

consists of a melody (H⁻) presented by the first violin with an accompaniment by the remaining three instruments. The melody contains one complete statement of the basic set (P_2) partitioned into four trichords. The accompaniment adds to each trichord of the melody three trichords that represent the three remaining trichords of the basic set. Each chord in the accompaniment, taken with the overlying trichord of the melody, forms a hexachord that is either a linear segment of the basic set or equivalent to one. Example 4.3, then, again displays two harmonic dimensions derived from the basic set. The primary dimension represents four complete statements of the same row form, while the secondary dimension binds together the melody and accompaniment by hexachords either identical or equivalent to linear segments of the basic set. As in Example 4.2, Schoenberg uses a secondary harmonic dimension to confirm the meter of the movement, in this case 4/4.

The next two examples show how Schoenberg can establish a meter through secondary harmonic dimensions between combinatorially related row forms. Example 4.4 shows the opening of *Unentrinnbar* op. 27 no. 1, a short canon for mixed chorus. The soprano sings the first hexachord of P_6 (mm.1-2) which the alto imitates with the first hexachord of I_{11} (mm.3-4). Although P_6 and I_{11} are combinatorially related, the hexachords in mm.3-4 contain the same pitch-classes and consequently do not form an aggregate. Instead, Schoenberg exploits the internal structure of these hexachords to create a secondary harmonic dimension that articulates the duration of each measure. The two voices sing only six pitches in m.3 and six in m.4, and in both instances these hexachords represent equivalent forms of the principal hexachord of the basic set (pc set 6-5). (In the following phrase, which does not

116   A Theory of Twelve-Tone Meter

Example 4.4   Four Pieces, op. 27 no. 1, Unentrinnbar

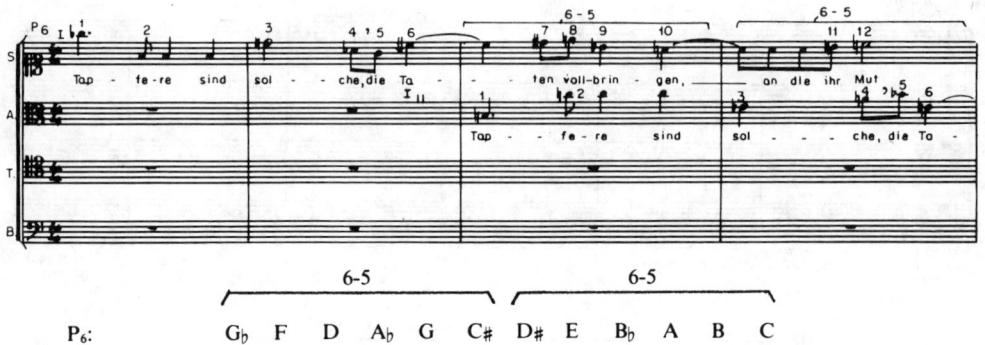

appear in this example, the same kind of structure pairs together the entrances of the tenor and bass.) Even within a texture whose coherence is insured by imitative counterpoint and the combinatorial property, Schoenberg derives a secondary harmonic dimension in order to articulate the duration of the measure. If we did not recognize this secondary harmonic dimension, we would have difficulty explaining why Schoenberg chose the 4/4 meter over other possibilities. Just as in tonal music, meter is not imposed upon Schoenberg's twelve-tone music, but rather evolves from its harmonic structure.

Example 4.5   Suite, op. 29, Gigue

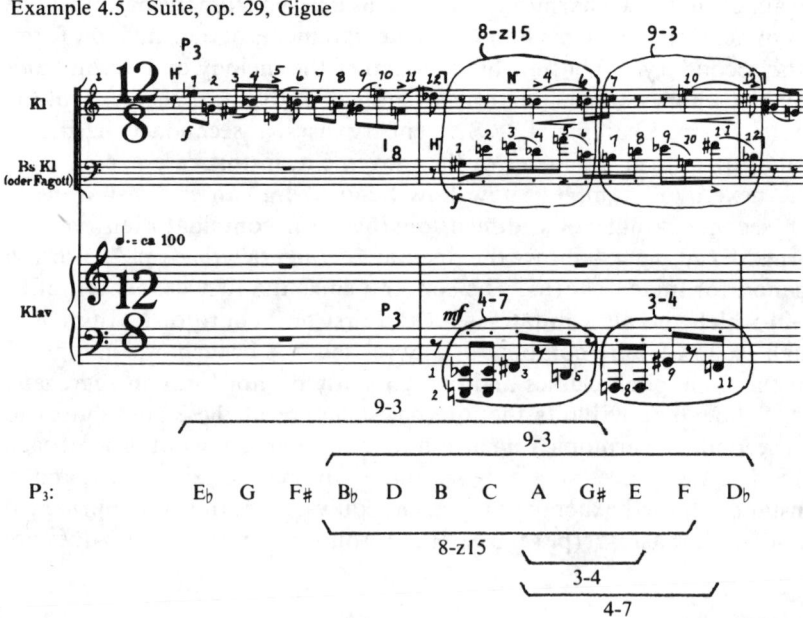

Again, in the opening theme of the Gigue op. 29 (Example 4.5), a secondary harmonic dimension establishes a meter typical of the Baroque gigue, 12/8. This example is somewhat more complex, for the secondary dimensions combine simultaneously with two aggregates between P_3 and I_8. Notice how the pc sets 8-z15 and 9-3 which contain pitches from both row forms serve to bind together the two melodic voices (H⁻, N⁻) and, more importantly, divide the twelve-beat measure into two six-beat groups. Each six-beat group, following a typical gigue formula, ends with what we would ordinarily call a metrical down-beat. A metrically complementary secondary dimension structures the piano accompaniment with pc sets 4-7 and 3-4. Because equivalent forms of all the pc sets in this secondary dimension appear as linear segments of the basic set, Schoenberg has in effect used a single basic set to derive a multidimensional harmonic structure, a structure which serves to integrate a complex musical texture harmonically as well as metrically.

The preceding examples should have clarified two of Schoenberg's structural techniques: first, all harmonic events are connected to the basic set through secondary dimensions in which occur harmonies equivalent to linear segments of the basic set, and second, these secondary harmonies organize the various events on the rhythmical surface of the composition metrically. Why Schoenberg employs at least two harmonic dimensions to provide rhythmic structure, and why this structure is defined by secondary and not primary harmonic dimensions, are complex issues. They will require a careful formulation of what we mean by "meter" in a twelve-tone context. As I maintain below, twelve-tone meter has much in common with tonal meter, for it depends upon harmonic structure and thus requires a concept of structural levels. In developing a model for twelve-tone meter, I am drawing concepts and categories from Maury Yeston whose *The Stratification of Musical Rhythm* goes far towards integrating a theory of tonal rhythm with Schenker's structural levels.[6] While Yeston deals only with tonal music, his elegant and useful theory also provides, with suitable modifications, an effective model for discussing Schoenberg's rhythm. The rhythmical structures both of tonal and of Schoenberg's twelve-tone music are, then, special cases in a general theory of rhythm, a brief exposition of which will be useful to introduce concepts and terms.

A Model for Twelve-Tone Meter

This general theory of musical rhythm deals with the regular recurrence of events. Rhythm is not abstract in this theory; one must speak of the rhythm of some events and those events must recur. Recurrence establishes a logical class of events in which the occurrence and its recurrence are both members, and some criterion must specify this logical class. Criteria include such features as quality of attack, dynamic level, timbre, pitch class, and pitch function. If events that belong to the same class recur at equal intervals of time, then they define a "rhythmic stratum"; they have a simple periodicity for which each recurrence begins a cycle that ends with the next recurrence. A rhythmic stratum thus contains more than one event; all its events recur at equal intervals of time; and all are defined by the same criterion.

The criteria that define recurrence in music fall into two broad categories. In the first, recurrence derives from such features as rhythmic notation, dynamics, timbre and texture. In the second, it derives from pitch differentiation and function. The two broad kinds of feature correspond to two broad kinds of rhythmical pattern produced. The first produces "purely rhythmic" patterns that are independent of the pitches they contain, but that, in a musical texture, will emphasize those pitches. The second produces "purely-pitch" patterns that give rhythmic significance to pitches according to their pitch function.

A perennial problem in theories of rhythm is confusion caused by failure to distinguish between these two kinds of features when analysing rhythmic structure. Circularity haunts analyses that assign importance to a pitch because of its rhythmic placement and then assert the importance of this rhythmic event because it includes the important pitch. One can avoid this sort of circular argument only by keeping the patterns formed by various rhythmic features separate—in effect expanding the surface of the composition into a structure of various levels or strata, one for each feature that defines recurrence. Only after isolating rhythmic strata in this way can one explore their interactions, see them as interrelated strata in the rhythmical structure of the piece.

One stratifies a piece of music in this way, first to keep its rhythmic features separate, but ultimately to see how they interact. Any pattern produced by a single feature—in other words, any one rhythmic stratum considered by itself—forms an "uninterpreted rhythmic stratum." A metronome, for instance, ticks out a regular pattern of equal durational pulses, unaccented and measured only by exact recurrence, but such a pattern, because it lacks accentual grouping or meter, can by itself have little significance. To create a more significant rhythmic structure, one must add a second stratum of musical motion which will interact with the first, thereby accenting and interpreting it. The resulting "interpreted rhythmic structure" may then be described according to whatever scheme of accents is produced, 3/4, 4/4 and so forth. But it is important to recognize that the scheme of accents does not produce the structure; the structure—the interaction of strata—creates the scheme of accents.

Pieces of music normally contain rhythmic strata more complex than the beats of a metronome, of course, often presenting what in prosody are called

Example 4.6

feet and what I shall call "rhythmical subpatterns"—repeated groups of varied durational values such as those shown in Example 4.6. If these patterns are considered independently of any internal grouping or metrical structure, then they too may be thought of as being uninterpreted rhythmic strata because they do not have strong and weak beats. Uninterpreted strata formed by repeating subpatterns are more complex than a metronome beat, however, because they offer more than one possible recurring pulse. The subpattern in Example 4.6 at A, for instance, allows either an eighth- or a quarter-note pulse.

The kind of analysis I am describing proceeds through three stages. First, one begins by expanding the rhythmic surface of the piece into a set of strata defined by the various kinds of recurrent features. Then one studies the uninterpreted pattern in each stratum by itself. Finally, one analyzes the ways in which the various strata interact to accent and interpret each other to form a rhythmic structure. It is important to understand that a stratum when it interprets another stratum does not collapse or disappear into it. A stratum may interact with several other strata, so that quite different interpreted patterns may share the same uninterpreted stratum.

Before presenting some of the criteria by which strata may be isolated within a composition, I need to introduce Yeston's terminology for describing rhythmic strata. The "attack-point" of an event is the point at which it begins. In a series of events, the interval of time between a pair of successive attack-points is called the associated "attack-point interval," and the succession of attack-point intervals determined by the series as a whole is termed the "attack-point rhythm." The attack-point interval measures the time between the beginnings of successive events and indicates nothing about the duration of the events themselves. If the attack-point interval remains constant over a series of events, then it indicates that the series contains at least one uninterpreted rhythmic stratum.

Attack-point rhythm is a useful criterion for establishing the equivalence of rhythmic strata. In Example 4.10b the attack-point rhythm of the subpattern that structures the cello and clarinets each considered separately is 1 3 1 3 1 3 1 3 (in eighth notes). Since the subpatterns of all three instruments have identical attack-point rhythms, they represent equivalent rhythmic strata. One can determine the attack-point rhythm for the strata simultaneously, however, and then it becomes 1 1 1 1 1 ... (in eighth notes). Attack-point rhythm, in this fashion, consequently can be a composite of more than one rhythmic stratum, in which case it may designate the time determined by the onset of recurring events in different strata combined.

The simplest features that define rhythmic strata in a piece are those that I have described as "purely rhythmic"—features independent of pitch differentiation and function, such as timbre, dynamic markings, density and pattern recurrence. A few examples will show how Schoenberg uses these features to form uninterpreted rhythmic strata.

Repeated dynamic markings frequently project rhythmic strata, as in Example 4.2 where the repeated accent marking "sf" in the melodic line (H⁻) forms a stratum with an attack-point rhythm of 3 3 3 3 (in eighth notes). Often a stratum consisting of single stresses like this one will intersect with other strata, as in this example, where it is closely related to the stratum defined by the recurring timbre of the winds.

Recurring changes in dynamic levels, such as crescendo and decrescendo markings, can also define rhythmic strata, and these changes can occur between different dynamic levels or within the same dynamic level. In Example 4.5, for instance, the crescendo markings project a rhythmic stratum with an attack-point rhythm of 6 6 (in eighth notes). The attack-point rhythm here marks the onset of equivalent changes in dynamic levels.

Recurrence of identical subpatterns, which I refer to as "pattern recurrence," often projects rhythmic strata. Each subpattern will contain as many attack-points as it contains discrete events, but when it recurs, it will also have a single attack-point for the subpattern as a unit. Each subpattern alone has an attack-point rhythm faster than the attack-point rhythm of the entire stratum. Example 4.7 includes two instances of pattern recurrence; the cello and viola each articulate a subpattern with the internal attack-point rhythm 1 1 1 1 8 (in thirty-second notes), and this pattern recurs at an attack-point interval of 3 (in eighth notes). The second instance of pattern recurrence occurs in the lower register of the piano. While the entire piano part presents recurring eighth notes, the lower register repeats a subpattern with the internal

A Theory of Twelve-Tone Meter 121

Example 4.7 Suite, op. 29, Overture

attack-point rhythm 2 1 (in eighth notes), recurring at an attack-point rhythm of 3 (in eighth notes). In both cases, the internal attack-point rhythm of the subpatterns is faster than the external attack-point interval of their recurrence.

Regular changes in density offer another criterion for isolating rhythmic strata. A simple instance of this occurs in Example 4.3 where the density of simultaneous attacks makes a subpattern with the attack-point rhythm of 1 3 (in quarter notes). The recurrence of this subpattern marks a stratum with an attack-point rhythm of 4 4 4 (in quarter notes). In Example 4.4 a different kind of density pattern defines a rhythmic stratum. Here, the imitative entrances of the voices mark off a regular increase in the density of simultaneous attacks. The attack-point interval of this stratum is 8 (in quarter notes).

Such features as dynamic markings, pattern recurrence, changes in density, and timbre all can recur, then, in ways that create rhythmic strata. As in tonal music, pitch functions can also create rhythmic strata in twelve-tone music, but before turning to them, it will be useful to describe more fully the interaction of uninterpreted rhythmic strata, from which will emerge a model for twelve-tone meter and for what can be called twelve-tone syncopation.

When an uninterpreted stratum interacts with a second stratum that accents and interprets it, it becomes metrical, since rhythmic strata by definition contain regularly recurring events. This second stratum necessarily moves at a slower rate. Meter evolves, then, through the interaction of two strata, the faster of which provides the rhythmic events, and the slower of which groups them. Thus, the accents of an interpreted stratum necessarily imply the existence of a second rhythmic stratum which coincides with the succession of accents.

The rhythmic surface of a piece, the rhythmic foreground, contains all the events of all the rhythmic strata, but unless one can isolate and hear a slower moving stratum in the middleground, one will not be able to hear meter. Consequently, metrical structure does not reside in the rhythmic foreground alone. Meter arises only through interpretation of a *foreground stratum* by a slower moving *middleground stratum*. Similarly, a middleground stratum, though it may interpret a foreground stratum, cannot itself become metrical unless it interacts with a yet slower moving stratum.

In this theory, a piece's time signature consequently designates two rhythmic strata. The faster stratum can occur either in the foreground or middleground, and the slower stratum can only occur in the middleground. The time signature, however, does not create meter. Rather, musical events on a middleground level shape the foreground in such a way that the time signature usually (but not always) describes the rhythmical structure.

There are two general ways that rhythmical strata may interact; they may be either "in-phase" or "out-of-phase." In-phase strata have attack-points that intersect and attack-point intervals that are integral multiples of one another;

Example 4.8

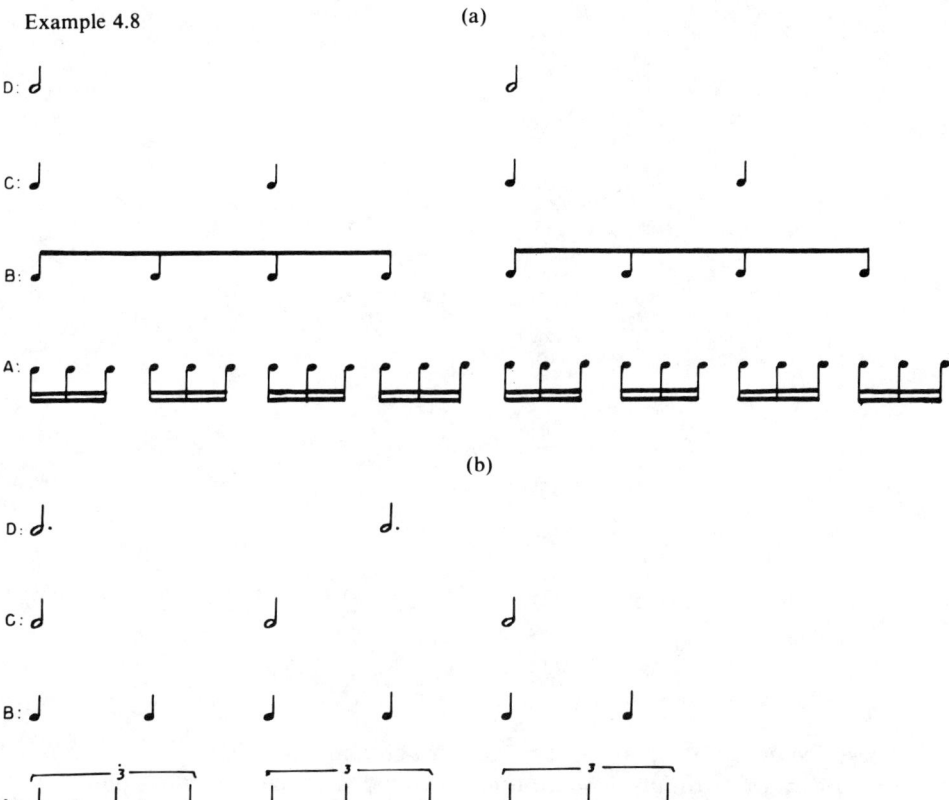

out-of-phase strata do not. By extension one may also speak of in-phase and out-of-phase structures. Example 4.8 provides a schematization of both types of structure. All of the strata are simple multiples of each other in Example 4.8a, which thus has an in-phase structure. The four stata offer six possible meters: between A:B, A:C, A:D, B:C, B:D and C:D. No stratum contradicts the accentuation of the foreground produced by any of the other strata. Example 4.8b shows an out-of-phase rhythmic structure. Its four strata offer only three possible meters—between A:C, B:D and B:C—because A:B, A:D and C:D are out-of-phase and therefore do not produce metrical accentuation.

The most frequent kind of out-of-phase rhythmic structure arises from division of the same interval of time into two parts in one stratum and three in another. Commonly referred to as "hemiola," it involves interaction of two middleground levels. In Example 4.9a a hemiola occurs between middleground strata B and C. Before this structure can be understood metrically, one

Example 4.9

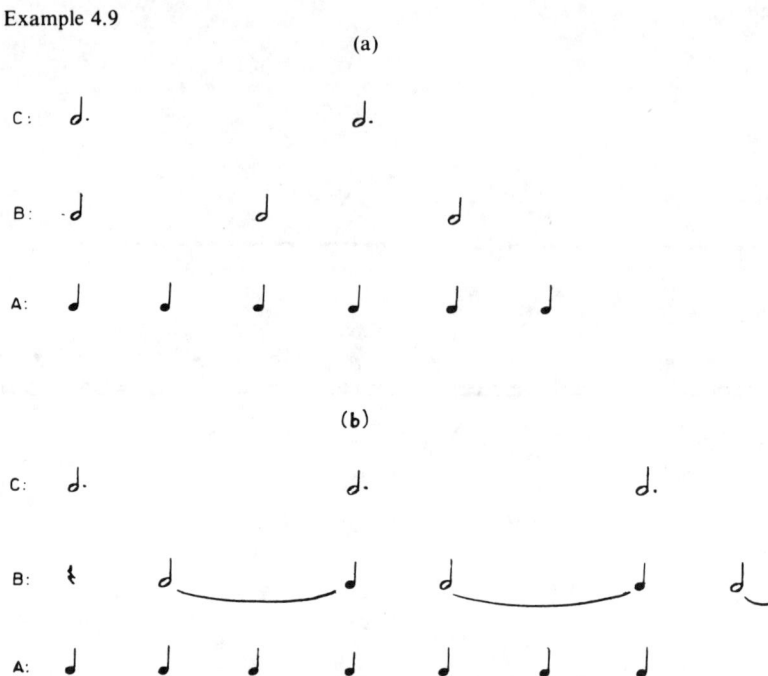

must decide from the musical context which middleground stratum is more significant. If two out-of-phase middleground strata are equally significant, then the structure has two clashing meters—in effect it has no meter at all. A structure with two equally significant out-of-phase strata produces what we commonly term syncopation.

A second type of syncopation involves not out-of-phase rhythmic strata, but rather the displacement of an in-phase stratum from the established metrical structure. In Example 4.9b, for instance, strata A:C establish a meter of 3/4. The attack-point rhythm of stratum C is 3 3 (in quarter notes). Stratum B has the same attack-point rhythm of 3 3, but its attack-points do not coincide with those of strata A or C. Stratum B thus does not represent a different division of time, but rather the same division displaced by a quarter beat.

So far I have been dealing with structure produced solely by rhythmic features, features independent of pitch values, function and differentiation. But Schoenberg's twelve-tone music also employs "purely pitch" features to organize rhythm, and as in tonal music, these features are more complex and often more important. Pitch function and differentiation generate rhythmic strata in two ways: by recurrence of identical pitches, or by recurrence of equally significant pitch events. The first type can easily be isolated, while the second requires analysis of the function of the pitch events to show their equivalence. In tonal music, well-defined principles determine the equivalence of pitch events and therefore regulate isolation of rhythmic strata derived from them. These tonal principles—such as the rules of voice-leading and harmonic progression, or the role of triadic structure—can produce middleground pitch events that recur regularly and make the chief source of rhythmic accent in tonal music. An analogous process operates in Schoenberg's twelve-tone music: structural principles determine the equivalence of pitch events, recurrence of these equivalent pitch events produces middleground rhythmic strata, and, as in tonal music, middleground strata make up the key source of rhythmic organization.

If an analogous process operates in both tonal music and Schoenberg's twelve-tone music, its details, nevertheless, differ radically. In Schoenberg, the middleground rhythmic strata inhere in secondary harmonic dimensions, and in contrast to tonal procedures, these secondary harmonic dimensions do not emphasize individual pitches, but rather unordered pitch-class sets that are equivalent to linear segments of the basic set. These unordered sets are determined mainly by interval-class content, rather than pitch-class content, so that by emphasizing them Schoenberg follows a major premise of his system—that all twelve tones of a basic set must be equally emphasized.

If we assert that secondary harmonic dimensions form middleground strata which metrically interpret the foreground, then we necessarily imply that these secondary dimensions move more slowly than the primary dimension—the ordered unfolding of the row. But it is not always apparent that secondary dimensions do move more slowly than the ordered unfolding of the row. Since the same pitches simultaneously present both the primary and secondary harmonies, the two dimensions might seem to move at the same speed. Or, alternatively, secondary dimensions might seem to move faster, since they often contain several events in the same duration as the single unfolding of the row. The secondary harmony 6-2 in Example 4.1, for instance, contains nonsuccessive pitches with order numbers 1, 2, 5, 6, 7 and 8, and would seem therefore to move as fast or faster than the unfolding of the row. If secondary dimensions can move as fast or faster than the row, it would be impossible to see them as middleground strata rhythmically interpreting a foreground. But the problem has even more serious consequences. A faster-moving secondary dimension necessarily must present some pitches out of the regular order of the row (as in Example 4.1); this premature repetition of a pitch would produce an emphasis that might lead to its being heard as a tonic. Precisely to avoid these effects, Schoenberg insisted upon the regular and ordered unfolding of the row.

The appearances are deceiving in Example 4.1, however. Schoenberg, we remember, justified using the tetrachords as independent small sets only because the "[basic] set has already become familiar," and this must mean, sufficiently familiar to be heard as an implied foreground against the reordered tetrachords. In general, the problem that secondary dimensions may seem to move as fast as primary ones derives from a misconception of the primary dimension. The primary diemnsion is formed by the regular unfolding of the basic set; however, it is not merely a sequence of pitches, but includes *all* the harmonies possible in that sequence. Secondary dimensions by definition involve joining nonsuccessive elements of a basic set, and thus the events in secondary dimensions necessarily move more slowly than *all* the harmonies of the basic set, which occupy the primary dimension. As the following examples show, these secondary dimensions often recur regularly and consequently represent the chief source of twelve-tone rhythmic accent.

Application of the Model for Twelve-Tone Meter

Several rather extended excerpts from the Suite should suffice to show the application of this model of twelve-tone meter and also to make clear two of Schoenberg's chief techniques for structuring twelve-tone rhythm: first, harmonic dimensions provide metrical organization, and second, metrical structure is repeated, developed and varied so as to become an essential motivic feature. This latter technique, as in the next example, often proves crucial in Schoenberg's extended musical forms.

The Theme with Variations from the Suite op. 29 is a simple but convincing example of how rhythmical structure can provide the basis for variation form. In line with his rather whimsical conception of the Suite, Schoenberg takes as a theme the tonal German folksong "Aennchen von Tharen." It first appears in the bass clarinet with its successive pitches extracted from the various row forms that make up the piano accompaniment (Example 4.10a). Someone who knows the origin of the theme will be surprised by its initial presentation because, with the accompaniment, it sounds both nontonal and nonmetrical. At first glance, it seems obvious how Schoenberg has created the rhythmical effect: he syncopates the theme by unfolding it primarily in dotted quarter-notes against an accompaniment emphasizing a quarter-note pulse. But closer analysis shows that these opposing surface rhythms complement a more important structural feature: all the harmonies—both horizontal and vertical—always contain pitch-classes adjacent in the basic set. Consequently, there appear to be no secondary harmonic dimensions to accent the rhythmic foreground.[7] Such a one-dimensional harmonic structure is rare in Schoenberg's twelve-tone music, and it seems likely, in light of the following variations, that the absence of rhythmic accent was precisely the effect he intended.

Example 4.10a Suite, op. 29, Theme with Variations (Theme)

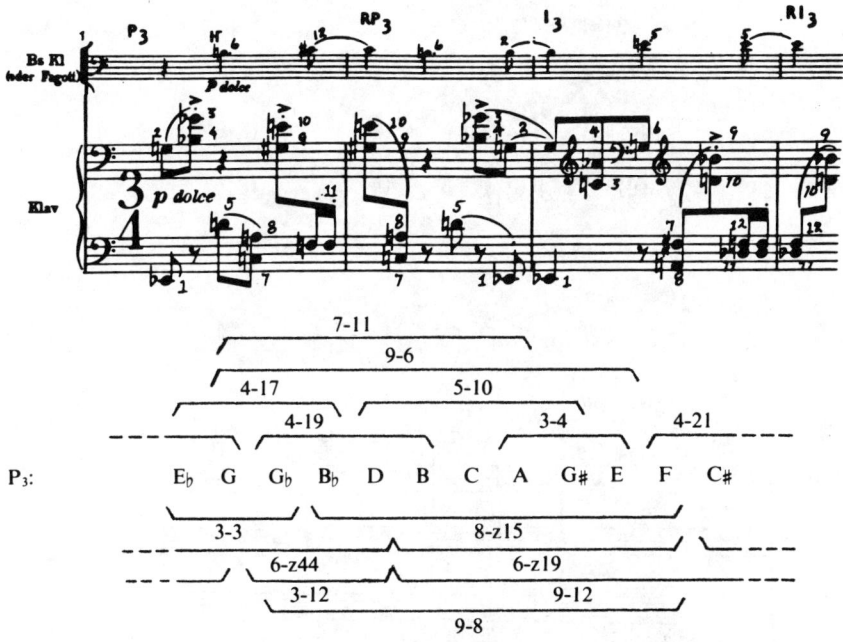

As a kind of answer to this one-dimensional theme, Schoenberg bases the variations on secondary harmonic dimensions and the metrical structures they create. In Variation I the theme appears in the bass (Example 4.10b). (In this variation and those following arrows mark the first four pitches of the theme.) Purely-rhythmic events crowd the foreground. Pattern recurrence, timbre and articulations in the violin and viola, clarinets, and cello all create strata with the same attack-point rhythm (2 2 2 2 in quarter notes). In addition, the slur and staccato articulations, which group the recurring eighth notes in the clarinets and cello, together form a stratum with the attack-point rhythm 1 1 1 1 1 1 1 1 (in quarter notes). As the diagram above Example 4.10b shows, these purely-rhythmic strata marked A and B, as well as others, form an in-phase rhythmic structure.[8]

Purely-pitch criteria create strata that extend this in-phase structure and organize it metrically. The primary harmonic dimension (I_3, P_1, RI_1, P_{11}) forms stratum C with an attack-point rhythm of 2 2 2 2 (in quarter notes). One secondary harmonic dimension is formed by the repeating complementary hexachords 6-z19/6-z44. These hexachords articulate stratum D with an attack-point rhythm of 2 2 2 2 (in quarter notes) which metrically groups the foreground into four measures of equal length—each containing two beats.

Example 4.10b Suite, op. 29, Theme with Variations (Var. I)

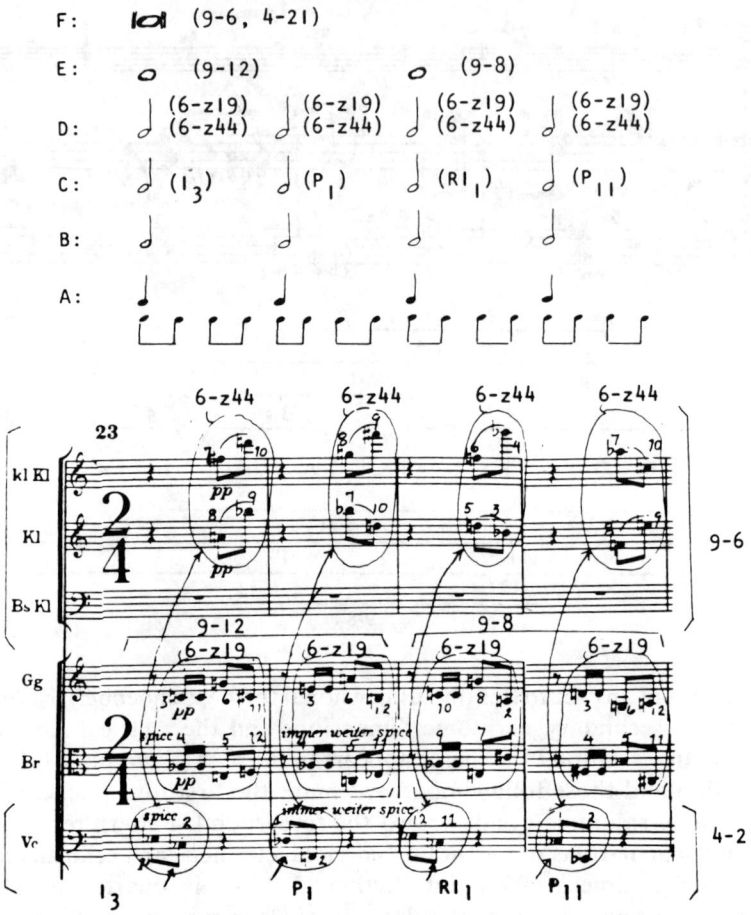

(The linear segments of the basic set equivalent to the secondary harmonies are all marked in Example 4.10a.) This secondary dimension thus creates the meter indicated by the time signature 2/4. A slower secondary dimension in the violin and viola joins successive measures with pc sets 9-12 and 8-9 and forms a stratum (E) with the attack-point rhythm 4 4 (in quarter notes). A last secondary dimension organizes the clarinets (pc set 9-6) and cello (pc set 4-21) and joins the four measures into a single phrase (stratum F).[9]

Example 4.10c Suite, op. 29, Theme with Variations (Var. II)

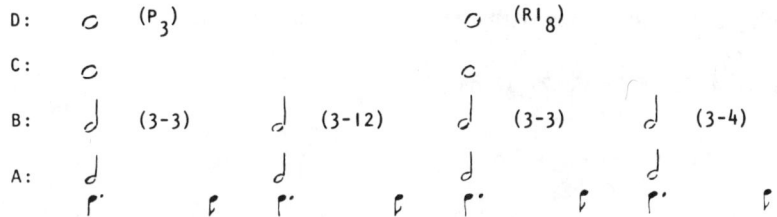

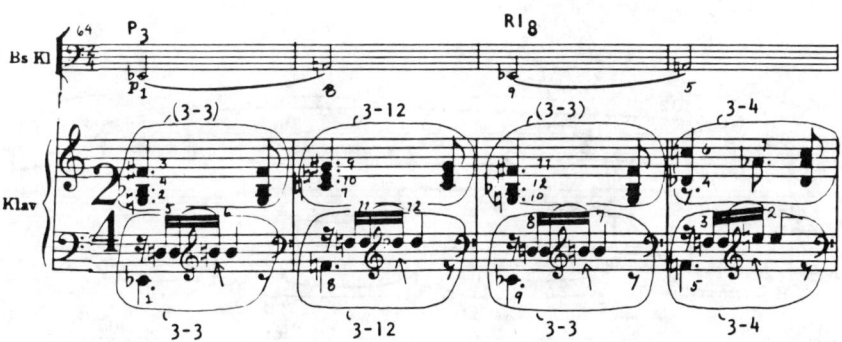

Variation II has a similar in-phase metrical structure, except that the secondary harmonic dimension that coincides with the notated time signature derives from trichords rather than hexachords (Example 4.10c). As in Variation I, numerous purely-rhythmic criteria fill the foreground. Pattern recurrence in the piano and bass clarinet, for instance, make foreground strata, both marked B, with the same attack-point rhythm (2 2 2 2 in quarter notes). Pattern recurrence articulated by pitch contour and slur articulations in the bass clarinet forms a slower stratum (C) with an attack-point rhythm of 4 4 (in quarter notes). Pitch criteria form an identical stratum (D), derived from the primary harmonic dimension (P_3, RI_8) and having an attack-point rhythm of 4 4 (in quarter notes). The secondary harmonic dimension consists of the trichords that appear in the left hand of the piano and span the duration

130   A Theory of Twelve-Tone Meter

of each measure. (The trichords in the right hand alternate between the primary and secondary dimensions.) This middleground stratum (B), then, has an attack-point rhythm 2 2 2 2 (in quarter notes) and metrically interprets the foreground. The rhythmical structure of Variation II, like Variation I, is in-phase and coincides with the notated time signature 2/4.

Example 4.10d   Suite, op. 29, Theme with Variations (Var. III)

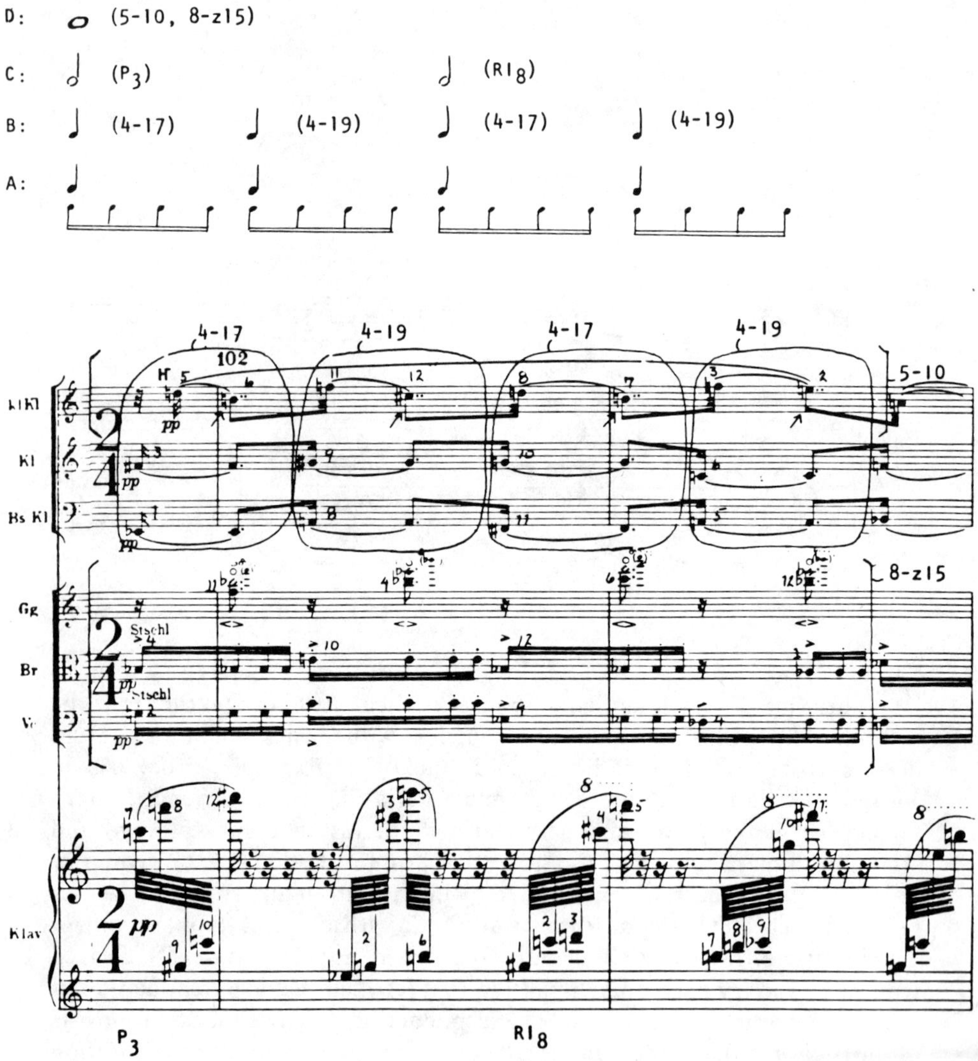

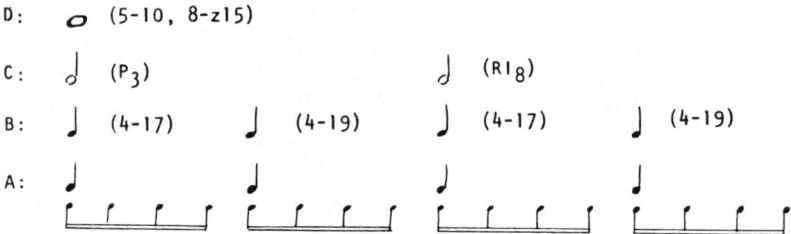

In Variation III Schoenberg uses a secondary dimension based on tetrachords to create a syncopated metrical structure (Example 4.10d). Exemplifying the second type of syncopation described above, it involves not out-of-phase middleground strata, but rather displacement of an in-phase middleground stratum from the established metrical structure. Unlike the previous examples, here the purely-rhythmic strata do not confirm the 2/4 meter, which derives instead from the harmonic strata and also carries over implicitly from Variation II. The primary dimension (P_3, RI_8) forms a stratum with the attack-point rhythm 2 2 (in quarter notes). The secondary harmonic dimension unfolds tetrachords in the clarinets and forms a stratum (B) with the attack-point rhythm 1 1 1 1 (in quarter notes). No single stratum structures the piano, because its harmonies alternate between the primary and secondary dimensions. A slower secondary dimension (D) unfolds in the H⁻ voice (pc set 5-10) which serves to join the two measures into a single phrase. The rhythmical structure formed by the primary and secondary dimensions establishes the meter 2/4, but it is displaced from the notated meter 2/4 by one sixteenth-note. This displacement creates an implied syncopation, as is common in tonal music, because the 2/4 meter established in Variation II is conceptually maintained through the beginning of Variation III.

As in the previous variations, purely-rhythmic events crowd the foreground. The fastest stratum (A) is formed by the repeating sixteenth notes in the viola and cello which has an attack-point interval of 1 (in sixteenth notes). Pattern recurrence in all parts, and recurring accents (viola and cello) project slower strata all with the same attack-point interval (1 in quarter notes). All of these strata are in-phase with the metrical structure formed by the primary and secondary dimensions, and thus are displaced one sixteenth-note from the notated meter. Schoenberg reinforces the implied syncopation by including in Variation III several strata that continue the established metrical pulse of Variation II; these strata, which have an attack-point interval of 1 (in quarter notes), are formed by the thematic pitches of the folk song (clarinet), and the harmonics and crescendo markings in the violin.

The final and most complex variation (Example 4.10e) uses secondary dimensions based on trichords and tetrachords to form a new kind of metrical structure (6/8). As in the previous variations, purely-rhythmic criteria form numerous foreground strata. Among the most prominent are those formed by pattern recurrence: the repeating subpatterns in winds and strings project strata (A) with an attack-point interval 3 (in eighth notes). The primary harmonic dimension (P_3:RP_3, I_8:RI_8) makes a stratum (C) which defines the measures and has an attack-point rhythm 6 6 (in eighth notes). Secondary dimensions, based upon trichords (3-3, 3-4, 3-11) and tetrachords (4-19) make a meter-defining middleground stratum (B) which has an attack-point rhythm 3 3 3 3 (in eighth notes) and coincides with the strata formed by pattern

132 A Theory of Twelve-Tone Meter

Example 4.10e Suite, op. 29, Theme with Variations (Var. IV)

recurrence.[10] As in Variation III, the entire theme marked H⁻(viola, clarinet) unfolds a slower secondary dimension (D) that groups the two measures into a single phrase (pc set 7-11). As in Variations I and II, the rhythmical structure is in-phase and creates the new, notated meter 6/8.

For this movement of op. 29, then, Schoenberg first designs a theme that lacks secondary dimensions and then interprets it both metrically and harmonically in the variations. Each variation sets up its own secondary dimensions that also form distinctive metrical structures. These examples from op. 29 thus make clear the important connection between metrical structure and motivic variation. Schoenberg varies and develops meter just as he does themes, and therefore regards rhythmical structure as an essential motivic feature.

The next example, again from the Suite op. 29, shows how Schoenberg uses multiple middleground strata both to group phrases (not merely measures) metrically and to create syncopation by hemiola. The complete phrase appears in Examples 4.7 and 4.11. Because the strata formed by rhythmic criteria in the first four measures (marked A in Example 4.7) were

A Theory of Twelve-Tone Meter   133

Example 4.11   Suite, op. 29, Overture

discussed above, discussion here can be limited to strata formed by pitch criteria. Four combinatorially-related row forms (P_9, I_2, I_4, P_{11}), each spanning one measure, represent the primary dimension and form a stratum (B) with the attack-point rhythm 3 3 3 3 (in eighth notes). Secondary dimensions form three different middleground strata. The first appears in the principal voice marked H^- and contains the secondary harmonies 4-7 and 3-4. (Indicated below Example 4.7 are the linear segments of the basic set equivalent to the secondary harmonies.) Like the primary dimension, this secondary dimension forms a stratum (C) with the attack-point rhythm 3 3 3 3 (in eighth notes). The third and slowest secondary dimension appears in the principal voice marked N^-, spans the entire four-measure phrase, and consists of a single occurrence of the principal hexachord 6-20. (An identical stratum is formed by the tetrachord 4-7 held invariant throughout the entire piano part.) Analysis of the final four measures will show that this slowest stratum (E) metrically divides the eight measures into two four-measure phrases. As the diagram in Example 4.7 indicates, all the strata form an in-phase rhythmic structure in accord with the meter indicated by the time signature, 3/8.

In the final four measures of this phrase (mm. 109-12, Example 4.11) Schoenberg creates syncopation by hemiola. Pattern recurrence in the piano and strings forms a stratum (A) with a new attack-point rhythm 2 2 2 2 2 2 (in eighth notes), as do the six successive row forms in the primary dimension (stratum B). As in the first four measures, the harmonic middleground contains three strata formed by secondary dimensions all of which are in-phase with the foreground strata. The first contains the successive horizontal trichords in the clarinets (mm. 109-10) and in the strings and winds (mm. 111-12), and makes a stratum (C) with the attack-point rhythm 2 2 2 2 2 2 (in eighth notes). Another secondary dimension unfolds in the principal voice marked H^- (pc sets 5-21, 4-19) and creates a stratum (E) with the attack-point rhythm 6 6 (in eighth notes). The third and slowest secondary dimension (comprising a single occurrence of the principal hexachord 6-20) again occurs in the principal voice marked H^- and spans the entire four-measure phrase. Completing the stratum begun by the principal voice marked N^- in mm. 104-8, it makes a stratum (F) with an attack-point rhythm 12 12 (in eighth notes). All strata in these measures are in-phase and create two possible meters, 3/4 or 6/8—neither of which is the meter (3/8) notated and established in the first four-measure phrase. Notice that both four-measure phrases have the same number and types of middleground strata, except that strata in the second phrase contain three events where in the same duration those in the first phrase contained only two. Middleground strata, then, divide the same interval of time first into two and then into three parts, so that the example as a whole has an out-of-phase, syncopated structure. By juxtaposing these two sets of clashing middleground strata, Schoenberg relies upon a common tonal technique for creating syncopation: the meter of the first four-measure phrase is implied through the second, creating syncopation by hemiola.

The rhythmic structure of the final four measures is still more complex, however. Schoenberg reinforces the implied syncopation with secondary dimensions that, unlike the ones already mentioned, are in-phase with the notated time signature 3/8. As Example 4.11 shows, the pc sets formed independently by the winds, strings, and piano span each measure and project the secondary harmonies 6-z10, 7-21, 8-19 and 9-12. This secondary dimension makes a stratum (D) with the attack-point rhythm 3 3 (in eighth notes). Because this stratum is out-of-phase with all other foreground strata, it remains covert, but works to reinforce the syncopation by continuing the meter established in the first four-measure phrase.

In this example, the slowest secondary dimension (N^-, mm.105-8; H^-, mm.109-12) creates a stratum that divides the eight measures into two four-measure phrases. This example is representative; both meter and phrase structure in Schoenberg's twelve-tone music derive from the same method of structuring harmony by secondary dimensions.[11] It is also important to understand how the combinatorial property affects the structure of this phrase. It does not form aggregates, as one might expect, but rather insures a maximum number of invariant segments among row forms. These invariants in turn provide the means by which Schoenberg limits the size of the secondary harmonic sets that form the slowest moving strata. Consider, for example, the voice marked H^- that defines the first four-measure phrase. Even though the melody contains fourteen pitches extracted from four row forms, it includes only six different pitch-classes, and thus unfolds only one form of the principal hexachord. (Because the principal hexachord of op. 29's basic set is all-combinatorial and has only four distinct forms, it lends itself well to this kind of phrase structure.) This example clearly shows, then, that invariants allow Schoenberg to limit the number of harmonies in a secondary dimension, which on the surface appears to move as fast as or faster than the primary dimension.

As I proposed at the beginning of this chapter, one test of a theory of meter for Schoenberg's twelve-tone music is its capacity to explain, at least in some contexts, why one meter is more appropriate than another. In the previous examples, secondary dimensions always make clear whether a passage has a douple or triple meter, but in-phase structures often offer several possible meters all of which may seem equally appropriate. As in tonal music, however, there are instances where only one meter works, and the last example will show how my model for twelve-tone meter can make clear a choice between two meters (2/4, 4/4) often considered interchangeable.

I have selected an example from Schoenberg's String Trio op. 45, one of his most difficult and experimental compositions. To end with this example

136   A Theory of Twelve-Tone Meter

from a late work seemed attractive for several reasons. First, it shows Schoenberg in a later, experimental composition refining the techniques for creating meter he had developed in earlier pieces. Second, it points towards the kinds of problems we confront when trying to analyze more extended rhythmical structures. In order to discuss this example, I need to describe briefly the basic set and the overall form of the Trio.

Schoenberg's row tables for the Trio (#1055, #1057) indicate that he uses two basic sets. The first and principal basic set contains eighteen pitches, and the second contains the usual twelve. In the eighteen-note set, the first and last hexachords contain identical pitches, but they are ordered differently. In his row tables, Schoenberg associates each prime form of the principal basic set with the row form that relates combinatorially by I_5, and these pairs of row forms always appear on the same system and unfold simultaneously. In addition, Schoenberg has stemmed separately the first and last pitches of every hexachord. The following diagram shows the basic set paired with its I_5 related row form and has arrows marking the pitches Schoenberg has stemmed separately.

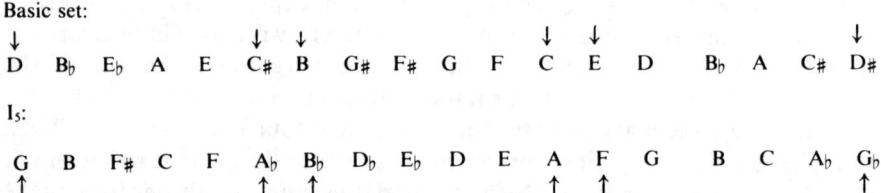

Schoenberg's separate stemming selects from each *pair* of row forms twelve pitch-classes, which may be termed the "derived basic set," for it contains many harmonies equivalent to those of the two basic sets. Because the derived basic set is formed by associating nonadjacent elements of combinatorially related row forms and duplicates many of their harmonies, it is, in effect, a secondary harmonic dimension. Not surprisingly, Schoenberg uses it as he does secondary dimensions in other pieces—to articulate middleground meter-defining strata. Unlike ordinary secondary dimensions, however, the derived basic set occasionally functions apart from the paired row foms from which it is derived—that is, as an *independent* basic set.

The String Trio consists of a single movement which is divided into five sections called Part I, Episode I, Part II, Episode II, and Part III, Schoenberg bases Parts I and II on the eighteen-note basic set and Episodes I and II on the twelve-tone basic set. Part III is based on both basic sets, for it presents an abbreviated "recapitulation" of the entire piece. Three tetrachords (4-1, 4-7, 4-9) which represent linear segments of the principal basic set are among the principal motivic materials of the Trio. (These tetrachords are marked on the

Example 4.12 String Trio, op. 45

6-5 6-5 6-5

P₂: D B♭ E♭ A E D♭ B A♭ G♭ G F C E D B♭ A D♭ E♭

4-9 4-1 4-7

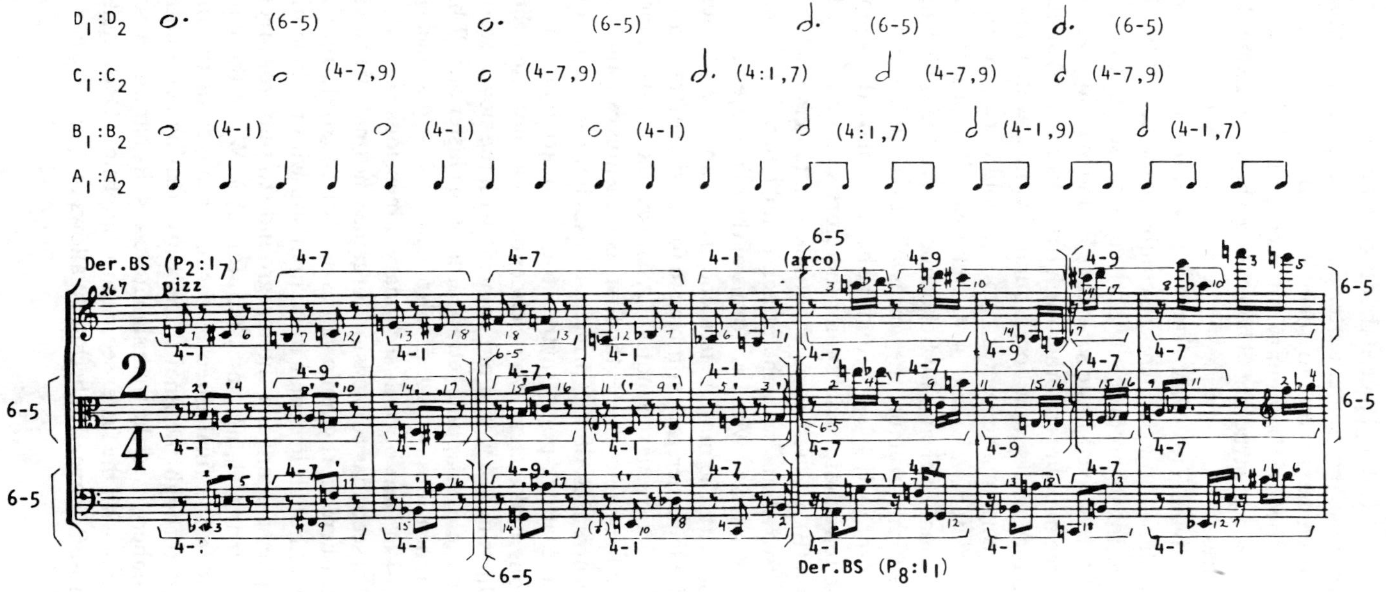

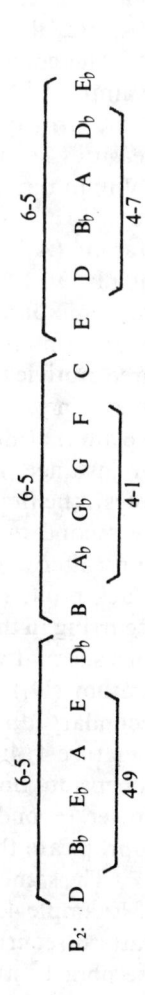

138   A Theory of Twelve-Tone Meter

basic set below Example 4.12.) A glance at the diagram above shows that these three tetrachords are those that remain after Schoenberg separates the first and last pitches of each hexachord to form the derived basic set. These tetrachords dominate the Trio's primary and secondary dimensions and control much of its metrical structure. The passage shown in Example 4.12 illustrates these features.

The coda of the String Trio (Part III) begins with the phrase shown in Example 4.12 which shows how Schoenberg combines the paired row forms of the principal basic set to produce the derived basic set: in the first six measures, a form of the derived basic set (from P_2 and RI_7) appears in the violin; in the final three measures another form (from P_8 and RI_1) appears in the cello. At first glance, the simple foreground rhythms, which suggest a stratum (A_1) of recurring quarter notes (violin), would seem to conform equally well to two meters, 2/2 and 4/4, but analysis of the secondary harmonic dimensions makes clear why Schoenberg gave the time signature 2/4. Secondary dimensions structure the voices with overlapping forms of the three motivic tetrachords (4-1, 4-7, 4-9), and the bar lines mark the beginnings of each new motivic tetrachord. Each voice therefore simultaneously forms two alternating strata (B_1, C_1) with identical attack-point intervals. The viola, for instance, forms two strata with the attack-point interval 4 (in quarter notes); the first begins in m.267 with two forms of the motivic tetrachord 4-1, the second in m.268 with the motivic tetrachords 4-9 and 4-7. Because the strata alternate with each other, they combine to form a single stratum with an attack-point interval 2 (in quarter notes). A slower secondary dimension occurring in the cello and viola divides the first six measures exactly in half. It consists of two occurrences of the principal hexachord 6-5 and forms a stratum (D_1) with the attack-point rhythm 6 6 (in quarter notes).[12] Both secondary dimensions make clear why Schoenberg has not used the time signature 4/4: bar lines in 4/4 would not coincide with the slower secondary dimension, nor with the overlapping tetrachords of the faster one. While the slower secondary dimensions would fit also with 6/4, 4/4 is clearly less appropriate than 2/4 in light of both secondary dimensions.

The same kind of secondary dimensions organize the final three measures of Example 4.12, but here all rhythmic values are halved (strata B_2, C_2, D_2). Pattern recurrence, although irregular in comparison with the beginning of the phrase, still implies a change in the foreground stratum from recurring quarter notes to recurring eighth notes (stratum A_2). While the harmony moves twice as fast in the final three mesures, the meter of the first six measures is implied through the final three, thus creating syncopation by hemiola. Had Schoenberg used the time signature 4/4, its bar lines would not have formed a hemiola with the faster secondary dimension. One might argue that Schoenberg chose 2/4 over 4/4 because it allows the phrase to end with a complete measure, but in light of the harmonic structure, that explanation seems trivial. A theory of meter based on Schoenberg's use of multiple harmonic dimensions does account, even in many ambiguous examples, for his choice of time signature.

As some readers may have noticed, besides being metrical my examples share two distinctive features: all of them are beginnings—either of movements or of principal sections within movements—and all, as beginnings, introduce important motives or themes. These two features were at first accidental; I did not choose to use only beginnings as examples, but rather looked for clear and distinctive metrical structures. Further analyses of complete movements show, however, that the occurrence of clear, distinctive metrical structures in beginnings is not accidental; it is essential to Schoenberg's rhythmical organization.

If we step back for a moment and think generally about beginnings, they seem to pose weighty problems for composers—problems often overlooked or minimized by analysts. Risking the obvious, one can make several generalizations about what an effective beginning does. First and most obvious, beginnings distinguish a piece of music from other pieces; they present the features that make a piece unique. Second, beginnings usually imply criteria for inclusion and exclusion. That is, they determine the compositional method—which techniques are admissible, and which are not—and if beginnings introduce such criteria, then they also create certain expectations for the listener. In other words, beginnings usually imply rules for prolonging and developing motives—explicit or implicit modes of continuation. One mark of an effective beginning, then, is its power to generate continuations that are distinctive to the particular work it introduces.

If we return from the safety of abstraction and consider Schoenberg's beginnings, they seem to illustrate these criteria for effective beginnings. First, Schoenberg introduces every piece in its uniqueness by requiring that all its melodies and harmonies derive from a unique basic set. Not surprisingly, his beginnings usually set forth the regular ordering of the basic set. While some beginnings make the ordering of the basic set ambiguous, rarely is the basic set unambiguously reordered. When it is, as in the minuet op. 25, Schoenberg has reasons to justify this irregularity. Similarly, only rarely do beginnings lack secondary dimensions; when they do the absence is usually developed in a special way, as for example in the Theme with Variations op. 29. The absence of irregularities or licenses at beginnings, then, helps a listener infer Schoenberg's criteria for inclusion and exclusion, and the clear use of secondary harmonic dimensions and metrical structures at beginnings creates expectations about the kind of harmonic and rhythmical structures that will organize and continue the piece. Schoenberg's principal technique for building extended forms—developing variation—in fact insures that continuations fulfill the expectations promised by the beginnings. It should not surprise us then, in light of the general function of beginnings and Schoenberg's own use of developing variation, that his beginnings often exhibit clear and distinctive metrical structures.

But if developing variation makes for rhythmical coherence in Schoenberg's twelve-tone music, it also makes Schoenberg's rhythmical structures hard to analyze, since their effect often depends greatly upon the listeners' expectations. Meter is bound to be slippery and elusive when it emerges from an interplay between what we expect and what we actually hear. One example will portray in miniature the kind of interplay I am talking about. The beginning of the phrase shown in Example 4.12 has an exceptionally clear metrical structure, one that depends little upon what has immediately preceded it—but the ending of the phrase is quite the opposite. If we analyzed only the ending, apart from the beginning, we would find its metrical structure only approximate, perhaps even questionable; variations in rhythmic subpatterns, as well as unsteady pattern recurrence threaten to disrupt the foreground rhythmic stratum. In isolation, moreover, nothing indicates that this slippery metrical structure creates syncopation by hemiola. Heard in context, however, the metrical effect is quite audible; the irregularities that seem to frustrate our theoretical model are heard as simple associations that our experience with tonal music has taught us to make. While this example hardly taxes our imagination, it does suggest the kinds of problems we confront when trying to analyze more extended rhythmical structures.

It may seem futile to outline a model for twelve-tone meter and then qualify it with some sort of elusive interplay, but in fact the program is neither futile nor insignificant. It partakes of the nature of all theoretical models. If the kind of interplay I have described resists definition or precise measurement, what remains important is that the interplay occurs. One can write rules for meter, but one cannot write rules for the interplay or tension of meter against other elements of musical texture, either in twelve-tone or tonal music. But this limitation of rules (or theoretical models) does not make them futile. Without the abstract patterns they imply, there could be no interplay between listeners' expectations, which depend upon internalizing or learning such patterns, and the free and unpredictable (though not irrational) inventions of the composer. There is a key difference, in other words, between simple absence of meter and a constant interplay or tension of meter (as an abstract norm or expectation) against the realized texture of the music.[13] Deviations are bound to occur with any theory of meter that is not uselessly vague, and they ought to be noticed and studied and talked about even if, in a particular case, one cannot and should not adjust the model to account for them. A model is not a machine to compose music without human art or genius; it is an abstraction to help us hear and analyze music already composed.

As an idea, interplay of meter with the other elements of musical texture is no doubt dangerous; it could be used to defend any model, however unhelpful, from challenge or modification. But one can control this danger by keeping interplay concrete, attached to particular contexts and demonstrable effects. I must therefore admit that although interplay explains many of the deviations that surface when my model is applied to an entire twelve-tone piece, it does not explain all. I want to conclude by suggesting why not and what our response ought to be.

Deviations from a prevailing metrical pattern that cannot be explained as interplay or tension with other musical elements arise, I think, from the fact that harmonic structure in Schoenberg's twelve-tone music derives from equivalencies that are not well defined as compared to those of tonal music. These equivalences are the properties that create harmonic structure— invariant segments, combinatoriality, row transpositions and inversions, inversional balance, and so forth, and they seem sometimes to substitute for or take precedence over metrical structure. Perhaps meter ought to be seen as only one among various kinds of equivalency in Schoenberg's repertoire of compositional devices, all functioning to the same end. If we could formulate a general principle of equivalency for Schoenberg's twelve-tone method we might arrive at a broader vision of our subject, but that broader vision, that more inclusive theory, will have to include the metrical effects Schoenberg achieved through the multiple dimensions of his harmonic structures.

Appendix

Prime Forms and Vectors of Pitch-Class Sets

Appendix

This Appendix is reproduced from Forte, *The Structure of Atonal Music* (New Haven and London: Yale University Press, 1973).

Name	Pcs	Vector	Name	Pcs	Vector
3-1(12)	0,1,2	210000	9-1	0,1,2,3,4,5,6,7,8	876663
3-2	0,1,3	111000	9-2	0,1,2,3,4,5,6,7,9	777663
3-3	0,1,4	101100	9-3	0,1,2,3,4,5,6,8,9	767763
3-4	0,1,5	100110	9-4	0,1,2,3,4,5,7,8,9	766773
3-5	0,1,6	100011	9-5	0,1,2,3,4,6,7,8,9	766674
3-6(12)	0,2,4	020100	9-6	0,1,2,3,4,5,6,8,10	686763
3-7	0,2,5	011010	9-7	0,1,2,3,4,5,7,8,10	677673
3-8	0,2,6	010101	9-8	0,1,2,3,4,6,7,8,10	676764
3-9(12)	0,2,7	010020	9-9	0,1,2,3,5,6,7,8,10	676683
3-10(12)	0,3,6	002001	9-10	0,1,2,3,4,6,7,9,10	668664
3-11	0,3,7	001110	9-11	0,1,2,3,5,6,7,9,10	667773
3-12(4)	0,4,8	000300	9-12	0,1,2,4,5,6,8,9,10	666963
4-1(12)	0,1,2,3	321000	8-1	0,1,2,3,4,5,6,7	765442
4-2	0,1,2,4	221100	8-2	0,1,2,3,4,5,6,8	665542
4-3(12)	0,1,3,4	212100	8-3	0,1,2,3,4,5,6,9	656542
4-4	0,1,2,5	211110	8-4	0,1,2,3,4,5,7,8	655552
4-5	0,1,2,6	210111	8-5	0,1,2,3,4,6,7,8	654553
4-6(12)	0,1,2,7	210021	8-6	0,1,2,3,5,6,7,8	654463
4-7(12)	0,1,4,5	201210	8-7	0,1,2,3,4,5,8,9	645652
4-8(12)	0,1,5,6	200121	8-8	0,1,2,3,4,7,8,9	644563
4-9(6)	0,1,6,7	200022	8-9	0,1,2,3,6,7,8,9	644464
4-10(12)	0,2,3,5	122010	8-10	0,2,3,4,5,6,7,9	566452
4-11	0,1,3,5	121110	8-11	0,1,2,3,4,5,7,9	565552
4-12	0,2,3,6	112101	8-12	0,1,3,4,5,6,7,9	556543
4-13	0,1,3,6	112011	8-13	0,1,2,3,4,6,7,9	556453
4-14	0,2,3,7	111120	8-14	0,1,2,4,5,6,7,9	555562
4-Z15	0,1,4,6	111111	8-Z15	0,1,2,3,4,6,8,9	555553
4-16	0,1,5,7	110121	8-16	0,1,2,3,5,7,8,9	554563
4-17(12)	0,3,4,7	102210	8-17	0,1,3,4,5,6,8,9	546652
4-18	0,1,4,7	102111	8-18	0,1,2,3,5,6,8,9	546553
4-19	0,1,4,8	101310	8-19	0,1,2,4,5,6,8,9	545752
4-20(12)	0,1,5,8	101220	8-20	0,1,2,4,5,7,8,9	545662
4-21(12)	0,2,4,6	030201	8-21	0,1,2,3,4,6,8,10	474643
4-22	0,2,4,7	021120	8-22	0,1,2,3,5,6,8,10	465562
4-23(12)	0,2,5,7	021030	8-23	0,1,2,3,5,7,8,10	465472
4-24(12)	0,2,4,8	020301	8-24	0,1,2,4,5,6,8,10	464743
4-25(6)	0,2,6,8	020202	8-25	0,1,2,4,6,7,8,10	464644
4-26(12)	0,3,5,8	012120	8-26	0,1,2,4,5,7,9,10	456562
4-27	0,2,5,8	012111	8-27	0,1,2,4,5,7,8,10	456553
4-28(3)	0,3,6,9	004002	8-28	0,1,3,4,6,7,9,10	448444
4-Z29	0,1,3,7	111111	8-Z29	0,1,2,3,5,6,7,9	555553
5-1(12)	0,1,2,3,4	432100	7-1	0,1,2,3,4,5,6	654321
5-2	0,1,2,3,5	332110	7-2	0,1,2,3,4,5,7	554331
5-3	0,1,2,4,5	322210	7-3	0,1,2,3,4,5,8	544431
5-4	0,1,2,3,6	322111	7-4	0,1,2,3,4,6,7	544332
5-5	0,1,2,3,7	321121	7-5	0,1,2,3,5,6,7	543342
5-6	0,1,2,5,6	311221	7-6	0,1,2,3,4,7,8	533442
5-7	0,1,2,6,7	310132	7-7	0,1,2,3,6,7,8	532353

Name	Pcs	Vector	Name	Pcs	Vector
5-8(12)	0,2,3,4,6	232201	7-8	0,2,3,4,5,6,8	454422
5-9	0,1,2,4,6	231211	7-9	0,1,2,3,4,6,8	453432
5-10	0,1,3,4,6	223111	7-10	0,1,2,3,4,6,9	445332
5-11	0,2,3,4,7	222220	7-11	0,1,3,4,5,6,8	444441
5-Z12(12)	0,1,3,5,6	222121	7-Z12	0,1,2,3,4,7,9	444342
5-13	0,1,2,4,8	221311	7-13	0,1,2,4,5,6,8	443532
5-14	0,1,2,5,7	221131	7-14	0,1,2,3,5,7,8	443352
5-15(12)	0,1,2,6,8	220222	7-15	0,1,2,4,6,7,8	442443
5-16	0,1,3,4,7	213211	7-16	0,1,2,3,5,6,9	435432
5-Z17(12)	0,1,3,4,8	212320	7-Z17	0,1,2,4,5,6,9	434541
5-Z18	0,1,4,5,7	212221	7-Z18	0,1,2,3,5,8,9	434442
5-19	0,1,3,6,7	212122	7-19	0,1,2,3,6,7,9	434343
5-20	0,1,3,7,8	211231	7-20	0,1,2,4,7,8,9	433452
5-21	0,1,4,5,8	202420	7-21	0,1,2,4,5,8,9	424641
5-22(12)	0,1,4,7,8	202321	7-22	0,1,2,5,6,8,9	424542
5-23	0,2,3,5,7	132130	7-23	0,2,3,4,5,7,9	354351
5-24	0,1,3,5,7	131221	7-24	0,1,2,3,5,7,9	353442
5-25	0,2,3,5,8	123121	7-25	0,2,3,4,6,7,9	345342
5-26	0,2,4,5,8	122311	7-26	0,1,3,4,5,7,9	344532
5-27	0,1,3,5,8	122230	7-27	0,1,2,4,5,7,9	344451
5-28	0,2,3,6,8	122212	7-28	0,1,3,5,6,7,9	344433
5-29	0,1,3,6,8	122131	7-29	0,1,2,4,6,7,9	344352
5-30	0,1,4,6,8	121321	7-30	0,1,2,4,6,8,9	343542
5-31	0,1,3,6,9	114112	7-31	0,1,3,4,6,7,9	336333
5-32	0,1,4,6,9	113221	7-32	0,1,3,4,6,8,9	335442
5-33(12)	0,2,4,6,8	040402	7-33	0,1,2,4,6,8,10	262623
5-34(12)	0,2,4,6,9	032221	7-34	0,1,3,4,6,8,10	254442
5-35(12)	0,2,4,7,9	032140	7-35	0,1,3,5,6,8,10	254361
5-Z36	0,1,2,4,7	222121	7-Z36	0,1,2,3,5,6,8	444342
5-Z37(12)	0,3,4,5,8	212320	7-Z37	0,1,3,4,5,7,8	434541
5-Z38	0,1,2,5,8	212221	7-Z38	0,1,2,4,5,7,8	434442
6-1(12)	0,1,2,3,4,5	543210			
6-2	0,1,2,3,4,6	443211			
6-Z3	0,1,2,3,5,6	433221	6-Z36	0,1,2,3,4,7	
6-Z4(12)	0,1,2,4,5,6	432321	6-Z37(12)	0,1,2,3,4,8	
6-5	0,1,2,3,6,7	422232			
6-Z6(12)	0,1,2,5,6,7	421242	6-Z38(12)	0,1,2,3,7,8	
6-7(6)	0,1,2,6,7,8	420243			
6-8(12)	0,2,3,4,5,7	343230			
6-9	0,1,2,3,5,7	342231			
6-Z10	0,1,3,4,5,7	333321	6-Z39	0,2,3,4,5,8	
6-Z11	0,1,2,4,5,7	333231	6-Z40	0,1,2,3,5,8	
6-Z12	0,1,2,4,6,7	332232	6-Z41	0,1,2,3,6,8	
6-Z13(12)	0,1,3,4,6,7	324222	6-Z42(12)	0,1,2,3,6,9	
6-14	0,1,3,4,5,8	323430			
6-15	0,1,2,4,5,8	323421			
6-16	0,1,4,5,6,8	322431			
6-Z17	0,1,2,4,7,8	322332	6-Z43	0,1,2,5,6,8	
6-18	0,1,2,5,7,8	322242			

Appendix

Name	Pcs	Vector
6-Z19	0,1,3,4,7,8	313431
6-20(4)	0,1,4,5,8,9	303630
6-21	0,2,3,4,6,8	242412
6-22	0,1,2,4,6,8	241422
6-Z23(12)	0,2,3,5,6,8	234222
6-Z24	0,1,3,4,6,8	233331
6-Z25	0,1,3,5,6,8	233241
6-Z26(12)	0,1,3,5,7,8	232341
6-27	0,1,3,4,6,9	225222
6-Z28(12)	0,1,3,5,6,9	224322
6-Z29(12)	0,1,3,6,8,9	224232
6-30(12)	0,1,3,6,7,9	224223
6-31	0,1,3,5,8,9	223431
6-32(12)	0,2,4,5,7,9	143250
6-33	0,2,3,5,7,9	143241
6-34	0,1,3,5,7,9	142422
6-35(2)	0,2,4,6,8,10	060603

Name	Pcs	Vector
6-Z44	0,1,2,5,6,9	
6-Z45(12)	0,2,3,4,6,9	
6-Z46	0,1,2,4,6,9	
6-Z47	0,1,2,4,7,9	
6-Z48(12)	0,1,2,5,7,9	
6-Z49(12)	0,1,3,4,7,9	
6-Z50(12)	0,1,4,6,7,9	

Glossary of Technical Terms

I am indebted for some of these defintions to Allen Forte, *The Structure of Atonal Music* (New Haven and London: Yale University Press, 1973), and Bo Alphonce, "The Invariance Matrix," Ph.D. dissertation (Yale University, 1974).

Aggregate. An aggregate contains partitioned segments from two or more combinatorially related row forms. It displays all the harmonies of the basic set within one or more harmonic dimensions. Between discrete harmonic dimensions there can be no invariant pitches. An aggregate thus contains the universal set and can include more than twelve elements.

Attack-point. The attack-point of an event is the point at which it begins. In a series of events, the interval of time between a pair of successive attack-points is called the associated *attack-point interval,* and the succession of attack-point intervals determined by the series as a whole is termed the *attack-point rhythm.* The attack-point interval measures the time between the beginnings of successive events and indicates nothing about the duration of the events themselves. If the attack-point interval remains constant over a series of events, then it indicates that the series contains at least one uninterpreted rhythmic stratum.

Basic set (P). In this study, basic set refers to an ordered set containing twelve pitch-classes. It is best described as a group of harmonies determined by an ordered set. The terms *basic set* and *twelve-tone row* are synonymous.

Cardinal number. Cardinal number refers to the number of pitch-class representatives within a pitch-class set.

Combinatoriality. Combinatoriality is the property by which the application of T, RT, I, or RI to a segment of P produces a new segment whose pitch content is exclusive of the original segment. The property depends upon the segmental pitch-class content but is completely independent of the ordering of elements within those segments. It allows for the formation of *secondary sets* and *aggregates* between two or more combinatorially related row forms. A secondary set represents the linear juxtaposition of the partitioned segments from discrete row forms. An aggregate is the simultaneous presentation of such segments. Both the aggregate and the secondary set contain the universal set.

Complement (of a pc set). The complement of a pc set S is a set T formed by all elements of the universal set that are not elements of S. For example, the complement of the pc set [0,1,5,9,10] is the pc set [2,3,4,6,7,8,11]. The *set-names of complementary sets* possess complementary cardinal numbers (mod 12) and identical ordinal numbers. Thus pc set 4–17 is the complementary set of pc set 8–17, and pc set 3–3 is the complementary set of pc set 9–3. The only exception involves some pc sets of cardinality 6. These are clearly indicated on the list of prime forms (see Appendix). It should not be assumed that the pc content of two sets with complementary set-names must necessarily comprise the universal set.

Equivalent pc sets. Two pc sets are equivalent if their normal order forms reduce to the same prime form by transposition, or inversion followed by transposition. In this study, two pc sets

148   Glossary

that are equivalent usually do not contain identical pitch-classes. If two pc sets contain identical pitch-classes they are termed *identical pc sets*.

Foreground pitch event.   A foreground pitch event is a harmonic event within the primary harmonic dimension.

Harmonic dimension.   An harmonic dimension contains one or more harmonic segments.

Harmonic segment.   An harmonic segment represents an harmonic event. It can be either a linear or nonlinear segment of the basic set. If it is a nonlinear segment it must be delineated by what Schoenberg referred to as the same spatial continuum.

Harmonies of a basic set.   The harmonies of a basic set include all linear segments that contain pitch-class sets of cardinality 3 through 9 (inclusive) and their complements. They are not restricted to a specific pitch-class content. They are identified primarily by their total interval-class content and not by the ordering of their pitches.

Ic.   See *interval-class*.

Interval.   If a and b are pc integers, then the interval formed by a and b is the absolute (positive) value of the difference of a and b. An interval is thus the number of semitones between two pitch-classes.

Interval class.   An interval class is one of the seven interval classes designated by the integers 0 through 6. Any interval greater than 6 is reducible to one of the classes 0 through 6 by replacing it with its *inverse*.

Interval content.   The interval content of a pc set refers to its total interval-content; the collection of interval-class representatives formed by taking the absolute value differences of all pairs of elements of a pc set.

Interval succession.   An interval succession designates the intervals formed by successive elements of an ordered pc set. If, for example, the set is [0,1,6,7], the interval succession is [1-5-1].

Interval vector.   An ordered array of numerals enclosed in square brackets represents the interval contents of a pc set and is called an interval vector. The first numeral gives the number of intervals of interval class 1, the second gives the number of intervals of interval class 2, and so on.

Invariant subset.   Two permutations (S and U) contain an invariant subset whenever a transformation (inversion, transposition) of S produces a permutation U which contains a segment identical to a segment of S. It should be noted that the preservation of the order positions of the segment is not a criterion for invariance, nor is the preservation of order relations, except that a segment is preserved in consecutive order positions.

Inverse.   If a is a pc integer and a' represents the inverse of a, then a' = 12 − a (modulo 12).

Inversion (I).   Inversion refers to the process by which each element e of a basic set is replaced by 12 − e.

Linear Segment. See *Segment*.

Middleground pitch-event.   A middleground pitch-event is a harmonic event within the secondary harmonic dimension.

Normal order.   A pc set is in normal order if all of its elements are distinct and in ascending order, and if the set is in that order which yields the smallest possible interval between the first and the last element. Out of these possible orderings of a pc set and its inversion (if distinct) that satisfy this criterion that one is in the *best normal order* where the intervals between the leftmost elements are the smallest possible. A *prime form* is a pc set in best normal order, transposed so that the first element is 0. For example, the pc set [11,7,3,2,3], rid of replication and arranged in ascending order, reads [2,3,7,11]. The inversion of this set, arranged in ascending order, is [1,5,9,10]. Of their cyclical reorderings the following four satisfy the normal order criterion: [7,11,14,15], [11,14,15,19], [5,9,10,13], [9,10,13,17]; these all span the interval 8 which is the smallest possible for this set. Comparing their respective interval successions 4-3-1, 3-1-4, 4-1-3, 1-3-4, the last one satisfies the criterion for best normal order. Then [9,10,13,17] with its elements reduced mod 12 and the set transposed at t = 3 yields the prime form [0,1,4,8].

Ordered set. An ordered set is a pc set in which the order of the elements is regarded as significant.

Order numbers. Order numbers refer to the position of pcs within a twelve-tone row. There are twelve positions numbered one through twelve. Order number 1 designates the initial pc of all prograde and inversion permutations. The ordering of positions is reversed in the retrograde permutations. That is, the first position of a retrograde permutation is always designated by order number 12, the second position by order number 11, and so on.

Pattern recurrence. Pattern recurrence indicates that there is a recurrence of identical rhythmic subpatterns. (See *rhythmic subpatterns.*)

Pc. See *pitch-class.*

Permutation. A twelve-tone row a is a permutation of a twelve-tone row b if b is related to a by I, RI, T, or RT.

Pitch-class (pc). Pitch-class denotes all pitches of the same relative position in all octave transpositions of a twelve-tone scale. The 12 pitch-classes are designated by the integers 0 through 11. Pitch-class 0 refers to all notated pitches C, B♯, and D♭. Pitch-class 1 refers to all notated pitches C♯, D♭, and B♯♯, and so on.

Pitch-class set (pc set). A pitch-class set is a set of distinct integers representing pitch-classes. The conventional notation for a pc set presents pc integers separated by commas; the whole set is enclosed in brackets; thus, the pc set containing pitch-classes C, D, F♯, G♯, is written [0,2,6,8].

Primary harmonic dimension. A primary harmonic dimension contains a linear harmonic segment of the basic set P and occurs with every statement of P.

Primary rhythmic dimension. The primary rhythmic dimension contains the regular recurrence of the linear harmonic segments of the basic set.

Prograde (P). The operation that does not alter the order between any two elements of the basic set is called prograde.

Retrograde (R). The operation that yields the exact reversal of the ordering of elements is called retrograde.

Rhythmic stratum. If events that belong to the same class recur at equal intervals of time, then they define a rhythmic stratum; they have a simple periodicity for which each recurrence begins a cycle that ends with the next recurrence. A rhythmic stratum thus contains more than one event; all its events recur at equal intervals of time; and all are defined by the same criterion. There are two general ways that rhythmical strata may interact; they may be either *in-phase* or *out-of-phase*. In-phase strata have attack-points that intersect and attack-point intervals that are integral multiples of one another; out-of-phase strata do not. Any stratum produced by a single criterion forms an *uninterpreted rhythmic stratum*. An *interpreted rhythmic structure* is formed by two rhythmic strata that are in-phase but move at different rates; one stratum must interact with the second, thereby accenting and interpreting it. The resulting interpreted rhythmic structure may then be described according to whatever scheme of accents is produced, 3/4, 4/4, and so forth.

Rhythmic subpatterns. Rhythmic subpatterns represent repeated groups of varied durational values. If these patterns are considered independent of any internal grouping or metrical structure, then they too may be thought of as being uninterpreted rhythmic strata because they do not have strong and weak beats. (See *pattern recurrence.*)

Row-form label. Row forms are labelled according to the transformation and the integer that represents the initial pitch-class of their prograde permutation. Transformations are designated by T (transposition), I (inversion) and R (retrograde). The integers that represent pitch-classes remain fixed; that is, pc 0 always represents the pitch C, pc 1 always represents D♭, and so on. For labels of transpositional forms of the basic set, the letter P often substitutes for the letter T. The label P_5, for example, designates the transposition of the basic set whose initial pitch is F; the label RP_5 represents the retrograde of the transposition of the basic set whose initial pitch is F. In other words, RP_5 represents the retrograde of the transpositional permutation labelled P_5.

Row table. If S is a twelve-tone row, a row table is a particular tabulation of all the possible permutations of S. In this study, the ordering of permutations is determined by the inversion of the row, i.e., P and transpositions of P are listed so that the succession of t-values is the same as the succession of pcs in the inverted row; similarly, the transpositions of the inversion are ordered according to the prime form (P) of the basic set. The first transposition of P that appears across the top of the row table represents the principal or initial form of the basic set. (In Example 2.0, for instance, P_3 represents the initial and most important row permutation in the first movement.)

Secondary harmonic dimension. A secondary harmonic dimension contains a nonlinear harmonic segment derived from one or more forms of the basic set. These nonlinear segments must represent secondary harmonic sets, that is, they must represent sets that are either identical or equivalent to the linear segments of the basic set.

Secondary rhythmic dimension. A secondary rhythmic dimension contains the regular recurrence of nonlinear harmonic segments of P that represent secondary harmonic sets.

Segment. In this text, segment always designates a linear segment. A *linear segment* denotes a subset S of a twelve-tone row P such that S is completely contained in consecutive order positions of P. *Linear set* and *linear segment* are synonymous. A *nonlinear segment* denotes a subset S of a twelve-tone row P such that S is not completely contained in consecutive order positions of P. A nonlinear segment may include elements from more than one permutation. *Nonlinear set* and *nonlinear segment* are synonymous.

Set name. Each prime form of the twelve-tone system has a unique set name of the form c-n where c is the cardinal number of the set and n is an ordinal number; e.g., the prime form [0,1,4,8] is associated with the set name 4-19. Ordinal numbers are established on Allen Forte's list of prime forms (see Appendix). The ordinal number may be preceded by a Z to indicate that the set is a member of a pair of *Z-related sets*, i.e., two pc sets that have the same interval vector without being reducible to the same prime form.

Secondary harmonic set. For a harmonic set to be designated a secondary harmonic set it must be equivalent to a harmony of the basic set *and* occur simultaneously in a primary and secondary harmonic dimension. This means that one statement of a secondary harmonic set contains pcs occupying contiguous order numbers in P, and the remaining statements must contain pcs occupying noncontiguous order numbers in P, or contain pcs from more than one permutation. The chief function of a secondary harmonic set is to integrate (that is interconnect) two or more dimensions of harmonic structure.

Subset. A set X is said to be a subset of a set Y if every element of X is an element of Y.

Superset. A set X is said to be a superset of a set Y if every element of Y is an element of X.

Transposition (T). Transposition of a basic set P consists of the addition (modulo 12) of some integer t to each element of P.

Universal set. The set containing all pitch-classes of the twelve-tone system is called the universal set. The universal set is unordered.

Unordered set. An unordered set is a pc set in which the order of the elements is regarded as insignificant.

Notes

Preface

1. Arnold Schoenberg, "Composition with Twelve Tones (1)" in *Style and Idea*, ed. Leonard Stein, trans. Leo Black (New York: St. Martins Press, 1975), p. 219; originally published in *Style and Idea* (New York: Philosophical Library, 1950).

Chapter 1

1. Arnold Schoenberg, "Composition with Twelve Tones (1)" (hereafter "Composition") in *Style and Idea*, ed. Leonard Stein, trans. Leo Black (New York: St. Martins Press, 1975), pp. 214-45; originally published in *Style and Idea* (New York: Philosophical Library, 1950).
2. Arnold Schoenberg, "Vortrag / 12 T K / Princeton" (hereafter "Vortrag"), ed. Claudio Spies, *Perspectives of New Music* 13/1 (1974): 58-136.
3. For example, in "Composition with Twelve Tones" Schoenberg explicitly states that in the Suite op. 25, he has transposed the basic set at the interval of a diminished fifth to avoid octave doubling. This obscures more important reasons for this particular transposition, reasons which are discussed in the following section. In the earlier version this precaution is not mentioned and consequently one feels freer to consider other possible reasons.
4. "Composition," p. 216.
5. Ibid.
6. Ibid., pp. 216-17.
7. Ibid., p. 217.
8. Ibid.
9. As the following chapters demonstrate, Schoenberg uses various procedures in his twelve-tone music that he developed for his atonal compositions during the twelve-year period preceding his first twelve-tone compositions. These procedures are described by Allen Forte in *The Structure of Atonal Music* (New Haven: Yale University Press, 1973).
10. "Composition," pp. 218-19.
11. Ibid., p. 220.
12. Ibid.
13. Ibid.

14. Ibid.
15. Ibid., p. 223.
16. Ibid.
17. Arnold Schoenberg, "Composition with Twelve Tones (2)" in *Style and Idea*, ed. Leonard Stein, trans. Leo Black (New York: St. Martins Press, 1975), pp. 246-47. This short essay is undated. But some references to retirement, renewed interest in composing *Die Jakobsleiter*, and work on *Structural Functions of Harmony* suggest that it was written after 1946 and perhaps as late as 1948.
18. "Vortrag," p. 85. This concept becomes clearer if we consider how we recognize harmonies within tonal melodies. If, for example, a major triad unfolds horizontally, we recognize its harmonic identity regardless of the ordering of its pitches. Thus, the third can appear first, followed by the fifth and the root, and we still recognize it as a major triad. Similarly, as we become more familiar with the harmonies of a specific basic set, Schoenberg stresses that they become easily recognizable regardless of the ordering of their pitches.
19. "Composition," p. 234.
20. "Vortrag," p. 83.
21. "Composition," p. 220.
22. Ibid., p. 225.
23. Ibid., p. 234.
24. "Vortrag," p. 99.
25. Schoenberg of course does not mean that tonal harmonies never occur horizontally, but rather that they are defined, unlike twelve-tone harmonies, by a specific vertical structuring of intervals.
26. "Vortrag," p. 83.
27. "Composition," p. 220.
28. Ibid., p. 219.
29. Ibid., p. 218.
30. "Vortrag," p. 93.
31. "Composition (2)," pp. 247-48.
32. "Vortrag," p. 99. The term "linear segment" designates a segment that is formed by pc representatives that are contiguous; the term "nonlinear segment" designates a segment that is formed by pc representatives that are not contiguous.
33. "Composition," p. 232. The designation of pc sets has been added to each of Schoenberg's examples. The pc set names are derived from the list given by Allen Forte in *The Structure of Atonal Music* (New Haven: Yale University Press, 1973). This list is reproduced in the Appendix.
34. "Vortrag," p. 101.
35. "Composition," p. 229.
36. Forte, *Atonal Music*, p. 77.

37. Ibid., p. 78.
38. "Vortrag," p. 99.
39. Ibid.
40. "Composition," p. 231.
41. Ibid., p. 230.
42. It is important to note that while some of these equivalent trichords duplicate the exact interval succession in the basic set, others do not. (Compare, for example, the respective occurrences of pc set 3-2.) Therefore, the equivalent harmonies must relate primarily by *total* intervallic content and not merely by a specific succession of intervals.
43. "Composition," pp. 238-39.
44. Ibid., p. 234.
45. Ibid., p. 236.
46. Ibid., p. 233.
47. "Composition (2)," p. 247.
48. "Composition," p. 219.
49. Ibid.
50. Schoenberg's claim that the basic set regulates all harmonic and structural elements has met with considerable skepticism. Skeptics assert that "licenses," such as reorderings, repetitions, and association of nonadjacent segments of the basic set, as well as the verticalization of ordered segments to form vertical harmonies, result in many events unrelated to the basic set and point toward serious weaknesses in his twelve-tone method. This skepticism began during Schoenberg's life and has continued until the present. The following can fairly represent it: Richard S. Hill, "Schoenberg's Tone-Rows and the Tonal System of the Future," *The Musical Quarterly* 22 (1936): 14-37; Ernst Krenek, "New Developments of the Twelve-Tone Technique," *Music Review* 4 (1943): 81-97; Peter Stadlen, "Serialism Reconsidered," *The Score* 22 (1958): 12-27; Seymour Shifrin, "A Note from the Underground," *Perspectives of New Music* 1/1 (1962): 152-53; George Perle, *Serial Composition and Atonality* (Berkeley and Los Angeles: University of California Press, 1963), pp. 61-110, and *Twelve-Tone Tonality* (Berkeley and Los Angeles: University of California Press, 1977), pp. 23-24. Various theorists and composers have refused to interpret these "licenses" as weaknesses, but have not succeeded in explaining how they are regulated by the basic set. See for example the responses to Stadlen's article by Walter Piston, Roberto Gerhard and Roger Sessions, all in *The Score* 23 (1958): 46-64. The inadequacies of these responses is aptly pointed out by George Perle, "Theory and Practice in Twelve-Tone Music," *The Score* 25 (1959): 58-64. George Rochberg in his review of Perle, *Serial Composition and Atonality*, harkens back to the earlier responses by ignoring entirely Schoenberg's theoretical claim while explaining away his "licenses" by appeal to creative genius (*Journal of the American Musicological Society* 16 [1963]: 413-18). René Leibowitz and Josef Rufer, on the other hand, tend to ignore the whole issue and merely describe uncritically Schoenberg's procedures and his use of classical forms. Babbitt comments tellingly on the superficiality of this approach in his review of Leibowitz, *Schoenberg et son école* (Paris: J.B. Janin, 1947) and *Qu'est ce que la musique de douze sons?* (Liège: Editions Dynamo, 1948) in *Journal of the American Musicological Society* 3 (1950): 57-60, as does Krenek in his remarks on Rufer, *Die Komposition mit zwölf Tonen* (Berlin: Max Hesses

154 Notes for Chapter 2

Verlag, 1952) appearing in "Is The Twelve-Tone Technique on the Decline?" *The Musical Quarterly* 39 (1953): 513-27; a more recent review of the twelve-tone harmonic problem appears in Peter Westergaard's "Toward a Twelve-Tone Polyphony," *Perspectives of New Music* 4/2 (1966): 90-112. Milton Babbitt and David Lewin are most prominent among those who have seriously considered the difficulties of twelve-tone harmonic structure. See especially Babbitt, "Some Aspects of Twelve-Tone Composition," *The Score* 12 (1955): 53-61; "Twelve-Tone Invariants as Compositional Determinants," *The Musical Quarterly* 46 (1960): 246-59; "Set Structure as a Compositional Determinant," *Journal of Music Theory* 5 (1961): 72-94; and Lewin, "A Theory of Segmental Association in Twelve-Tone Music," *Perspectives of New Music* 1/1 (1962): 89-116; "A Study of Hexachord Levels in Schoenberg's Violin Fantasy," *Perspectives of New Music* 6/1 (1967): 18-32; "Inversional Balance as an Organizing Force in Schoenberg's Music and Thought," *Perspectives of New Music* 6/2 (1968): 1-21.

51. George Perle, *Serial Composition and Atonality* (Berkeley and Los Angeles: University of California Press, 1963). (Hereafter page references will appear in text.)

52. "Composition," p. 230.

53. "Vortrag," p. 97.

Chapter 2

1. My analyses assume to some extent familiarity with these compositional procedures. For a fair review of these procedures, see especially the articles by Milton Babbitt and David Lewin listed in the Bibliography.

2. The sketches analyzed in this chapter represent hitherto unpublished sketch material in the Arnold Schoenberg Institute, University of Sourthern California, Los Angeles, California. They are included in *Filmfile No. 5 — Chamber Music,* "Manuscripts of Arnold Schoenberg," Suite op. 29, Reihentabellen (#1179-88), Skizzen (#1189-1206) and in *Skizzenbuch V,* Suite op. 29. The dates for the individual movements appear in *Skizzenbuch V*. All the sketches appearing in Chapter 2 are xerographic copies of the original sketches except for several which would not reproduce well and have been transcribed. In those few cases, I have indicated that the sketch represents a transcription of the original. In several instances it has been necessary to darken the copies of the original sketches to ensure reproduction.

3. "Vortrag," p. 83.

4. "Composition," p. 220.

5. For an explanation of the *row table* and the system I use for *order-numbers* and *row-form labels* see the Glossary. The reader should review these conventions, for they conform most closely to Schoenberg's method but are not typical of current usage.

6. This is a transcription of a sketch appearing on #1185. I have added set names, order numbers and brackets.

7. Milton Babbitt, "Some Aspects of Twelve-Tone Composition," *The Score* 12 (1955): 53-61. See also "Twelve-Tone Invariants as Compositional Determinants," *The Musical Quarterly* 46 (1960): 246-59 and "Set Structure as a Compositional Determinant," *Journal of Music Theory* 5 (1961): 72-94.

Notes for Chapter 3   155

8. This sketch represents only one of several sketches appearing on #1188. In most of the following examples the sketches similarly represent only part of the material contained on each numbered sketch.

9. Daniel Starr and Robert Morris, "A General Theory of Combinatoriality and the Aggregate (Part I)," *Perspectives of New Music* 16/1 (1978): 3-4.

Chapter 3

1. See "complement" in Glossary.

2. Example 3.1 shows a transcription of a sketch appearing on #1185. Set names, order numbers and brackets have been added.

3. As the row table for op. 29 shows (Example 2.0), each row form shares three invariant tetrachords with exactly one other row form, and these tetrachords appear in the same order. Thus, in Example 3.7 the simultaneous presentation of the tetrachordal segments of P could represent equally well two different row forms. The row forms I have chosen to indicate are in accordance with those indicated by Schoenberg in *Skizzenbuch V*.

4. Joseph Rufer, *Composition with Twelve Notes*, trans. Humphrey Searle (New York: Macmillan Company, 1954), p. 70. I have chosen to cite Rufer rather than more contemporary theorists because, despite his association with Schoenberg, his description of Schoenberg's techniques is still incomplete, a fact that reinforces again our impression that Schoenberg kept secret his compositional procedures from friends and critics alike. Future page references will appear in the text.

5. The sketches for op. 29 contain numerous examples that show Schoenberg working out the trichordal derivations of 6-20 (see Examples 2.2b and 2.22). A three-dimensional harmonic structure similar to Example 3.8 appears in Example 2.6.

6. Even though one trichord in the accompaniment appears in retrograde form (order numbers 1, 2, 3), the accompaniment as a whole uses order numbers that represent a harmony of P, since it represents the complement of the linear segment marked pc set 5-2.

7. Schoenberg's markings in *Skizzenbuch V* indicate that he regarded this passage as a single row permutation containing multiple repetitions rather than four repetitions of the same permutation.

8. "Composition," p. 225.

9. Perle, *Serial Composition*, p. 101.

10. Ibid., p. 105.

11. As in Chapter 2, I describe two or more row forms as being combinatorially related when their hexachords contain identical pcs. In some cases individual row forms may require the application of the R operation to conform to the strict definition of combinatoriality. I am using the term "combinatoriality" in this broader sense because in op. 29 the primary feature Schoenberg uses to associate row forms is their inclusion of such hexachords, that is, their membership in one of the two groups of twelve row forms whose hexachords contain identical pc contents; in general, their potential for forming aggregates is a less crucial consideration. Consequently, when I describe row forms as being combinatorially related, individual permutations may require the R operation to fulfill the strict definition of combinatoriality.

12. In *Skizzenbuch V* Schoenberg first includes the E of P_7 (m.43) in the right hand of the piano part, a position which accentuates the intended secondary harmony 4-19. He erases this, however, and places it in the left hand probably to make it technically easier.

13. See, for example, Starr and Morris, "Theory of Combinatoriality (I)," pp. 3-4.

14. A sketch containing a similar type of harmonic configuratin appears in Example 2.12. In this sketch, however, Schoenberg associates equivalent rather than identical hexachords. In both cases, dyads occupying corresponding order positions in P_3 and I_8 are associated to form a succession of tetrachords equivalent to linear segments of P.

15. Schoenberg's interest in harmonic structures of this type is indicated by the sketches appearing in Example 2.11, Example 2.13 and Example 2.14.

16. This does not represent a complete analysis of the harmonic structure of this passage, but merely points out this single feature of the accompaniment.

17. Starr and Morris, "Theory of Combinatoriality (I)," pp. 3-4.

18. Rufer, *Composition with Twelve Tones*, p. 95.

19. "Composition," p. 234.

20. "Vortrag," p. 95.

21. Brian Fennelly, "Twelve-Tone Techniques" in *Dictionary of Contemporary Music*, ed. John Vinton (New York: E.P. Dutton, 1974), p. 774.

22. Perle, *Serial Composition*, p. 140.

23. Ibid., pp. 74-75.

24. Milton Babbitt, "Some Aspects," p. 57.

25. "Composition," p. 226.

26. Schoenberg, "Epilogue, December 1949" in *The String Quartets of Schoenberg, Berg, and Webern: A Documentary Study*, ed. Ursula v. Rauchhaupt (Hamburg: Deutsche Grammophon Gesellschaft mbH, 1971), p. 65.

27. Malcolm MacDonald, *Schoenberg* (London: J.M. Dent & Sons, 1976), p. 8.

28. Schoenberg, "How One Becomes Lonely," in *Style and Idea*, p. 38.

29. Schoenberg, "Epilogue, December 1949," p. 65.

Chapter 4

1. See, for example, Pierre Boulez, "Schoenberg Is Dead," *The Score* 6 (1952): 18-22, and *Notes Of An Apprenticeship* (New York: Alfred A. Knopf, Inc., 1968), pp. 368-75.

2. "Composition," pp. 234-35.

3. Other ways of segmenting this or any phrase would lead to alternate harmonic dimensions, but these would be hard to hear because they lack the emphasis that repetition accords dimensions equivalent to segments of the basic set.

4. In this example and those following, the basic set often contains more than one linear segment that is equivalent to a secondary harmony. In such instances I mark on the basic set as many of its linear segments as space and clarity permit.

Notes for Chapter 4   157

5. In Example 4.2 I point out only one aspect of its complex rhythmic structure. A more complete analysis must consider the exact succession of tetrachords, for Schoenberg has ordered them to articulate successive groups comprised of three eighth-notes and larger groups comprised of six eighth-notes. As the following diagram shows, the groups are treated as unordered segments.

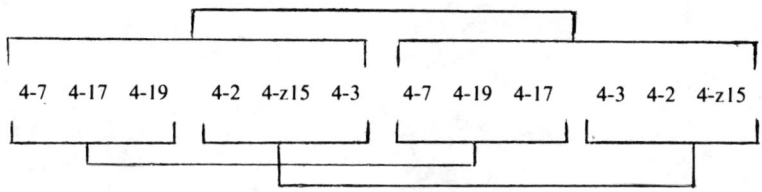

6. Maury Yeston, *The Stratification of Musical Rhythm* (New Haven and London: Yale University Press, 1976).

7. Repetition of row forms does form a stratum, but in light of the following variations, it provides only a superficial source for metrical accent.

8. Because of limitations in space, my diagrams of purely-rhythmic strata in this example and those following are not exhaustive; I have merely indicated some of the more prominent ones.

9. With very few exceptions, the pc sets marked in the examples all contain nonadjacent elements of the basic set and thus represent secondary harmonies; in the few instances where I have marked primary harmonies, the set names are enclosed in parentheses.

10. Perhaps because the principal hexachord of op. 29 can be derived in three different ways from the trichord 3-11, Schoenberg uses this trichord as a secondary harmony throughout op. 29 even though it does not occur as a linear segment of the basic set.

11. For further discussion of how Schoenberg uses secondary dimensions to generate phrase structure, see my article "The Roots of Form In Schoenberg's Sketches," *Journal of Music Theory* 24 (1980):1-36.

12. The harmonic scheme of the secondary dimensions and especially the repeating pitch-contour patterns indicate that the viola and cello have been mistakenly switched in m.271 (Example 4.12). I have therefore emended the published edition and given the correct pitches in parentheses.

13. I am indebted for several ideas and some phrasing in this paragraph to W.K. Wimsatt and Monroe K. Beardsley, "The Concept of Meter: An Exercise in Abstraction," in *Hateful Contraries: Studies in Literature & Criticism* (Lexington: University of Kentucky Press, 1966), pp. 108-45.

Selected Bibliography

Alphonce, Bo Harry. "The Invariance Matrix." Ph.D. dissertation, Yale University, 1974.
Babbit, Milton. "Set Structure as a Compositional Determinant." *Journal of Music Theory* 5: 72-94.
———. "Some Aspects of Twelve-Tone Composition." *Score* 12: 53-61.
———. "Three Essays on Schoenberg." In *Perspectives on Schoenberg and Stravinsky,* edited by Benjamin Boretz and Edward T. Cone. New York: W.W. Norton, 1972.
———. "Twelve-Tone Invariants as Compositional Determinants." *Musical Quarterly* 46: 246-59.
Beach, David. "Segmental Invariance and the Twelve-Tone System." *Journal of Music Theory* 20: 157-84.
Epstein, David M. "Schoenberg's *Grundgestalt* and Total Serialism: Their Relevance to Homophonic Analysis." Ph.D. dissertation, Princeton University, 1968.
Fennelly, Brian. "Twelve-Tone Techniques." In *Dictionary of Contemporary Music,* edited by John Vinton. New York: E.P. Dutton, 1974.
Forte, Allen. "The Basic Interval Patterns." *Journal of Music Theory* 17: 234-73.
———. "Sets and Nonsets in Schoenberg's Atonal Music." *Perspectives of New Music* 11/1: 43-64.
———. *The Structure of Atonal Music.* New Haven and London: Yale University Press, 1973.
Howe, Hubert. "Some Combinatorial Properties of Pitch Structures." *Perspectives of New Music* 4/1: 45-61.
Hyde, Martha M. "The Roots of Form in Schoenberg's Sketches." *Journal of Music Theory* 24: 1-36.
———. "The Telltale Sketches: Harmonic Structure in Schoenberg's Twelve-Tone Method." *Musical Quarterly* 66: 560-80.
Kassler, Michael. "Toward a Theory that is the Twelve-Note-Class System." *Perspectives of New Music* 5/2: 1-80.
Lewin, David. "Inversional Balance as an Organizing Force in Schoenberg's Music and Thought." *Perspectives of New Music* 6/2: 1-21.
———. "Moses und Aron: Some General Remarks, and Analytic Notes for Act I, Scene I." *Perspectives of New Music* 6/1: 1-17.
———. "On Partial Ordering." *Perspectives of New Music* 14/2: 252-57.
———. "A Study of Hexachord Levels in Schoenberg's Violin Fantasy." *Perspectives of New Music* 6/1: 18-32.
———. "A Theory of Segmental Association in Twelve-Tone Music." *Perspectives of New Music* 1/1: 89-116.
Maegaard, Jan. "A Study in the Chronology of Op. 23-26 by Arnold Schoenberg." *Dansk Aarbog for Musikforskning,* 1962.

———. "Schoenbergs Zwölftonreihen." *Die Musikforschung* 29: 385-425.
———. *Studien zur Entwicklung des dodekaphonen Satzes bei Arnold Schönberg.* Copenhagen: Wilhelm Hansen, 1972.
Martino, Donald. "The Source Set and Its Aggregate Formations." *Journal of Music Theory* 5: 224-73.
Perle, George. *Serial Composition and Atonality.* Third ed. Berkeley and Los Angeles: University of California Press, 1972.
Rochberg, George. "The Harmonic Tendency of the Hexachord." *Journal of Music Theory* 3: 208-30.
Rothgeb, John. "Some Ordering Relationships in the Twelve-Tone System." *Journal of Music Theory* 11: 176-97.
Rufer, Josef. "Arnold Schönbergs Nachlass." *Österreichische Musikzeitschrift* 13: 96-106.
———. *Das Werk Arnold Schönbergs.* Kassel: Bärenreiter, 1959. Reprinted 1971. *The Works of Arnold Schoenberg: a catalogue of his compositions, writings, and paintings.* Translated by Dika Newlin. London: Faber and Faber, 1962.
———. *Komposition mit zwölf Töne.* Berlin: Hesse, 1952. *Composition with Twelve Notes Related to One Another.* Translated by H. Searle. New York: Macmillan Co., 1954.
Schoenberg, Arnold. *Sämtliche Werke.* Edited by Josef Rufer et al. Vienna: Universal Edition, 1966-.
———. *Style and Idea.* Edited by Leonard Stein, translated by Leo Black. New York: St. Martins Press, 1975.
Spies, Claudio. " 'Vortrag/ 12 T K /Princeton.' " *Perspectives of New Music* 13/1: 58-136.
Starr, Daniel, and Robert Morris. "A General Theory of Combinatoriality and the Aggregate (I)." *Perspectives of New Music* 16/1: 3-35.
———. "A General Theory of Combinatoriality and the Aggregate (II)." *Perspectives of New Music* 16/2: 50-84.
Westergaard, Peter. "Toward a Twelve-Tone Polyphony." *Perspectives of New Music* 4/2: 90-112.
Yeston, Maury. *The Stratification of Musical Rhythm.* New Haven and London: Yale University Press, 1976.

Index

Aggregate, 58-60, 75-76, 83-100
   definition, 97

Boulez, Pierre, 156 n. 1
Babbitt, Milton, 33, 101, 153-54 n. 50, 154 n. 1
Basic set, 3-5
   cyclical rotation of, 9-11, 19-22, 67-68
   harmonies of, 8-11
   pitch repetitions and doublings, 69-74, 85-86
   reordering of, 55-58, 100-108

Combinatoriality, 33, 58-60, 75-76, 83-100
   described by Schoenberg, 75
"Composition with Twelve Tones," 1-23, 69, 83, 98-99, 108-109, 111-12

Forte, Allen, 151 n.9
Four Pieces for mixed chorus op. 27, 115-16

Harmony, twelve-tone, 1-23
   definition, 7-8
   past views, 18-23, 153-54 n.50

Invariant segments, 74-76, 85-86

Krenek, Ernst, 153 n.50

Leibowitz, René, 153 n.50
Lewin, David, 153-54 n.50, 154 n.1
Linear segment, 30, 152 n.32

Meter, twelve-tone, 111-41
   attack-point, 119-20
   in-phase and out-of-phase strata, 122-23
   interpreted rhythmic structure, 118
   model, 117-26
   recurrence criteria, 118

   rhythmic stratum, 118
   rhythmic subpatterns, 118-19
   syncopation, 123-24, 134-35, 138-39
   uninterpreted rhythmic stratum, 118

Perle, George, 18-23, 32, 75, 98, 100-101, 153-54 n.50
Piston, Walter, 153 n.50
Pitch-class sets, 143-45
   complements of, 9-11
Primary harmonic dimension, 31
Primary harmonic set, 31

Rochberg, George, 153 n.50
Rufer, Josef, 32, 70, 74-76, 98, 100, 109, 153-54 n.50, 155 n.4
   letter from Schoenberg, 99

Secondary harmonic dimension, 31
Secondary harmonic set, 31
Stein, Erwin, 108
String Quartet no. 4 op. 37, 37, 114-15
String Trio op. 45, 101, 135-39, 140
Suite for piano op. 25, 5, 15-16, 101, 111-13
Suite op. 29 (Septett):
   compositional sketches, 25-60, 105, 154 n.2
   row table, 28
   secondary harmonic sets, 35-36
   structure of basic set, 33-36

Variations for orchestra op. 31, 13-16

Westergaard, Peter, 153-54 n.50
Wind Quintet op. 26, 9-13, 19-22

Yeston, Maury, 117